**Colloquial**
# Cantonese

## THE COLLOQUIAL SERIES
### Series Adviser: Gary King

The following languages are available in the Colloquial series:

| | | |
|---|---|---|
| Afrikaans | German | Romanian |
| Albanian | Greek | Russian |
| Amharic | Gujarati | Scottish Gaelic |
| Arabic (Levantine) | Hebrew | Serbian |
| Arabic of Egypt | Hindi | Slovak |
| Arabic of the Gulf | Hungarian | Slovene |
| Basque | Icelandic | Somali |
| Bengali | Indonesian | Spanish |
| Breton | Irish | Spanish of Latin America |
| Bulgarian | Italian | Swahili |
| Cambodian | Japanese | Swedish |
| Cantonese | Korean | Tamil |
| Catalan | Latvian | Thai |
| Chinese (Mandarin) | Lithuanian | Turkish |
| Croatian | Malay | Ukrainian |
| Czech | Mongolian | Urdu |
| Danish | Norwegian | Vietnamese |
| Dutch | Panjabi | Welsh |
| English | Persian | Yiddish (forthcoming) |
| Estonian | Polish | Yoruba |
| Finnish | Portuguese | Zulu (forthcoming) |
| French | Portuguese of Brazil | |

## COLLOQUIAL 2s series: *The Next Step in Language Learning*

| | | |
|---|---|---|
| Chinese | German | Russian |
| Dutch | Italian | Spanish |
| French | Portuguese of Brazil | Spanish of Latin America |

All these Colloquials are available in book & CD packs, or separately. You can order them through your bookseller or via our website www.routledge.com.

# Colloquial
# Cantonese

## The Complete Course for Beginners

Dana Scott Bourgerie, Keith S.T. Tong, and Gregory James

LONDON AND NEW YORK

First edition by Keith S.T. Tong and Gregory James
Published 1994 by Routledge

This edition first published 2010
by Routledge
2 Park Square, Milton Park, Abingdon, Oxon OX14 4RN

Simultaneously published in the USA and Canada
by Routledge
270 Madison Ave, New York, NY 10016

*Routledge is an imprint of the Taylor & Francis Group, an informa business*

© 1994 Keith S.T. Tong and Gregory James
© 2010 Dana Scott Bourgerie, Keith S.T. Tong, and Gregory James

Typeset in Avant Garde and Helvetica by
Graphicraft Limited, Hong Kong
Printed and bound in Great Britain by
TJ International Ltd, Padstow, Cornwall

All rights reserved. No part of this book may be reprinted or reproduced or utilized in any form or by any electronic, mechanical, or other means, now known or hereafter invented, including photocopying and recording, or in any information storage or retrieval system, without permission in writing from the publishers.

*British Library Cataloguing in Publication Data*
A catalogue record for this book is available from the British Library

*Library of Congress Cataloging in Publication Data*
Bourgerie, Dana Scott.
  Colloquial Cantonese : the complete course for beginners / Dana Scott Bourgerie, Keith S.T. Tong and Gregory James.—2nd ed.
  p. cm. — (The colloquial series)
  English and Chinese.
  Includes bibliographical references and index.
  1. Cantonese dialects—Textbooks for foreign speakers—English.  2. Chinese language—Textbooks for foreign speakers—English.  3. Cantonese dialects—Sound recordings for English speakers.  4. Chinese language—Sound recordings for English speakers.  5. Cantonese dialects—Computer-assisted instruction for English speakers.  6. Chinese language—Computer-assisted instruction for English speakers.  I. Tong, Keith S.T.  II. James, Gregory.  III. Title.
  PL1733.B88 2010
  495.1'727—dc22
  2009033172

ISBN13: 978-0-415-47886-1 (pbk)
ISBN13: 978-0-415-47888-5 (audio CDs)
ISBN13: 978-0-415-47887-8 (pack)
ISBN13: 978-0-415-56970-5 (MP3)
ISBN13: 978-0-203-85476-1 (ebk)

# Contents

Acknowledgments    vii

**Introduction**    1

1. **Gāaujai**    15
   Meeting people
2. **Máaih-yéh**    30
   Shopping
3. **Sihou**    45
   Interests and leisure activities
4. **Sìhgaan**    62
   Telling the time
5. **Ngoihbíu**    77
   Physical appearances
6. **Gachìhn**    94
   Prices
7. **Fāan-gūng**    112
   Commuting
8. **Kéuihdeih jouh-gán mātyéh?**    130
   What are they doing?
9. **Bōng ngóh jouh dī yéh**    144
   Can you help me?
10. **Hái bīndouh?**    157
    Where is it?
11. **Giu yéh sihk**    174
    Ordering food
12. **Tīnhei**    188
    The weather

| | | |
|---|---|---|
| 13 | **Yīfuhk**<br>The clothes we wear | 203 |
| 14 | **Léuihhàhng gīngyihm**<br>Traveling experiences | 215 |
| 15 | **Dá-dihnwá**<br>On the telephone | 228 |

| | |
|---|---|
| **Translations of dialogues** | 241 |
| **Key to the exercises** | 254 |
| **Cantonese–English glossary** | 268 |
| **English–Cantonese glossary** | 280 |
| **Further reading** | 291 |
| **Appendix** | 292 |
| **Index of grammatical structures** | 294 |

# Acknowledgments

The first and most obvious acknowledgment goes to the authors of the first edition of *Colloquial Cantonese*, Keith S.T. Tong and Gregory James, on whose work this second edition is based. I would like to acknowledge also the help of Samily Kwok, who helped collect and edit updated material for this edition. I would especially like to thank Danielle Kessie, who provided invaluable support with numerous aspects of this project, including help with exercises, locating material, and general editing, as well as the creation of the audio script and index. Thanks also to Shu Ying Poon for her work with the character audio script and final proofing.

I am indebted as well to the many people at Routledge for guiding me though the process of this edition, especially Samantha Vale Noya and Sarah Mabley. They showed great patience and professionalism at all stages of the project.

Lastly, I would like to thank my wife, Kathryn, for her constant support in this and all endeavors.

# Introduction

## Cantonese: language or dialect?

The "Chinese language" is extremely diverse, yet the speakers of the different varieties of Chinese do not regard themselves as members of different linguistic communities. All the varieties of Chinese look toward a common "standard" model, fundamentally the linguistic standards of the written language. In modern China, linguistic standards for speech have been based on the pronunciation of the capital, Beijing, and the national language of the People's Republic of China is called Putonghua, "the common language," or Mandarin. Cantonese is that variety of Chinese that is spoken in wide areas of the southern coastal provinces of Guangdong (capital Guangzhou, or Canton) and Guangxi (capital Nanning), and in some neighboring places such as Hong Kong and Macao, as well as in numerous places in Southeast Asia outside China proper, such as Cambodia, Indonesia, Malaysia, Singapore, Thailand, and Vietnam. The latter half of the twentieth century witnessed a great deal of accelerated emigration of Cantonese speakers, notably to Australia, Canada, New Zealand, the United Kingdom, and the United States, and Cantonese is the dominant form of Chinese spoken in many families of the "chinatowns" of the major cities in these countries. Indeed, in the United States, many of the early Chinese immigrants also trace their ancestry not only to Guangdong Province, but to one particular rural district, Taishan (about ninety kilometers southwest of Guangzhou), whose accessible harbor was used by American ships which came to recruit cheap labor along the Chinese coast in the middle of the nineteenth century.

Traditionally, Cantonese has been considered a "dialect" of Chinese. However, this term is misleading, and tends to have more socio-political than linguistic significance. Over the four thousand and more years of the history of Chinese, the language has developed in different ways in the various regions of China. In particular, the regional varieties of the language that have emerged have been marked by their individual sound systems. Many of the varieties of modern Chinese are mutually incomprehensible when spoken, yet because of the uniformity of the written characters of the language, communication can often be effected successfully through the medium of writing. The situation, generalized throughout the language, is similar to, say, a Spanish speaker not understanding an English speaker saying the word "five," yet comprehending fully the written figure "5."

Some varieties of Chinese—like some varieties of English—enjoy more prestige in the language community than others. Ever since the Ming dynasty (1368–1644), by which time the Pearl River delta had become an important economic and cultural center, the Cantonese of Guangzhou has been an important variety of Chinese, and even the medium for an extensive vernacular literature, including ballads, epic poetry, and some fiction writing. Although these styles are regarded as rustic by purists, their popularity has given rise to the generation of special written forms for Cantonese colloquialisms. Indeed, Cantonese is the only variety of Chinese (besides Mandarin) with widely recognized non-traditional written characters for such colloquial words and expressions. Such "dialect writing" is disapproved of in the People's Republic of China, but is kept alive in the Cantonese press and other publications in Hong Kong and elsewhere. Many of the non-traditional characters of Cantonese are known throughout China—at least in the urban areas. In the north the use of Cantonese colloquialisms, because of the association of this variety of Chinese with the West, through Hong Kong, adds a touch of exoticism or raciness to one's speech.

Cantonese is thus more than simply a dialect. It is a regional standard, with a national and an international prestige and currency not enjoyed by any other variety of Chinese, except Mandarin. In spite of the special written characters that have emerged, Cantonese remains essentially a spoken language, with no universally recognized written form. The language has several geographical dialects, distinguished largely by their phonological characteristics, but the "Colloquial Cantonese" used in this book would be accepted by native speakers as a standard form of the language, as spoken in Hong Kong. Within this standard, there are levels of formality and informality in expression. We have aimed for a neutral style in speech, appropriate to a wide range of social and professional situations. In one or two instances, where the formal–informal distinction is significant, for example where the use of particular words in public broadcasting differs from the corresponding words that would be used in conversation, this has been pointed out.

## Cantonese grammar

From several points of view, the grammar of Cantonese is extremely straightforward. Verbs do not conjugate for person or number, nor are there different forms for tense, mood, or voice. Nouns and adjectives do not decline, and have no number, gender, or case. There is no subject-verb or adjective-noun agreement. In short, Cantonese is free of the challenges with which learners of European languages are so familiar.

However, superficial simplicity of form does not mean that there is any less functional capability in the language. One can say in Cantonese anything that one would wish to say in English, or any other language; but the relationships between words and meanings that are made formally in English by, for example, inflection or agreements are expressed in different ways in Cantonese. Word order is especially important, and subject to more rigid regulation than in English. Cantonese also possesses a series of "classifiers," which identify objects largely by shape, and a rich repertoire of "particles" which are used to express mood, emotion, attitude, etc. There are many multifunctional words, which can act as nouns, adjectives, or verbs, depending upon the context (compare the various functions a word such as "right" has in English); indeed, even the formal distinction between nouns, verbs, and adjectives in Cantonese is often extremely blurred.

The varieties of Chinese show a great deal of syntactic uniformity. Yet there do exist some significant differences amongst them. Cantonese and Mandarin, for example, differ in word order in certain constructions. In Cantonese the direct object precedes the indirect object, whereas the opposite obtains in Mandarin:

| | |
|---|---|
| Cantonese: | **béi syū ngóh** |
| | give + book + (to) me |
| Mandarin: | **géi wô shū** |
| | give + (to) me + book. |

Certain adverbs (such as **sīn** "first") which precede the verb in Mandarin follow the verb in Cantonese (as in **heui sīn** "go first" vs. Mandarin **xiān qù** "first go"). Often the differences are more subtle: a Mandarin sentence pattern in Cantonese will sometimes be understood by native Cantonese speakers, but will nevertheless not be accepted as truly idiomatic. Conversely, colloquial Cantonese has a number of patterns that would not be linguistically acceptable in Mandarin.

## Cantonese vocabulary

Cantonese, like all varieties of Chinese, is generally considered to be monosyllabic: almost every syllable carries meaning. Although there are many monosyllabic words (words of one syllable), it is by no means true that every word is made up of one syllable: there are many words which are made up of two, or three, syllables, such as:

| | |
|---|---|
| **sáubīu** | wristwatch |
| **syutgwaih** | refrigerator |
| **fēigēichèuhng** | airport |
| **láahngheigēi** | air conditioner |

Whereas syllables in English are often individually meaningless (e.g. "*syl-la-ble*," "*car-ries*"), syllables in Cantonese are largely individually meaningful:

| | |
|---|---|
| **sáubīu** | **sáu** = "hand" + **bīu** = "watch" |
| **syutgwaih** | **syut** = "snow" + **gwaih** = "cupboard" |

This is not always the case, and Cantonese has examples of "bound" syllables, which carry meaning or express function only when they occur with other syllables, but these forms are often the result of foreign borrowing:

| | |
|---|---|
| **bōlēi** | glass |
| **pùihwùih** | to linger |

Neither **bō** nor **lēi** nor **pùih** nor **wùih** carries any meaning apart from in these combinations. Similar examples in English are "cranberry" or "kith and kin." The syllables "cran-" and "kith" have no individual meanings—that is, they cannot occur meaningfully alone—but they do have meaning when they occur with "-berry" and "and kin" respectively.

While most Cantonese vocabulary is the same as other varieties of Chinese, in some cases words that are common in everyday Cantonese are seen as archaic and literary in Mandarin, for example:

| | |
|---|---|
| **mihn** | face |
| **hàahng** | walk |
| **sihk** | eat |
| **wah** | say |

There are also examples where the meanings of words differ or are even reversed in Cantonese and Mandarin. The word for "house" in in Cantonese, **ūk** (Mandarin **wū**), typically means "room" in Mandarin. Conversely, Cantonese **fòhng** (Mandarin **fáng**), that ordinarily means "room" in Cantonese, refers to "house" in Mandarin.

At the same time, in recent history, Cantonese has, because of its socio-cultural contacts, borrowed a large number of words from other languages, especially English:

| | |
|---|---|
| **jyūgūlīk** | chocolate |
| **nèihlùhng** | nylon |
| **wàihtāmihng** | vitamin |
| **wāisihgéi** | whisky |

## The sound system of Cantonese

The romanization adopted in this book, and in *Cantonese: A Comprehensive Grammar*, also published by Routledge, is the Yale system, which is a widely used and convenient learning tool. Note, however, that this is not the system generally found in official transliterations of personal and place names, where there has been little standardization over the centuries.

Below we list the various sounds of Cantonese, as they are transcribed in the Yale romanization. Two terms may need explanation:

"aspirated" and "unreleased." Aspirated consonants are pronounced with a puff of air, as in English "p" in "pan" and "lip." In some cases, such as, in English, after "s" ("span," "spill"), the same consonants lose the puff of air and are unaspirated. At the end of a word they may not even be completed: the lips close to form the sound but do not open again to make the sound "explode"; such sounds are termed "unreleased."

A more elaborate description of the Cantonese phonological system can be found in *Cantonese: A Comprehensive Grammar*.

##  Consonants (CD1; 2)

**b** resembles the (unaspirated) "p" in "span," "spill"; to an unaccustomed ear, an initial unaspirated *p* can often sound like "b" in "bill."

**d** resembles the (unaspirated) "t" in "stand," "still."

**g** resembles the (unaspirated) "c" in "scan," and "k" in "skill."

**gw** resembles the "qu" in "squad," "square." There is some evidence that this sound is becoming simplified over time, and words transcribed with **gw-** in this book may actually be heard, in the speech of some native speakers, as beginning with **g-**. As a learner, you are advised to follow the pronunciation of the transcription.

**j** an unaspirated sound something between "ts" in "cats" and "tch" in "catch."

**p** in initial position resembles the (aspirated) "p" in "pat," "pin"; in final position, that is, at the end of a syllable, "p" is unreleased.

**t** in initial position resembles the (aspirated) "t" in "top," "tin"; in final position, "t" is unreleased.

**k** in initial position resembles the "k" in "kick," "kill"; in final position, "k" is unreleased.

**kw** a strongly aspirated plosive, resembles the "qu" in "quick," "quill."

**ch** resembles the (aspirated) "ch" in "cheese," "chill."

**f** resembles the "f" in "fan," "scarf."

**s** resembles the "s" in "sing," "sit."

**h** (only in initial position in the syllable) resembles the "h" in "how," "hand." (Where it appears later in the syllable, "h" is explained under Tone, below.)

l   resembles the "l" in "like," "love."
m   resembles the "m" in "man," "stem."
n   resembles the "n" in "now," "nice." There is a widespread tendency, particularly amongst the younger generation of Cantonese speakers, to replace an initial **n** by **l**, and there is consequently some variation in pronunciation: many words which are transcribed with an initial letter *n* in this book may be heard as beginning with *l*, for instance **néih** "you," may be heard as **léih**. As a learner, you are advised to follow the pronunciation of the transcription.
ng  resembles the southern British English pronunciation of "ng" as in "sing" (that is, without pronouncing the "g" separately). This sound occurs only after vowels in English, but in Cantonese it can also occur at the beginning of syllables. However, many native speakers do not pronounce this sound initially. And, just as in English, a final **-ng**, particularly after the long vowel **aa**, is often replaced by **-n**, although this variation does not have the social connotation it has in British English (cf. "runnin' and jumpin' ").
y   resembles the "y" in "yes," "yellow."
w   resembles the "w" in "wish," "will."

## Vowels (CD1; 3)

a   resembles the "u" in the southern British English pronunciation of "but."
aa  resembles the southern British English "a" in "father." When this sound is not followed by a consonant in the same syllable, the second **a** of the **aa** is omitted in writing: **fā** is pronounced as if it were "faa."
e   resembles the "e" of "ten."
eu  resembles the French "eu" as in "feu," or the German "ö" as in "schön." It is pronounced like the "e" of "ten," but with rounded lips.
i   resembles the "ee" of "deep."
o   resembles the "aw" in "saw."
u   resembles the "u" in the southern British English "put."
yu  resembles the French "u" as in "tu," or the German "ü" as in "Tür." It is pronounced like the "ee" of "deep," but with the lips rounded instead of spread.

## Diphthongs (CD1; 4)

The diphthongs consist of the vowels in different combinations:

- **ai**   **a** + **i**, a combination of "a" plus "i," a very short diphthong, much shorter than the sound of "y" in "my."
- **aai**   **aa** + **i**, resembling the "ie" in "lie."
- **au**   **a** + **u**, resembling the "ou" in "out."
- **aau**   **aa** + **u**, resembling a long "ou" in "ouch!"
- **eui**   **eu** + **i**, a combination of "eu" plus "i," something like the hesitation form "er" in English (without the "r" sound) followed by "ee": "e(r)-ee."
- **iu**   **i** + **u**, a combination of "i" plus "u," something like "yew" in English.
- **oi**   **o** + **i**, resembling the "oy" in "boy."
- **ou**   **o** + **u**, resembling the "oe" in "foe."
- **ui**   **u** + **i**, resembling the "ooey" in "phooey."

## Tone (CD1; 11)

Cantonese is a *tone language*. This means that the same syllable pronounced on different pitches, or with different voice contours, carries different meanings. Consider first an example from English. To agree with someone, you might say simply, "Yes." The voice tends to fall, from a mid-level to a low pitch. If, however, the answer "Yes" to a question is unexpected, you may repeat it as a question: "Yes?" meaning: "Did you really say 'yes'?" The voice tends to rise from a mid-level to a high pitch, the span of the rise depending upon the amount of surprise you want to convey. A further example might be the answer "Yes!" as an exclamation, to show surprise or amazement, with the voice tending to fall from a high to a mid-level pitch, again with the span of the fall depending on the intensity of the exclamation. These instances demonstrate that, in English, syllables can be pronounced on different pitches and with different voice contours to express different attitudes. The fundamental meaning of the syllable remains the same; "yes" means "yes" whatever the pitch. However, the variations in pitch indicate whether "yes" is a statement "yes," a questioning "yes?," an exclamatory "yes!," etc. In English the combinations of the sounds in individual words carry the formal meanings of the words, that is, what the words *denote*. The pitch, or intonation, variations indicate the speaker's attitudes or emotions, that is, what the words *connote*.

Another example: if you asked, in English, "What day is it today?" the answer might be "Monday." Normally, this would be said with the voice falling from mid-level to a lower level. Such an intonation contour indicates a plain statement of fact in English. If the answer were to be given with a rise at the end, it might be interpreted as insecurity on the part of the speaker ("[I'm not sure. Is it] Monday?"), or perhaps not even understood. On the other hand, a strongly stressed first syllable with a high pitch, followed by an unstressed second syllable on a lower pitch ("*Mon*day!") might indicate the speaker's surprise at being asked the question at all, perhaps expressing something like "Don't you know it's Monday?" The differences in pitch contours indicate differences in the speaker's attitude, the *connotation* of the answer. However, in Cantonese, a similar question **Gāmyaht sīngkèih géi?** "What day is it today?" might be answered **Sīngkèih yāt**, with the first syllable high, the second syllable a low fall and the third syllable high. This would mean, "Monday." With one change, from a relatively high pitch to a lower level pitch on the last syllable, **Sīngkèih yaht**, the meaning becomes "Sunday"! The pitch, or tone, variation, indicates a change in the *denotation* of the word: it means something different—in this case, a different day of the week. Every syllable has to be said on a particular pitch for it to carry meaning, and the same syllable said on a different pitch has a different *denotational* meaning.

*Connotation*, which in English is conveyed by pitch variation in the voice, is often indicated in Cantonese by individual syllables, usually particles which occur at the end of the sentence, such as **gwa** or **lō**, as in the Cantonese equivalents to the answers discussed above:

**Sīngkèih yāt gwa**  = I'm not sure. Is it Monday?
**Sīngkèih yāt lō**   = *Mon*day! I'm surprised you asked me.

How many tones are there in Cantonese? Analyses vary: some say six, some seven, some even nine. In this book, we distinguish six tones, not simply because this is the minimum with which to operate comprehensibly and successfully in Cantonese, but because further distinctions actually depend on fine theoretical linguistic arguments.

Native Cantonese speakers appear nowadays to be confining themselves to these six definitive pitch differentiations in their speech, with any minor tonal variations beyond these certainly not being significant from the point of view of someone beginning an acquaintance with the language.

Actual pitch does not matter—everyone's voice is different in any case—but relative pitch is important. There are three levels of tones: *high*, *mid*, and *low*, and as long as a distinction is made from one level to another, comprehensibility is enhanced.

The *mid* level is the normal level of one's voice in conversation, and is the point of reference for the other levels.

The *high* level is a pitch somewhat higher than the mid level.

The *low* level is a pitch somewhat lower than the mid level.

Cantonese has words which are distinguished by pitch at each level, such as:

| | | |
|---|---|---|
| (high) | **mā** | mother |
| (mid) | **ma** | *question particle* |
| (low) | **mah** | to scold |
| (high) | **sī** | poetry |
| (mid) | **si** | to try |
| (low) | **sih** | a matter |

It is important to note the transcription adopted here. A macron (ˉ) is used to indicate a high-level tone (**mā, sī**). The absence of any such diacritic indicates a mid-level tone (**ma, si**) or a low-level tone (**mah, sih**), with the latter having an **h** following the vowel to indicate the low-level tone. The letter **h** is pronounced as in "how" or "hand" *only* when it occurs in initial position in the syllable; elsewhere it is merely a marker of low-level tone, and is not pronounced separately.

In addition to words said on a fixed level—high, mid, or low—there are three tone combinations: two rising, and one falling. For some speakers of Cantonese there is a second falling tone, the high falling, which is merged with the high level in most speakers.

The *high rising* tone is a rise from mid to high, rather like asking a question on one word in English: "Monday?"

The *low rising* tone is a rise from low to mid, again like asking a question, but rather suspiciously.

The *low falling* tone is a fall from mid to low, somewhat like an ordinary statement in English.

Note the transcription: an acute accent mark (´) is used for a rising tone, and a grave accent mark (`) is used for a falling tone. Again, remember that the letter **h**, when not in initial position, indicates low level.

Look at the following lists of words, in which the pairs are contrasted by tone only. Try to ensure that you make the tonal distinctions between each pair of words. Return to this exercise often, so as to practice these differences—they *are* important!

| High level | **tāu** (to steal)<br>**sīng** (star)<br>**tōng** (soup)<br>**chīm** (to sign) | Low falling | **tàuh** (head)<br>**sìhng** (city)<br>**tòhng** (sugar)<br>**chìhm** (to dive under water) |
|---|---|---|---|
| High level | **dāng** (lamp)<br>**fān** (to divide)<br>**jēui** (to chase)<br>**gām** (gold) | Mid level | **dang** (chair)<br>**fan** (to sleep)<br>**jeui** (drunk)<br>**gam** (to ban) |
| Mid level | **gin** (to see)<br>**si** (to try)<br>**seun** (letter)<br>**yim** (to loathe) | Low level | **gihn** (*classifier for* clothes)<br>**sih** (a matter)<br>**seuhn** (smooth)<br>**yihm** (to test) |
| High rising | **séui** (water)<br>**sáu** (hand)<br>**dím** (a point)<br>**séi** (to die) | Mid level | **seui** (years of age)<br>**sau** (thin)<br>**dim** (shop)<br>**sei** (four) |

For further information on tone see Appendix, p. 292.

## Comparison to the Mandarin tone system

In comparison to Mandarin, the Cantonese tone system is more complex and more closely reflects the system of earlier historical periods of Chinese. Although the tone values differ, there exists a mostly predictable correlation between the tone categories. Note that coming from Mandarin, one can often only narrow the possibilities to one of two Cantonese tones.

| Mandarin | Cantonese |
|---|---|
| first tone (high-level tone) | high level, high falling |
| second tone (high-rising tone) | low falling |
| third tone (dipping tone) | low rising |
| | high rising |
| fourth tone (falling tone) | mid level, low level |

Also, note that when a Cantonese word ends with **-p**, **-t**, or **-k** (the historical entering tone or 入聲 category) the correspondence is greatly complicated. In these cases, the table does not predict the correspondence. For example, the mid-level word 白 **baak** in Cantonese is a second tone (rising) in Mandarin.

## Using this book

This book is divided into fifteen units. Each unit has a similar format. At the head of each unit, you will find a short list of the objectives which the unit material aims to help you achieve.

The basic vocabulary of the unit is introduced in the *Vocabulary* sections. Look through the list of words. Read each item aloud, paying particular attention to the tone of every word. If you have the audio material, you can model your pronunciation on the recording.

The *Dialogues* are short, realistic exchanges preceded by questions. Read the questions, and then read or listen to each dialogue in order to find the answers to the questions. If you have the audio recordings, listen to the dialogues and answer the questions before reading the texts. It is not necessary to understand every word of the dialogue to be able to answer these questions. At this stage, just concentrate on answering the questions, and do not worry about the rest. As the units progress, material presented in earlier units is recycled, for consolidation.

The *Idioms and structures* sections give explanations of the idiomatic expressions used in the dialogues, as well as comprehensive usage notes, covering all the grammatical constructions introduced. Review these sections carefully, referring to the dialogues for the examples of usages.

You will find a series of *Exercises* to give you practice in using the vocabulary and structures introduced in the unit. You will also find a selection of *Communicative activities* toward the end of each unit. These are intended as extension exercises to allow you to put your newly acquired language skills into practice with the help of a partner or Cantonese-speaking friend.

Each unit ends with some related Chinese characters for recognition purposes, followed by a *Cultural point* section to provide a sense of the rich environment in which Cantonese is spoken, especially Hong Kong.

## Special conventions of the Yale transcription

1 The tone mark on a diphthong always falls on the first written vowel, e.g. **yáuh, móuh**, but the tone is a characteristic of the diphthong as a whole.

2 In the syllable **ńgh**, which has no vowel letters, the tone mark is written over the **g**, but the tone is characteristic of the whole syllable.

3 When **aa** is *not* followed by a consonant in the same syllable, the second **a** is dropped from the written form. Thus, **fā**, for example, is pronounced as if it were **faa**.

## Conventions used in this book

1 The apostrophe is used to indicate elision of numerals, as in **y'ah** (the elided form of **yih-sahp**), **sā'ah** (the elided form of **sāam-sahp**), etc. See Unit 5, p. 86.

2 The hyphen is used to indicate:

   (a) numbers above ten, e.g. **ńgh-sahp, sei-baak** (see Unit 2, p. 33);
   (b) verb-object constructions, e.g. **tái-syū, dá-dihnwá** (see Unit 3, p. 47);

(c) reduplicated forms of nouns and adjectives, e.g. **fèih-féi-déi, gōu-gōu-sau-sau** (see Unit 5, p. 80);
(d) comparative adjectives, e.g. **fèih-dī, gwai-dī** (see Unit 6, pp. 82 and 103);
(e) verbs with special markers, e.g. **sihk-jó faahn, cheung-gán gō** (see Unit 6, pp. 100 and 137);
(f) days of the week and months, e.g. **sīngkèih-yāt, gáu-yuht** (see Units 3 and 12, pp. 52 and 194).

3 The negative prefix for verbs, **m-**, becomes **-mh-** in choice-type questions (see Unit 1, p. 21), e.g. **mhaih/haih-mh-haih, msái/sái-mh-sái**. No tone mark is used on **m-** or **-mh-**, but the syllable is always pronounced on the low falling tone.

4 The asterisk is used to indicate sentences or structures that are not grammatically correct, but are for illustration only.

# Unit One
# Gāaujai

Meeting people

### In Unit 1 you will learn about:

- introducing yourself and others
- greeting people
- enquiring about someone
- the verbs "to be" and "can"
- forming negative statements
- forming choice-type questions and questions with question-words
- naming conventions, names of countries, languages, and nationalities

## Dialogue 1

**(CD1; 12)**

John and Carmen are at a gathering of the Cantonese Students' Club, where foreigners learning Cantonese meet and practice their Cantonese. Carmen is talking to Richard.

(a) What country does Carmen come from?
(b) What country does Richard come from?

| | |
|---|---|
| CARMEN: | Néih hóu, ngóh haih Carmen. |
| RICHARD: | Néih hóu, Carmen. Ngóh haih Richard. Carmen, néih haih bīndouh yàhn a? |
| CARMEN: | Ngóh haih Náusāilàahn yàhn. |
| RICHARD: | O, néih haih Náusāilàahn yàhn. |
| CARMEN: | Gám néih nē, Richard? |
| RICHARD: | Ngóh haih Méihgwok yàhn. |

| | |
|---|---|
| CARMEN: | How are you? I am Carmen. |
| RICHARD: | How are you, Carmen? I am Richard. Where are you from? |
| CARMEN: | I am a New Zealander. |
| RICHARD: | Oh, you are a New Zealander. |
| CARMEN: | And how about you, Richard? |
| RICHARD: | I am an American. |

## Dialogue 2

**(CD1; 14)**

John is talking to Emily.

(a) Where does John come from?
(b) What languages does he speak?
(c) Where does Emily come from?
(d) What languages does she speak?

| | |
|---|---|
| JOHN: | Néih hóu. Ngóh giujouh John. Néih giu mātyéh méng a? |
| EMILY: | Néih hóu. Ngóh giujouh Emily. Haih nē, John, néih haih-mh-haih Yīnggwok yàhn a? |

Unit 1: *Meeting people*

JOHN: Mhaih. Ngóh haih Oujāu yàhn. Ngóh sīk góng Yīngmán tùhng Dākmán.
EMILY: Ngóh haih Gānàhdaaih yàhn. Ngóh sīk góng Yīngmán tùhng síusíu Faatmán.

---

JOHN: How are you? My name is John. What is your name?
EMILY: How are you? My name is Emily. By the way, John, you are English, right?
JOHN: No, I am Australian. I speak English and German.
EMILY: I am Canadian. I speak English and a little French.

## Dialogue 3

**(CD1; 16)**
Carmen is introducing her friend Grace to John.

(a) Where does Grace come from?
(b) What languages can she speak?

---

CARMEN: Dáng ngóh lèih gaaisiuh. Nīgo haih Grace. Nī go haih John.
GRACE: Néih hóu, John.
JOHN: Néih hóu, Grace.
CARMEN: Grace haih Yahtbún yàhn. Kéuih sīk góng Yahtmán, Yīngmán tùhng Póutūngwá.
JOHN: Ngóh tùhng Carmen sīk góng síusíu Gwóngdōngwá, bātgwo ngóhdeih msīk góng Póutūngwá. Haih nē, chéhng mahn Grace néih gwai sing a?
GRACE: Ngóh sing Sawada.

---

CARMEN: Let me make an introduction. This is Grace. This is John.
GRACE: How are you, John?
JOHN: How are you, Grace?
CARMEN: Grace is Japanese. She speaks Japanese, English, and Mandarin.
JOHN: Carmen and I speak a little Cantonese, but not Mandarin. By the way, Grace, what is your surname?
GRACE: My surname is Sawada.

## Vocabulary

### Countries (CD1; 18)

Below is a list of some of the countries in the world. Try reading each item aloud. Practice pronouncing each word, using the audio recording if available.

| | | | |
|---|---|---|---|
| **Yīnggwok** | Britain, the UK | **Fēileuhtbān** | the Philippines |
| **Méihgwok** | the U.S. | **Yahtbún** | Japan |
| **Gānàhdaaih** | Canada | **Hòhngwok** | Korea |
| **Oujāu** | Australia | **Yandouh** | India |
| **Náusāilàahn** | New Zealand | **Bāgēisītáan** | Pakistan |
| **Faatgwok** | France | Of course, we must not forget: | |
| **Dākgwok** | Germany | **Hēunggóng** | Hong Kong |
| **Yidaaihleih** | Italy | **Jūnggwok** | China |
| **Sāibāanngàh** | Spain | | |

**Gwok** literally means "country." Hence **Yīng*gwok*** is "Britain," and **Faat*gwok*** is "France," **Dāk*gwok*** is "Germany," etc. The Cantonese names for some other countries are rough phonetic equivalents, for example: **Gānàhdaaih** for "Canada," **Náusāilàahn** for "New Zealand," **Yandouh** for "India," and **Bāgēisītáan** for "Pakistan." Sometimes the transliteration is based on the Mandarin readings of the Chinese characters and so is less obvious still.

To refer to the inhabitants of different countries, the word **yàhn**, which literally means "person(s)," is added to the name of a country. For example, a "Briton" is **Yīnggwok yàhn**, an "Australian" is **Oujāu yàhn**, "Indians" are **Yandouh yàhn**, and "Chinese" are **Jūnggwok yàhn**.

Now try reading out the list of countries again, but this time for each item add the word **yàhn** to the name of the country.

### Languages (CD1; 19)

| | | | |
|---|---|---|---|
| **Yīngmán** | English | **Yidaaihleihmán** | Italian |
| **Faatmán** | French | **Yahtmán** | Japanese |
| **Dākmán** | German | **Hòhnmán** | Korean |

> **Mán, wá, and yúh**
>
> **Mán** means "language," which usually implies both the spoken and written forms. There is another word in Cantonese, **wá**, which refers only to the spoken form of a language. Thus, for the languages spoken by Filipinos, Indians, and Pakistanis, which Cantonese-speaking people may hear being used but will probably never learn to read or write, **wá** is used instead. Hence, they use the vague term **Fēileuhtbānwá** for all languages spoken by Filipinos including Tagalog, **Yandouhwá** for all languages spoken by Indians, and **Bāgēisītáanwá** for all languages spoken by Pakistanis.
>
> Lastly, **yúh** is used for language as well but in a more general and more formal way. Note that with **Gwokyúh** below you cannot substitute **wá** or **mán** for **yúh**, but for national languages you often can. For example, **Faatyúh** for **Faatmán** "French" and **Yīngyúh** for **Yīngmán** "English."

**Jūngmán** refers to Chinese in general, including written Chinese and a spoken form of it, while **wá** refers to individual varieties or dialects spoken in different parts of China. Although technically **Jūngmán** refers to the written form of the language, it is widely used to refer to the language as a whole. Hence:

| | |
|---|---|
| **Gwóngdūngwá/** | Cantonese |
| **Gwóngjāuwá** | |
| **Seuhnghóiwá** | Shanghainese |
| **Chìuhjāuwá** | The Chiu Chow dialect |
| **Póutūngwá** | Putonghua (lit. "the common language"), Standard Mandarin |
| **Gwokyúh** | Standard Mandarin (lit. "the national language") |
| **Wàh gúh** | Standard Mandarin (outside of Greater China) |

# Idioms and structures

The items in the list below appear in the dialogues above. The *italicized* items are *new* items. In the notes, numbers in brackets refer to the expressions listed below.

| | | |
|---|---|---|
| 1 | *Néih hóu* | *How are you?* |
| 2 | *Ngóh haih* **Carmen** | *I am* Carmen. |
| 3 | *Néih haih bīndouh yàhn a?* | *Where are you from?* |
| 4 | *Ngóh giujouh* **John.** | *My name is* John.<br>(lit. "I am called John.") |
| 5 | *Néih giu mātyéh méng a?* | *What is your name?* |
| 6 | *Gám, néih nē?* | *So, what about you?* |
| 7 | *Haih nē,* | *By the way,* |
| 8 | *Néih haih-mh-haih* **Yīnggwok** *yàhn a?* | *Are you* British? |
| 9 | *Mhaih.* | *No, I'm not.* |
| 10 | *Ngóh sīk góng ...* | *I can speak ...* |
| 11 | *Yīngmán tùhng* **Dākmán** | *English and* German |
| 12 | *síusíu* **Faatmán** | *a little* French |
| 13 | *Dáng ngóh lèih gaaisiuh.* | *Let me introduce you.* |
| 14 | *Nī go haih* **Grace.** | *This is* Grace. |
| 15 | *bātgwo* | *but* |
| 16 | *chéhng mahn* **Grace** *néih gwai sing a?* | Grace, *may I know what your surname is?* |

## Greetings (1)

**Néih hóu** is a slightly formal greeting expression, which is used at all times of the day and which can be translated into "How are you?" in English, except that it is not a question and the usual response is the same: **Néih hóu**. In practice, it is more akin to saying "hello."

## Haih (2)

The verb **haih** is a copula in Cantonese, meaning it is used to equate (A=B). For example, He **is** Chinese. Note that, unlike the English "to be," **haih** is not a state verb and is not used with adjectivals. For example, the English "She is tall" is rendered **Kéuih gōu** (lit. "s/he tall").

## Questions with question-words (3, 5)

Like "wh" questions in English (why, where, who, etc.), many questions in Cantonese are formed with a question-word. However, the question-word in Cantonese is not put at the beginning of the sentence like the question-word in English, but occupies the position taken by the required information in the answer. Thus, the word order in a Cantonese question is essentially the same as that of a statement. For example, to ask where someone is from you use the question-word **bīndouh** "where" and say: **Néih haih *bīndouh* yàhn a?**, which literally means "You are where person?" The answer **Ngóh haih Náusāilàahn yàhn** literally means "I am New Zealand person." To ask someone their name you use the question-word **mātyéh** "what" and say: **Néih giu *mātyéh* méng a?**, which means "You are called by what name?," and the answer **Ngóh giujouh Emily** means "I am called Emily."

## Nē (6)

**Nē** is a final particle used to ask how the topic at hand relates to a certain subject. So if we were discussing what languages people speak, then **neih nē?** would mean "and what languages do you speak?" Alternatively, if we were asking how people are doing, then **Neih nē?** would mean "And how are you doing?" or "And you?" Put another way, it is like saying "Regarding the topic at hand, how do you relate to it?"

## Choice-type questions (8)

**Néih haih-mh-haih Yīnggwok yàhn a?** is a "choice-type" question, which is a common structure in Cantonese for "yes/no" questions. The question here literally means "Are you or are you not British?" The positive answer to the question is **Ngóh haih Yīnggwok yàhn** or **Haih** for short. The negative answer is **Ngóh mhaih Yīnggwok yàhn** or **Mhaih** for short.

Choice-type questions are formed by reduplicating the verbal form and inserting the negative prefix **m-** in the middle. (In the romanization used here the **m-** is written as **-mh-** in these types of structures.) In the choice-type question **Néih haih-mh-haih Yīnggwok yàhn a?**, the verb "to be," **haih**, is repeated. In the choice-type question **Néih sīk-mh-sīk góng Faatmán a?**, "Can you speak French?," the modal verb **sīk**, "can, know how to," is repeated.

## Negatives (9)

Negatives in Cantonese are often formed by inserting the negative prefix **mh** before a verb or an adjective. For example, **Ngóh haih Jūnggwok yàhn** means "I am Chinese" while **Ngoh mhaih Jūnggwok yàhn** means "I am *not* Chinese."

## Classifiers for people (14)

**Nī wái** is an honorific and polite way of referring to a person. Here **Nī go haih Grace** "this is Grace" would do if Grace is a peer student, for example. **Nī wái** is more polite than **Nī go** and as such would be the classifier to persons to whom you want to pay special respect. One normally never uses the classifier **wái** to refer to oneself, as it is a marker of respect to other people.

## Introducing by surname (16)

To ask for someone's surname, the rather formal expression **néih gwai sing a?** is used. **Sing** is a verb, which means "to be surnamed," while **gwai** is an adverb meaning "honorable." So **néih gwai sing a?** translates into English as "What is your honorable surname?" The respectful expression **chéhng mahn** further heightens the degree of formality. Note that, because **gwai** is an honorific form, it is never applied to one's own surname. Moreover, because **gwai sing** always refers to others, it becomes by default a question, even without a question particle at the end.

On formal occasions, it is very common for Chinese people to introduce themselves by surname, such as:

**Ngóh sing Léih.**   My (sur)name is Lee.

This situation nearly always would call for a response with a title such as *sīnsāang* "Mr."

**Léih *sīnsāang*, néih hóu.**   How are you, Mr. Lee?

Unit 1: *Meeting people* 23

Alternatively, the word **síu** "small, insignificant" is sometimes added to **sing** when referring to one's own surname to be especially polite, as in **Ngoh síu sing Léih**. Politeness would also dictate that you would never use **síu sing** when referring to another person. When introducing somebody else on a formal occasion, you may choose to do so on a last-name basis. In such a circumstance you do not use the verb **sing**, but instead introduce the person as Mr. X or Miss X:

**Nī wái haih Wòhng síujé.**    This is Miss Wong.

---

**Names in Cantonese**

Naming practices in Cantonese are complex, especially in Hong Kong Cantonese. Many, if not most, of the educated and professional classes in Hong Kong take English given names at some point, though they are given Chinese names at birth. It is common to use an English name even when speaking Cantonese. However, certain segments of society (the less educated and older people) are not as likely to use an English name even if they have one. When a person has a Chinese and an English name they will sometimes use both in formal situations such as authorship (for example, Jimmy LÀUH Gwok Sìhng).

Chinese names always take the form of surname first and given name second, though some people reverse that order when speaking English. For example, with the name **LÀUH Gwok Sìhng** that appears in Unit 4, Dialogue 2, **LÀUH** is the surname (or family name) and **Gwok Sìhng** is the given name. Brothers or sisters often share the same first character (in this case, **Gwok**). Note that using a Chinese person's given name alone is much more intimate than using an English given name. The functional equivalent of the English given name in Cantonese is the full name (for example, **LÀUH Gwok Sìhng**).

## Chéhng mahn (16)

**Chéhng mahn**, also pronounced **Chíng mahn**, is a polite and respectful way of prefacing a question, which can be translated as "Could I ask ... please?" in English, with **Chéhng** meaning "please" and **mahn** meaning "ask" by themselves. The expression can be freely added to a question to raise the level of politeness. For example, you can say **Chéhng mahn Touhsyugun hai bindouh a?** to ask directions to a library or **Chéhng mahn néih giu mātyéh méng a**? to ask somebody's name.

## Exercise 1 Comprehension

Read the following questions. Then go back to the three dialogues and find the answers. You can listen to the dialogues again if you have the audio recording.

(a) Who takes the initiative to greet the other person and then introduce himself or herself in Dialogue 1?

 (i) Carmen
 (ii) Richard

(b) What nationality does Emily presume John to be in Dialogue 2?

 (i) English
 (ii) Australian
 (iii) American

(c) How much French does Emily claim to speak in Dialogue 2?

 (i) A lot
 (ii) A little
 (iii) None

(d) According to Dialogue 3, do John and Carmen speak Putonghua?

 (i) Yes, both John and Carmen
 (ii) No, neither John nor Carmen
 (iii) Only John
 (iv) Only Carmen

## Exercise 2 Introducing yourself

Imagine you are at a social gathering. Provide the information asked for by completing the following conversation.

STRANGER: Néih hóu. Ngóh giujouh Sam, néih nē?
YOU:
STRANGER: Néih haih bīndouh yàhn a?
YOU:
STRANGER: Ngóh haih Oujāu yàhn. Haih nē, néih sīk-mh-sīk góng Póutūngwá a?
YOU:

## Exercise 3 Introducing others

Below is some information about six individuals. Imagine you have to introduce these people to some friends in Cantonese. Practice the language of introduction by yourself. The first one has been done for you. Then try introducing some of your real friends.

(a) *Name*: Jimmy Walkman
 *Nationality*: American
 *Languages spoken*: English, German

**Kéuih giujouh Jimmy Walkman. Kéuih haih Méihgwok yàhn. Kéuih sīk góng Yīngmán tùhng Dākmán.**

(b) *Name*: Pierre Gagnon
 *Nationality*: French
 *Languages spoken*: French, Spanish

**Kéuih giujouh Pierre Gagnon ...**

(c) *Name*: Paola Giannini
 *Nationality*: Italian
 *Languages spoken*: Italian, French, English

(d) *Name*: KIM Yoo Sung
 *Nationality*: Korean
 *Languages spoken*: Korean, Japanese, English

## Exercise 4 Information gathering

Read the two conversations in which four people introduce themselves saying where they come from and what languages they speak. Use the information you extract from the reading or listening to answer the questions that follow. You may find it useful to complete the table.

| RAUL: | Néih hóu, ngóh haih Raul. |
|---|---|
| JANE: | Néih hóu, ngóh giujouh Jane. |
| RAUL: | Ngóh haih Fēileuhtbān yàhn. Néih nē? |
| JANE: | Ngóh haih Oujāu yàhn. |
| RAUL: | Ngóh sīk góng Yīngmán, Sāibāanngàhmán tùhng Fēileuhtbānwá. Néih nē? |
| JANE: | Ngóh sīk góng sāam júng wá, Yīngmán, Faatmán tùhng síusíu Yidaaihleihmán. |

| BRUCE: | Néih giujouh mātyéh méng a? |
|---|---|
| ANTONIA: | Ngóh giujouh Antonia. Néih nē? |
| BRUCE: | Ngóh giujouh Bruce. Ngóh haih Méihgwok yàhn. |
| ANTONIA: | Ngóh haih Gānàhdaaih yàhn. Ngóh sīk góng Yīngmán, Faatmán tùhng Yidaaihleihmán. Néih nē? |
| BRUCE: | Ngóh sīk góng Yīngmán, Dākmán, Faatmán tùhng Sāibāanngàhmán. |

|  | *Nationality* | *Languages spoken* |
|---|---|---|
| Raul |  |  |
| Jane |  |  |
| Bruce |  |  |
| Antonia |  |  |

(a) How many different countries do the four people come from?
(b) How many different languages do they speak altogether?
(c) Who speaks the most languages?
(d) Which language is spoken by all four people?
(e) Which languages are spoken by *two* of the four people?
(f) Which languages are spoken by only *one* of the four people?

# Recognizing Chinese characters

| | |
|---|---|
| 英國人 | Briton, British |
| 美國人 | American |
| 法國人 | French |
| 德國人 | German |
| 韓國人 | Korean |
| 日本人 | Japanese |
| 印度人 | Indian |
| 菲律賓人 | Filipino |
| 巴基斯坦人 | Pakistani |
| 意大利人 | Italian |
| 西班牙人 | Spaniard, Spanish |
| 加拿大人 | Canadian |
| 澳大利亞人，澳洲人 | Australian |

The character

人

which appears in each item is pronounced **yàhn** and means "person," so a

英國人　　**(Yīnggwok yàhn)**

is a "British person," and a

日本人　　**(Yahtbún yàhn)**

is a "Japanese person." The character

國

which appears in the first five items is pronounced **gwok** and means "country," and so

法國　　**(Faatgwok)**

is "the country of France" while

韓國　　**(Hòhngwok)**

is "the country of Korea." The character

洲

is pronounced **jāu** and means "continent," and

澳洲　**(Oujāu)**

means "the continent of Australia." The remaining ones are all straight transliterations (i.e., the rendering is based on the sound of the source language) of the countries' names read in English. For example,

意大利

is pronounced **Yidaaihleih** and represents "Italy." (Note that the transliteration for Italy comes through the Mandarin **Yidali**, which is a closer match to the sound.)

## Communicative activities

> 1  Interview a Cantonese-speaking friend or study partner about his or her family and circle of acquaintances. Find out the name of each acquaintance and country of origin.
> 2  Do you have friends from other countries? If so, use your new language to describe that circle of friends. Where are they from exactly? What languages do they speak?

## Cultural point

### Chinese maps

See if you can find the names of the countries that you have learned on the following maps.

# Unit 1: *Meeting people*

Map of Asia

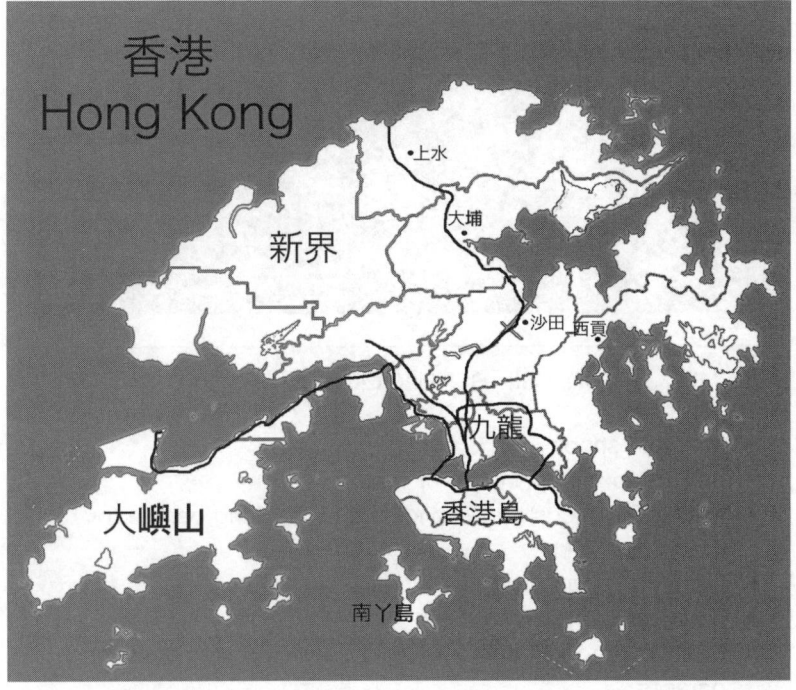

Map of Hong Kong

# Unit Two
# Máaih-yéh
## Shopping

### In Unit 2 you will learn about:

- prices in shops
- buying goods by weight or item
- asking for goods and services, and thanking people for them
- terms for payment and change
- personal pronouns
- forming simple statements, and questions with question phrases

Unit 2: *Shopping*

## Dialogue 1

**(CD1; 21)**
LAM Fong Ling is at a fruit-stall, asking the hawker about prices of fruit.

(a) What fruit did LAM Fong Ling buy?
(b) How many did she buy?
(c) How much did she pay for them?

| | |
|---|---|
| HAWKER: | Hóu leng ge sāanggwó. Máaih dī lā, síujé. |
| LAM FONG LING: | Dī mōnggwó dím maaih a? |
| HAWKER: | Dī mōnggwó ńgh mān yāt go. |
| LAM FONG LING: | Ngóh yiu sei go. |
| HAWKER: | Sei go mōnggwó, yih-sahp mān lā. |
| LAM FONG LING: | Nīdouh yih-sahp mān. |
| HAWKER: | Dōjeh. |
| LAM FONG LING: | Mhgōi. |

| | |
|---|---|
| HAWKER: | Very fresh fruit. Would you like to buy some, Miss? |
| LAM FONG LING: | How much for the mangoes? |
| HAWKER: | Mangoes are five dollars each. |
| LAM FONG LING: | I would like four. |
| HAWKER: | Four mangoes, that's 20 dollars. |
| LAM FONG LING: | Here is 20 dollars. |
| HAWKER: | Thank you. |
| LAM FONG LING: | Thank you. |

## Dialogue 2

**(CD1; 23)**
LAM Fong Ling's partner, John, is at a fruit-stall, talking to the hawker.

(a) What fruit did John buy?
(b) How many did he buy?
(c) How much did he pay for them?

| | |
|---|---|
| HAWKER: | Sīnsāang, máaih dī sāanggwó lā. |
| JOHN: | Dī cháang géidō chín yāt go a? |

| | |
|---|---|
| HAWKER: | Sahp mān sei go. |
| JOHN: | Mhgōi béi luhk go ā. |
| HAWKER: | Luhk go cháang, dōjeh sahp-ńgh mān. |
| JOHN: | Nī douh yih-sahp mān. |
| HAWKER: | Jáau fāan ńgh mān. Dōjeh. |
| JOHN: | Mhgōi. |

| | |
|---|---|
| HAWKER: | Sir, how about some fruit? |
| JOHN: | How much for each orange? |
| HAWKER: | Four for ten dollars. |
| JOHN: | Six please. |
| HAWKER: | Six oranges … 15 dollars please. |
| JOHN: | Here is 20 dollars. |
| HAWKER: | Your change is five dollars. Thank you. |
| JOHN: | Thanks. |

## Dialogue 3

**(CD1; 24)**
LAM Fong Ling is buying fruit from a hawker.

(a) What fruit did LAM Fong Ling buy?
(b) How much did she buy?
(c) How much did she pay for it?

| | |
|---|---|
| LAM FONG LING: | Tàihjí dím maaih a? |
| HAWKER: | Sahp-yih mān yāt bohng. |
| LAM FONG LING: | Jauh yiu yāt bohng lā. |
| HAWKER: | Yāt bohng tàihjí, dōjeh sahp-yih mān lā. |
| LAM FONG LING: | Nīdouh sahp-yih man. Mhgōi. |

| | |
|---|---|
| LAM FONG LING: | How much for the grapes? |
| HAWKER: | 20 dollars a pound. |
| LAM FONG LING: | I will take one pound then. |
| HAWKER: | One pound of grapes … 12 dollars please. |
| LAM FONG LING: | Here is 12 dollars. Thank you. |

Unit 2: *Shopping*

## Vocabulary

Below is a list of the fruit commonly found in a Hong Kong market. The list is followed by the cardinal numbers 1–100. Try reading each item aloud, paying special attention to the tones. Model your pronunciation on the audio recordings if available.

### Types of fruit (CD1; 26)

| | | | |
|---|---|---|---|
| sāanggwó | fruit | léi | pear |
| mōnggwó | mango | sāigwā | water-melon |
| cháang | orange | muhkgwā | papaya |
| pìhnggwó | apple | bōlòh | pineapple |
| hēungjīu | banana | laihjī | lychee |
| tàihjí | grape | kèihyihgwó | kiwifruit |
| boulām | plum | | |

### Numbers (CD1; 27–28)

| | | | | |
|---|---|---|---|---|
| yāt | 1 | yih-sahp | 20 |
| yih | 2 | yih-sahp yāt | 21 |
| sāam | 3 | yih-sahp yih | 22 |
| sei | 4 | yih-sahp sāam | 23 |
| ńgh | 5 | yih-sahp sei | 24 |
| luhk | 6 | yih-sahp ńgh | 25 |
| chāt | 7 | yih-sahp luhk | 26 |
| baat | 8 | yih-sahp chāt | 27 |
| gáu | 9 | yih-sahp baat | 28 |
| sahp | 10 | yih-sahp gáu | 29 |
| sahp-yāt | 11 | sāam-sahp | 30 |
| sahp-yih | 12 | sei-sahp | 40 |
| sahp-sāam | 13 | ńgh-sahp | 50 |
| sahp-sei | 14 | luhk-sahp | 60 |
| sahp-ńgh | 15 | chāt-sahp | 70 |
| sahp-luhk | 16 | baat-sahp | 80 |
| sahp-chāt | 17 | gáu-sahp | 90 |
| sahp-baat | 18 | yāt-baak | 100 |
| sahp-gáu | 19 | | |

Note that there are two forms of the word "two" in Cantonese. When "two" is used as a nominal number, such as in a room number or telephone number, **yih** is used. But when it is used as a measure or to indicate quantity, as in "two times" or "two pounds of bananas," then **léuhng** is used instead.

## Classifiers and measures

| | |
|---|---|
| yāt *go* cháang | an orange |
| yāt *dā* cháang | a dozen oranges |
| yāt *bohng* hēungjīu | a pound of bananas |
| yāt *mān* | one dollar |

In Cantonese, a noun is preceded by a classifier or a measure when it is preceded by a number or specifier (**nī** "this," or **go** "that"). For example, **bohng** is a measure meaning "pound," so **yāt bohng hēungjīu** means "one pound of bananas." (This is the imperial pound, in other words 454 g.) On the other hand, **go** is the classifier for oranges, so **yāt go cháang** means "an orange." There are many classifiers in Cantonese, the choice of which depends mainly on the shape, size, or function of the object referred to. For example, **go** is used for roundish objects such as oranges and apples, though its use also extends to other "objects" such as "people"—thus *yāt* **go yàhn** is "a person." **Tìuh** precedes nouns that are perceived as long and narrow in shape, such as **gāai** "street," *léngtāai* "necktie," or even **lùhng** "dragon." However, other long, narrow things such as pens and other writing implements take the classifier **jī**, while long things with handles (such as knives, swords, and umbrellas) take the classifier **bá**. In general, more specific classifiers take precedence over more broad ones. More classifiers will be introduced gradually with the nouns they accompany.

## Idioms and structures (CD1; 29)

The items in the list below appear in the same order as they do in the dialogues above. The *italicized* items are *new* items. In the notes, numbers in brackets refer to the expressions listed below.

Unit 2: *Shopping* 35

| | | |
|---|---|---|
| 1 | **hóu leng ge sāanggwó** | *very fresh fruit* |
| 2 | **máaih dī lā** | *please buy some* |
| 3 | **síujé** | *Miss* (a polite way of addressing a young woman) |
| 4 | **dī** **mōnggwó** | *the* mangoes |
| 5 | **dím maaih a?** | *what's the price?* |
| 6 | **ńgh mān yāt go** | *five dollars each* (lit. "five dollars one") |
| 7 | **Ngóh yiu sei go.** | *I would like four.* |
| 8 | **Sei go mōnggwó, yih-sahp mān lā.** | *Four mangoes, that's twenty dollars.* |
| 9 | **Nī douh yih-sahp mān.** | *Here's twenty dollars.* |
| 10 | **Dōjeh.** | *Thank you* (for the money). |
| 11 | **Mhgōi.** | *Thank you* (for the favor). |
| 12 | **sīnsāang** | *Mr.* (a polite way of addressing a man) |
| 13 | **géidō chín yāt go a?** | *how much each* (lit. "for one")? |
| 14 | **Mhgōi béi luhk go ā.** | *Please give (me) six.* |
| 15 | **dōjeh sahp-ńgh mān** | *fifteen dollars, please* |
| 16 | **Jáau fāan ńgh mān.** | *Here's five dollars change.* |
| 17 | **Jauh yiu yāt bohng lā.** | *Then I'll have one pound.* |

## Indefinite pronoun dī (2)

The indefinite pronoun **dī** functions as a pronoun referring to an unspecified number or amount of people or things. It is invariable, and is usually translated as "some" in English. For example, **Dī mōnggwó** in Dialogue 1 can mean "some fruit."

## Particles (2, 14; 5, 13)

Cantonese has a system of particles, which speakers use to express moods and achieve certain rhetorical functions. The **lā** in the expression **máaih dī lā** is a particle which helps convey the mood of a cordial invitation. On the other hand, the **lā** in **Mhgōi béi luhk go ā** has a slightly different connotation of giving an affirmation rather than making a cordial invitation. Note that **lā** always occurs at the *end* of a sentence, so we refer to it as a sentence-final particle. Other particles are used, for example, in questions and polite requests (see below).

## Definite determiner (4)

In this context, **dī** functions as a *definite determiner* used before plural or uncountable nouns to specify people or objects. It translates into "the" or "those" (for plural countable nouns) or "that" (for uncountable nouns) in English.

## Questions (5, 13)

**Dím maaih a?** is a general question one would use to ask about prices that fluctuate, such as prices of fruit and vegetables in the market, which depend on the quantity and quality of supply and also vary with individual sellers. Another way to ask such a question is to say **Géidō chín yāt go a?** Note that both questions contain a question phrase, namely, **dím maaih** (lit. "how sold?") and **géidō chín** (lit. "how much money?"), and end with the interrogative, or question, particle **a**.

## Personal pronouns (CD1; 30) (7)

| | | | |
|---|---|---|---|
| **ngóh** | I, me | **ngóhdeih** | we, us |
| **néih** | you (singular) | **néihdeih** | you (plural) |
| **kéuih** | he, him, she, her, it | **kéuihdeih** | they, them |

## Topic-comment constructions (8)

In Cantonese, a sentence is often made up of a *topic* followed by a *comment*, the two of which are not joined by any grammatical parts, such as a verb. This type of construction can serve to highlight and make definite the topic. This sentence from Dialogue 1 is typical:

> **Sei go mōnggwó, yih-sahp mān lā.**
> (lit.) Four mangoes, twenty dollars.

In this case **sei go mōnggwó** is the topic, and **yih-sahp mān lā** is the comment about it. This construction is common among questions, too. The questions used when asking for prices are good examples:

**Dī mōnggwó dím maaih a?**
(lit.) The mangoes, how (are they) sold?

**Dī cháang géidō chín yāt go a?**
(lit.) The oranges, how much money for one?

## Expressing thanks (10, 11)

Cantonese distinguishes between two kinds of thanks. We say **dōjeh** to someone for a gift or a treat, but **mhgōi** to someone for a favor or a service rendered. Thus, at the fruit-stall, the hawker will say **dōjeh** to thank the customer for the money paid for the fruit, while the customer will say **mhgōi** to the hawker for his service. In practice, it is not always necessary for the customer to say thank you. Another more colloquial way to say thanks for a favor to a friend (not in a service situation) is to feign how much trouble you have been to the person. For example, if a friend picks you up at the airport, you might say: **Màhfàhn néih!** "(I) troubled you!" To which the friend responds politely **móuh màhfàhn** "no trouble."

## Polite requests (14, 15)

The **mhgōi** and **dōjeh** in these two cases are interjections used as a polite way of making a request. The **mhgōi** in *Mhgōi béi luhk go ā* is a request made by the customer for a service by the hawker, while the **dōjeh** in *dōjeh sahp-ńgh mān* is a request from the hawker for payment by the customer. (In a similar vein, in English a salesperson might say "Five dollars, thank you" in order to solicit payment, that is, in anticipation of receipt, rather than in acknowledgment of it.) The **ā** in **Mhgōi béi luhk go ā** is a particle, conveying here the mood of a polite request.

## Exercise 1 Comprehension

Practice the dialogues, using the audio recordings if available. Then find the answers to the following questions.

(a) How much does the hawker say the fruit is in Dialogue 1?

   (i) $5 each

   (ii) $5 a pound

   (iii) $10 for two

(b) How much does the hawker say the fruit is in Dialogue 2?

   (i) $10 each
   (ii) $10 a pound
   (iii) $10 for four

(c) In Dialogue 2, how much change did the hawker give back to John?

   (i) $5
   (ii) $10
   (iii) $15

(d) How much does the hawker say the fruit is in Dialogue 3?

   (i) $20 each
   (ii) $20 a pound
   (iii) $20 for four

## Exercise 2 Asking about prices

Imagine you are at a fruit-stall. Ask about the price of each kind of fruit with **a dím maaih a** question. Then guess whether the hawker will give the price for **yāt go** or **yāt bohng**.

(a) **léi**
YOU: _____ dím maaih a?
HAWKER: Sei mān _____

(b) **sāigwā**
YOU: _____ dím maaih a?
HAWKER: Sāam mān _____

(c) **muhkgwā**
YOU: _____ dím maaih a?
HAWKER: Sei mān _____

(d) **bōlòh**
YOU: _____ dím maaih a?
HAWKER: Sahp mān _____

(e) **laihjī**
YOU: _____ dím maaih a?
HAWKER: Sahp-yih mān _____

Unit 2: *Shopping*

## Exercise 3 Giving prices

Imagine you are a hawker selling fruit in the market. The table shows your prices in Hong Kong dollars.

| Apples | Lychees | Papayas | Oranges | Water-melons | Pineapples | Pears |
|---|---|---|---|---|---|---|
| $10 for 3 | $12/lb | $20 for 3 | $10 for 4 | $4/lb | $9 each | $5 each |

How would you answer the following enquiries about prices?

(a) Dī sāigwā dím maaih a?

(b) Dī léi dím maaih a?

(c) Dī muhkgwā dím maaih a?

(d) Dī cháang dím maaih a?

(e) Dī bōlòh dím maaih a?

## Exercise 4 Making a sale

Now complete the following conversations, using the prices from Exercise 3.

(a) CUSTOMER 1: Dī pìhnggwó dím maaih a?
    YOU:
    CUSTOMER 1: Ngóh yiu yāt dā pìhnggwó.
    YOU:
    CUSTOMER 1: Géidō chín a?
    YOU:
    CUSTOMER 1: Nī douh sei-sahp mān. Mhgōi.
    YOU:

(b) CUSTOMER 2: Dī laihjī dím maaih a?
    YOU:
    CUSTOMER 2: Ngóh yiu sāam bohng.
    YOU:
    CUSTOMER 2: Géidō chín a?
    YOU:
    CUSTOMER 2: Nī douh sei-sahp mān.
    YOU:
    CUSTOMER 2: Mhgōi.
    YOU:

Exercise 5 Comparing prices

Mrs. Wong is doing some shopping. She wants to buy two pounds of bananas, a dozen oranges and half a dozen apples, and she wants to buy all the fruit at one stall. She asks about the prices of bananas, oranges and apples at two different stalls. Practice modeling the two conversations she has at the two stalls and then decide at which one she gets the better deal.

*At Stall A*:

MRS. WONG: Dī cháang dím maaih a?
HAWKER A: Sāam mān yāt go.
MRS. WONG: Dī pìhnggwó nē?
HAWKER A: Pìhnggwó sei mān yāt go.
MRS. WONG: Hēungjīu yau dím maaih a?
HAWKER A: Hēungjīu sahp-sāam mān yāt bohng.

*At Stall B*:

MRS. WONG: Dī hēungjīu dím maaih a?
HAWKER B: Dī hēungjīu sahp-yāt mān yāt bohng.
MRS. WONG: Dī pìhnggwó nē?
HAWKER B: Pìhnggwó sāam mān yāt go.
MRS. WONG: Dī cháang nē?
HAWKER B: Dī cháang sei mān yāt go.

(a) Which hawker offers a better deal to Mrs. Wong?

(b) How much does she have to pay if she takes this deal?

# Exercise 6 What are the prices?

Read the conversation and then fill in the prices in the picture of the fruit-stall.

| CUSTOMER: | Dī tàihjí dím maaih a? |
|---|---|
| HAWKER: | Dī tàihjí sahp-ńgh mān yāt bohng. |
| CUSTOMER: | Gám, dī kèihyihgwó nē? |
| HAWKER: | Dī kèihyihgwó sāam mān yāt go. |
| CUSTOMER: | Dī pìhnggwó nē? |
| HAWKER: | Pìhnggwó dōou haih sāam mān yāt go. |
| CUSTOMER: | Dī muhkgwā dím maaih a? |
| HAWKER: | Muhkgwā baat mān yāt bohng. |
| CUSTOMER: | Gám, sāigwā nē? |
| HAWKER: | Sāigwā léuhng mān yāt bohng. |
| CUSTOMER: | Dī cháang yauh dím maaih a? |
| HAWKER: | Dī cháang sahp mān sei go. |
| CUSTOMER: | Gám, dī léi nē? |
| HAWKER: | Dī léi dōu haih sahp mān sei go. |

## Exercise 7 Ordering fruit

Imagine you are on the telephone ordering some fruit from a grocery store. Give your order in Cantonese, according to the information shown in the table. The first item has been done for you as an example.

| Fruit | Place of origin | Quantity |
| --- | --- | --- |
| (a) apples | Australia | 10 |
| (b) oranges | the U.S. | 20 |
| (c) grapes | the U.S. | 2 lb |
| (d) pineapples | the Philippines | 3 |
| (e) mangoes | the Philippines | 8 |
| (f) pears | Australia | 12 |

(a) **Ngóh yiu sahp go Oujāu pìhnggwó.**

(b)

(c)

(d)

(e)

(f)

## Recognizing Chinese characters

In the local market sometimes the prices are written in a mix of Arabic numerals and Chinese characters (see photo at the beginning of this unit), but sometimes they are in Chinese characters only. The Chinese characters for the numbers one to ten are as follows:

| | | | |
| --- | --- | --- | --- |
| 一 | 1 | 六 | 6 |
| 二 | 2 | 七 | 7 |
| 三 | 3 | 八 | 8 |
| 四 | 4 | 九 | 9 |
| 五 | 5 | 十 | 10 |

The Chinese character for "dollar" is

元.

# Unit 2: Shopping

Thus, one dollar is written as

一元.

This is pronounced as **yāt māan** in colloquial Cantonese.
The classifier for "roundish" fruits is **go**, and is written as

個 or 个

in Chinese characters. Thus, "three dollars each" is written as

三元一个

and "five dollars each" is written as

五元一个.

The Chinese character for the measure "pound" is

磅.

"Eight dollars a pound" is thus

八元一磅

and "ten dollars per pound" is

十元一磅.

## Communicative activities

> If you have a Cantonese speaking friend or tutor, see if you can use what you have learned in this unit to do the following activities.
>
> 1 With a partner, take turns playing the roles of vendor and customer. Try to haggle down the price a bit (**pèhng síuíu** "a little cheaper") by first arguing that the quality is not too good (**mleng**). Use whatever props you have handy.
> 2 Follow the patterns above to describe to your partner what you bought on a market trip. Tell them what it cost for each item.

Cultural point

## Open markets in Hong Kong and China

Despite modernization and the increasing popularity of Western-style supermarkets in Hong Kong and elsewhere in China, open vegetable markets are still a popular place to buy fresh produce and meats. In these kinds of markets, the prices can fluctuate daily and one can often bargain according to quality and amount. Indoor supermarkets on the other hand typically have fixed priced labels.

In addition to the food markets, there are numerous other open street markets in the Cantonese-speaking world. Hong Kong's Tung Choi Street and Temple Street night markets are widely popular with tourists seeking bargains on clothes, watches, toys, etc. Haggling for the best price is expected for most items here.

# Unit Three
# Sihou

Interests and leisure activities

In Unit 3 you will learn about:

- discussing interests and leisure activities
- more question-words
- discussing how often you do things
- expressing likes and dislikes
- verb-object constructions
- the uses of **yáuh** "to have" and "to exist"
- the uses of **hái** "(to be) in/at"

## Dialogue 1

**(CD1; 31)**
John and Carmen are having tea with their two new friends at the Cantonese Students' Club.

Carmen is talking to Richard about her own interests and Richard's.

(a) What does Richard like to do in his spare time?
(b) What about Carmen?

| CARMEN: | Richard, néih yáuh dī mātyéh sihou a? |
|---|---|
| RICHARD: | Ngóh yáuh hóu dō sihou. Ngóh jūngyi yàuh-séui tùhng dá-móhngkàuh. Hái ngūkkéi jauh jūngyi tēng-yām-ngohk. Gám, néih nē, Carmen? |
| CARMEN: | Ngóh dōu jūngyi tēng-yāmngohk. Ngóh yauh jūngyi tái-syū tùhng tái-dihnsih. |

| CARMEN: | Richard, what kind of hobbies do you have? |
|---|---|
| RICHARD: | I have many hobbies. I like to swim and play tennis. At home I like to listen to music. And how about you, Carmen? |
| CARMEN: | I like to listen to music too. I also like reading and watching television. |

## Dialogue 2

**(CD1; 33)**
WONG Git is talking to Emily.

(a) What does Emily like to do in her spare time?
(b) What about WONG Git? What does he say his likes and dislikes are?

| WONG GIT: | Emily, néih dākhàahn yáuh dī mātyéh jouh a? |
|---|---|
| EMILY: | Ngóh jungyi hàahng-gāai tùhng tái-hei. |
| WONG GIT: | Ngóh dōu jungyi tái-hei, bātgwo ngóh mjūngyi hàahng-gāai. Kèihsaht ngóh jeui jūngyi heui-léuihhàhng, yānwaih ngóh hóu jūngyi yíng-séung. |

Unit 3: *Interests and leisure activities*

WONG GIT: Emily, what do you like to do in your free time?
EMILY: I like window-shopping and watching movies.
WONG GIT: I like watching movies too, but I don't like window-shopping. In fact, I most like traveling, because I like taking photos.

## Vocabulary

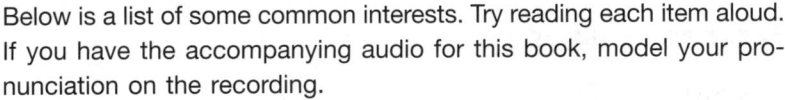

### Interests and leisure activities (CD1; 34)

Below is a list of some common interests. Try reading each item aloud. If you have the accompanying audio for this book, model your pronunciation on the recording.

| | |
|---|---|
| tái-dihnyíng/tái-hei | to watch a movie |
| tái-dihnsih | to watch television |
| heui-léuihhàhng | to go traveling |
| yíng-séung | to take pictures |
| tēng-yāmngohk | to listen to music |
| tēng-sāuyāmgēi | to listen to the radio |
| dá-móhngkàuh | to play tennis |
| dá-làahmkàuh | to play basketball |
| tek-jūkkàuh | to play soccer |
| cháai-dāanchē | to ride a bicycle |
| yàuh-séui | to swim |
| páau-bouh | to run |
| cheung-gō | to sing |
| tái-syū | to read |
| tái-boují | to read the newspaper |
| hàahng-gāai | to go window-shopping |
| wáan-yàuhheigēi | to play electronic games |

### Verb-object constructions

The leisure activities given above are all expressed in *verb-object constructions*, and are thus hyphenated. The first six largely parallel their English counterparts in structure and meaning. The next two (**dá-móhngkàuh, dá-làahmkàuh**) use the Cantonese verb **dá** (lit. "to hit"), which is common for games where there is contact with an object using the hands. By contrast **tek-jūkkàuh** is literally "kick-(a)-football." And then **cháai-dāanchē** is "pedal-(a)-bicycle," **yàuh-séui** is "swim-(in)-water," and **páau-bouh** is "run-paces"; **cheung-gō** is "sing-(a)-song"; **tái-syū** is "read-(a)-book," while **tái-boují** is "read-(the)-newspaper"; **hàahng-gāai** is "walk-(along-the)-street"; **wáan-yàuhheigēi** is "play-game-machine."

## Expressing likes

| **jūngyi** | to like |
| **héifūn** | to like |

Thus, "I like playing tennis" can be expressed as:

**Ngóh jūngyi dá-móhngkàuh.**
or **Ngóh héifūn dá-móhngkàuh.**

### Jūngyi **and** héifūn

The modal verbs **jūngyi** and **héifūn** are identical in meaning, but **héifūn** ranks higher on the level of formality and it is also used in Mandarin as well as in written Chinese, while **jūngyi** is only used in colloquial Cantonese. Of the two words **jūngyi** is more commonly used in daily conversations.

## Idioms and structures

The items in the list below appear in the same order as they do in the dialogues above. The *italicized* items are *new* items. In the notes, numbers in brackets refer to the expressions listed below.

1 **sihou** *hobbies/interests*

2 **Néih** *yáuh* **dī mātyéh sihou a?** What hobbies do you *have*?

Unit 3: Interests and leisure activities

| | | |
|---|---|---|
| 3 | **Ngóh yáuh hóu *dō* sihou.** | I have *many* hobbies. |
| 4 | *hái ngūkkéi* | at home |
| 5 | **Ngóh hái ngūkkéi *jauh* jūngyi ...** | (When I'm) at home *then* I like ... |
| 6 | **Ngóh *dōu* jūngyi tēng-yāmngohk.** | I like listening to music *too*. |
| 7 | **Ngóh *yauh* jūngyi tái-syū** | I *also* like reading |
| 8 | *dākhàahn* | free, not busy |
| 9 | **néih dākhàahn yáuh dī mātyéh *jouh* a?** | What do you *do* in your leisure time? |
| 10 | **bātgwo ngóh *mjūngyi* hàahng-gāai** | but I *don't like* window-shopping |
| 11 | ***Kèihsaht*** | *In fact* |
| 12 | **ngóh *jeui* jūngyi heui-léuihhàhng** | I like traveling *most* |
| 13 | *yānwaih* | *because* |

## Verbal yáuh (2, 3)

**Yáuh** is a verbal form, which denotes both *possession* and *existence*. In Dialogue 1, **Ngóh yáuh hóu dō sihou** ("I have many hobbies") denotes possession; whereas a sentence like **Yáuh pìhnggwó** ("There are apples") denotes existence. Note that the negative of **yáuh** is **móuh**, not *myáuh. For example, **Ngóh móuh sihou** is "I don't have any hobbies," while **Móuh pìhnggwó** means "There are no apples."

## Indefinite pronoun (2, 9)

**Dī** here is used as an indefinite pronoun referring to an unspecified number of things. Used in this context it is usually translated as "some" in English. (See Unit 2, p. 35.) Thus, **Néih yáuh *dī* mātyeh sihou a?** more directly translates into "What are some of the hobbies that you have?" while **Néih dākhàahn yáuh *dī* mātyeh jouh a?** can be translated as "What are some of the things you do in your leisure time?"

## Locative marker (4)

**Hái** is a marker of location: it is used in statements about where things are. It can be either *verbal* or *prepositional*. When it is verbal, it means "to be at/in." For example, **Kéuih *hái* sāanggwódong** means "He *is at* the fruit-stall." But in another sentence, **Ngóh *hái* sāanggwódong maaih sāanggwó** ("I sell fruit *at* a fruit-stall"), **hái** is used as a preposition, denoting *where* I sell fruit. In the longer sentence **Ngóh *hái* ngūkkéi jauh jūngyi tēng-yāmngohk** ("When I am at home I like listening to music"), **hái** is verbal. The condition **ngóh *hái* ngūkkéi** ("when I am at home") specifies the location where the action denoted by the main verb **tēng-yāmngohk** takes place.

## Conditional marker (5)

**Jauh** is a very common adverb used to state a condition. It is put before the main clause rather than the conditional clause, thus meaning "then" rather than "if." For example, **Ngóh hái ngūkkéi *jauh* jūngyi tēng-yāmngohk** specifies that the preferred activity **tēng-yāmngohk** ("listening to music") takes place under the condition **ngóh hái ngūkkéih** ("I'm at home").

## Dōu (6)

**Dōu** is an adverb used in a response to indicate a *shared* fact: in the context of this lesson, a *common hobby*. For example, to **Ngóh jūngyi dá-móhngkàuh** ("I like playing tennis") one says **Ngóh *dōu* jūngyi dá-móhngkàuh** ("I like playing tennis, too"). Here the adverb **dōu** qualifies the *subject* of the sentence, **ngóh**, and the use is similar to saying "Me too" in response to "I like playing tennis" in English.

## Yauh (7)

**Yauh** is an adverb used to introduce a further item on a list (not to be confused with **dōu** above, which is used to respond to what somebody else has said). For example, one can say **Ngóh jūngyi dá-móhngkàuh. Ngóh *yauh* jūngyi tek-jūkkàuh.** ("I like playing tennis. I also like playing soccer.") Here the adverb **yauh** qualifies the *object* of the sentence, **tek-jūkkàuh**, and the use is similar to adding "And soccer too" to "I like playing tennis" in English.

## Varying degrees of likes and dislikes (10)

To express dislikes, the negative prefix **m-** is used before the modal verb. Thus, "I don't like swimming" is **Ngóh mjūngyi yàuh-séui** or **Ngóh mhéifūn yàuh-séui**. To express varying degrees of likes and dislikes, the following adverbs can be used *before* the modal:

| | |
|---|---|
| **hóu** | very much |
| **géi** | quite (a lot) |
| **màh-má-déi** | so-so |
| **mhaih géi** | not that much |

For example:

| | |
|---|---|
| **Kéuih hóu jūngyi tái-hei.** | He likes watching movies very much. |
| **Kéuih géi jūngyi tái-hei.** | He quite likes watching movies. |
| **Kéuih màh-má-déi jūngyi tái-hei.** | He doesn't like watching movies that much. |
| **Kéuih mhaih géi jūngyi tái-hei.** | He doesn't like watching movies very much. |

Note that as both **màh-má-déi** and **mhaih géi** are already inherently negative in meaning, the modal remains *positive* to express a negative sentence meaning.

## Exercise 1 Likes and dislikes

Express the following English sentences in Cantonese. The first one has been done for you as an example.

(a) I like taking pictures very much.
   **Ngóh hóu jūngyi yíng-séung.**
(b) He doesn't like swimming.
   **Kéuih mjūngyi ...**
(c) She quite likes reading.
(d) We don't enjoy watching television that much.
(e) They don't like singing.

## Vocabulary

**(CD1; 35)**
### Days of the week

In Cantonese, a "week" is known as either **sīngkèih** or **láihbaai**. **Sīngkèih** is more common in writing and **láihbaai** is more common in speech. Here are the seven days of the week in Cantonese:

| | | |
|---|---|---|
| sīngkèih-yāt | or láihbaai-yāt | Monday |
| sīngkèih-yih | or láihbaai-yih | Tuesday |
| sīngkèih-sāam | or láihbaai-sāam | Wednesday |
| sīngkèih-sei | or láihbaai-sei | Thursday |
| sīngkèih-ńgh | or láihbaai-ńgh | Friday |
| sīngkèih-luhk | or láihbaai-luhk | Saturday |
| sīngkèih-yaht | or láihbaai-yaht | Sunday |

Note that the pronunciation of "Sunday" (**sīngkèih-yaht/láihbaai-yaht**) differs from that of "Monday" (**sīngkèih-yāt/láihbaai-yāt**) *in tone only*. Remember that the tone for **yaht** (as in "Sunday") is *low level*, and is much lower than that for **yāt** (as in "Monday"), which is *high level*.

### Time expressions

| | |
|---|---|
| yāt yaht | a day |
| yāt go láihbaai | a week |
| yāt go yuht | a month |
| yāt nìhn | a year |

Note that in Cantonese weeks and months take the classifier **go** (the same classifier as for apples, oranges, and people), but days and years do not need any classifiers.

| | |
|---|---|
| yāt chi | once |
| léuhng chi | twice |
| sāam chi | three times |
| sei chi | four times |

Note also that **yāt** can mean "a" or "one" in the expressions above.

Unit 3: *Interests and leisure activities*

## Dialogue 3

**(CD1; 36)**
Carmen is talking to Richard about his hobbies.

(a) How often does Richard play tennis?
(b) On what day(s) of the week does he play?

CARMEN: Richard, néih jūngyi dá-móhngkàuh. Gám, néih géinoih dá yāt chi móhngkàuh a?
RICHARD: Ngóh yāt go láihbaai dá yāt chi móhngkàuh. Ngóh fùhng sīngkèih-luhk dá.

CARMEN: Richard, you like playing tennis … so how often do you play?
RICHARD: I play tennis once a week. I play every Saturday.

## Dialogue 4

**(CD1; 37)**
John is talking to Emily about hobbies.

(a) How often does Emily watch a movie?
(b) How often does John go traveling?

JOHN: Emily, néih daaihyeuk géinoih tái yāt chi hei a?
EMILY: Ngóh hóu héifūn tái-hei. Ngóh daaihyeuk yāt go láihbaai tái léuhng chi hei. Gám, John, néih géinoih heui yāt chi léuihhàhng a?
JOHN: Ngóh yáuh chèuhng gakèih jauh heui-léuihhàhng. Daaiyeuk yāt nìhn heui léuhng chi léuihhàhng.

JOHN: Emily, about how often do you watch a movie?
EMILY: I really like watching movies. I watch a movie about twice a week. So John, how often do you go traveling?
JOHN: Whenever I have a long holiday, I go on a trip. I go about twice a year.

Idioms and structures

The items in the list below appear in the same order as they do in the dialogues above. The *italicized* items are *new* items. In the notes, numbers in brackets refer to the expressions listed below.

1  **Néih *géinoih* dá *yāt chi* móhngkàuh a?**
   *How often* do you play tennis?
2  **Ngóh *yāt go láihbaai* dá *yāt chi* móhngkàuh.**
   I play tennis *once a week*.
3  **Ngóh *fùhng sīngkèih-luhk* dá.**
   I play (tennis) *every Saturday*.
4  ***daaihyeuk***         *roughly, approximately*
5  ***chèuhng gakèih***    *long holiday*

### Asking about frequency                                         (1)

In a question about frequencies of activities, the question phrase **géinoih … yāt chi** is used. **Géinoih** is used to ask about the interval between occurrences, while **yāt chi** literally means "one time." Thus **géinoih … yāt chi?** is equivalent to asking "how often?" in English. However, as most activities are expressed in verb-object constructions, always remember the special word order involved in such expressions of frequency, namely, the verb must be put *before* **yāt chi** while the object is put *after* it. For example, "to watch a movie once" is expressed as **tái *yāt chi* hei**, and "how often do you watch a movie?" is **néih *géinoih* tái *yāt chi* hei a?** Similarly, "how often do you play tennis?" is **néih *géinoih* dá *yāt chi* móhngkàuh a?**

### Expressing frequency (CD1; 39)                                 (2)

To say how often an activity happens, an adverbial phrase of frequency is often used. This is typically formed by combining a phrase expressing a period of time and one expressing the number of occurrences in it.

| | |
|---|---|
| yāt yaht yāt chi | once every day |
| yāt go láihbaai yāt chi | once a week |
| yāt go yuht léuhng chi | twice a month |
| yāt nìhn sāam chi | three times a year |

Unit 3: *Interests and leisure activities*

Again, as leisure activities are often expressed in verb-object constructions (**tek-jūkkàuh**), the verb and object in the construction are *separated* in a sentence expressing frequency, and the following word order is used:

| Subject | Period of time | Verb | Number of times | Object |
|---|---|---|---|---|
| Ngóh | yāt go yuht | tek | léuhng chi | jūkkàuh. |
| Ngóh | yāt go láihbaai | dá | yāt chi | móhngkàuh. |

## Regular activities (3)

For regular activities that take place on the same day every week, the word **fùhng** can be used. For example:

**fùhng sīngkèih-yaht**   every Sunday
**fùhng sīngkèih-yih**   every Tuesday and Thursday
**tùhng (sīngkèih-)sei**

Thus, **Ngóh fùhng sīngkèih-yaht tek-jūkkàuh** is "I play soccer every Sunday," while **Ngóh fùhng sīngkèih-luhk dá-móhngkàuh** is "I play tennis every Saturday." Note that in Cantonese the time expression always *precedes* the verb.

## Exercise 2 "Jack of all sports"

Your friend Jack is a great sportsman. He likes many sports. Look at the picture and write about his interests and his busy schedule.

*Example*:
Jack yáuh hóu dō sihou. Kéuih jūngyi dá móhngkàuh. Kéuih fùhng sīngkèih-yāt dá móhngkàuh. Kéuih yauh jūngyi …

## Exercise 3 Comprehension

Read the following questions. Then go back to the dialogues and find the answers. If you have the audio recordings, listen to the dialogues first.

(a) According to Dialogue 1, what hobby do Richard and Carmen share?

(i) swimming
(ii) playing tennis
(iii) listening to music
(iv) reading
(v) watching TV

(b) According to Dialogue 2, what is WONG Git's favorite hobby?

(i) shopping
(ii) going to watch a movie
(iii) traveling
(iv) photography

(c) According to Dialogue 4, when does John go traveling?

(i) whenever he has money
(ii) whenever he has a long holiday

## Exercise 4 How often?

Express the following English sentences in Cantonese. The first one has been done for you as an example.

(a) I play soccer once a week.
   **Ngóh yāt go láihbaai tek yāt chi jūkkàuh.**
(b) I take a walk twice a week.
   **Ngóh yāt go láihbaai …**
(c) I go to watch a movie twice a month.

(d) I go swimming three times a week.
(e) I go traveling four times a year.

## Exercise 5 Your hobbies

At a social gathering with your Cantonese Club friends, someone asks you: **Néih yáuh dī mātyéh sihou a?** How would you answer?

## Exercise 6 Common interests

The table summarizes the likes and dislikes of Richard, Carmen, Emily, John, and WONG Git. Write in your own likes and dislikes in the fifth column. Then write some sentences to describe the common likes and dislikes. Try reading the sentences aloud.

|  | Richard | Carmen | Emily | John | WONG Git | You |
|---|---|---|---|---|---|---|
| listening to music | ✔ | ✔ | | | | |
| watching movies | | | ✔ | | ✔ | |
| watching TV | | ✔ | | | | |
| traveling | | | | ✔ | ✔ | |
| taking pictures | | | | | ✔ | |
| playing tennis | ✔ | | | | | |
| playing soccer | ✗ | ✗ | ✗ | ✗ | | |
| swimming | ✔ | | | | | |
| singing | ✗ | ✔ | ✔ | ✗ | | |
| reading | | ✔ | | | | |
| window-shopping | | | ✔ | | ✗ | |

*Example*:
**Richard tùhng Carmen dōu jūngyi tēng-yāmngohk.**
**Richard, Carmen, Emily tùhng John dōu mjūngyi tek-jūkkàuh.**

# Recognizing Chinese characters

Of the two Cantonese words for "week," **sīngkèih** is written as

星期

Thus, for Monday, which is the first day of the week, we write

星期一

and for Tuesday, the second day of the week, we write

星期二

and for Sunday, we write

星期日,

where

日

is the character for "the sun." Below is a full list of the seven days of the week written in Chinese characters.

| | |
|---|---|
| 星期一 | Monday |
| 星期二 | Tuesday |
| 星期三 | Wednesday |
| 星期四 | Thursday |
| 星期五 | Friday |
| 星期六 | Saturday |
| 星期日 | Sunday |

## Communicative activities

1 Interview a Cantonese-speaking acquaintance about his or her recreational practices, asking about activities he or she does at various times (once a week, once a month, twice a year and such).
2 Ask a conversation partner or friend about likes and dislikes. What kind of hobbies does he or she have? Switch roles and repeat.

## Cultural points

### Calendars

In modern times China uses the same calendar as the West, though sometimes with Chinese numbers. However, for observance of traditional holidays (Chinese New Year, Moon Festival, etc.) the Chinese use the lunar calendar. The Chinese zodiac also follows the lunar calendar.

Unit 3: *Interests and leisure activities*

Western numbered calendar with lunar calendar dates

The large character on the top, pronounced *fuk* in Cantonese, means "blessing(s)." Above the large character is the expression 年年有運, meaning "may you be fortunate throughout the year."

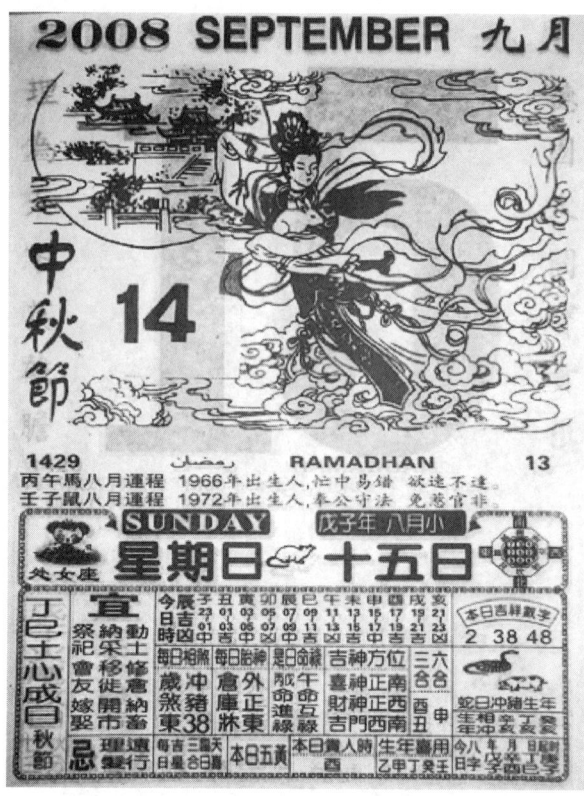

Traditional lunar calendar

This calendar acts as both a lunar calendar and a kind of almanac in the Chinese culture. Although most of the calendar uses Chinese, notice some of the numbering is in Arabic numerals and there are a couple of English words as well. This kind of mixing is especially common in Hong Kong. Note that the word Ramadhan next to the Arabic appears in the middle of the calendar. Because China has a significant Muslim minority, references to Muslim holidays are often included along with the traditional Han Chinese holidays such as the one featured on the page above. To the left of the number 14 are the Chinese characters 中秋節, Chung Chau Jit, meaning Mid-Autumn Festival (or Moon Festival), one of the most important traditional Chinese holidays.

Unit 3: *Interests and leisure activities*

## Some traditional Chinese holidays

| Name | Calendar date | Chinese name | Notes |
|---|---|---|---|
| Spring Festival (Chinese New Year) | Begins with the first day of the first moon of the lunar calendar. | 春節 *Chung Jit* | The most important of the traditional Chinese holidays, this festival lasts for two weeks, though the first few days are the most important. Celebrations involve fireworks, buying new clothes, eating special foods, and visiting family and friends. |
| Ching Ming Festival (Tomb Sweeping Day) | April 5 (April 4 in leap years) | 清明節 *Ching Mihng Jit* | A day for paying respects to one's ancestors by sweeping the tombs and offering food sacrifices. |
| Dragon Boat Festival | Fifth day of the fifth moon (lunar calendar) | 端午節 *Dun Nǵh Jit* | Usually occurs in June of the Western calendar. People may celebrate by eating *Jung* (rice cakes) and holding dragon boat races. The festival is said to have its origins in the death of the famous Chinese poet, Chu Yuan. |
| Mid-Autumn Festival (Lantern Festival) | Fifteenth day of the eighth moon (lunar calendar) | 中秋節 / 翌日 *Jung Chau Jit/ Dang Yaht* | Usually occurring in September, this celebration is a harvest festival. Activities include lighting of lanterns and eating moon cakes. |
| Chung Yeung Festival | Ninth day of the ninth moon (lunar calendar) | 重陽節 *Chung Yeung Jit* | Usually occurs in October of the Western Calendar and is a day for honoring the elderly and the deceased. Chinese often celebrate with mountain climbing and paying respects to ancestors by visiting gravesites. |

# Unit Four
# Sìhgaan

Telling the time

> In Unit 4 you will learn about:
>
> - asking and telling the time
> - discussing daily routines
> - discussing what time things happen
> - **yiu** as a modal verb, "to have to"

 Dialogue 1

 **(CD1; 40)**
John is talking to Emily at a Cantonese Students' Club gathering. Emily is about to leave.

(a) What time is it now?
(b) What time is Emily seeing a movie?

Unit 4: *Telling the time*

EMILY: Yìhgā géidímjūng a, John?
JOHN: Yìhgā sei dím bun.
EMILY: Gám ngóh yiu jáu la. Ngóh yiu heui tái-hei a.
JOHN: Néih géidímjūng tái-hei a?
EMILY: Ngóh ńgh dím bun tái-hei.

EMILY: What time is it now, John?
JOHN: It is 4:30 (now).
EMILY: Well, I need to leave now. I am going to see a movie.
JOHN: What time is the movie?
EMILY: I will see the movie at 5:30.

## Dialogue 2

**(CD1; 42)**
LÀUH Gwok Sìhng is talking to Jack, the all-round sportsman.

(a) What time does Jack play tennis on Monday?
(b) What time does he go biking on Saturday?
(c) What time does he play soccer on Sunday?

LÀUH GWOK SÌHNG: Jack, néih sīngkèih-yāt géidímjūng dá-móhngkàuh a?
JACK: Ngóh sīngkèih-yāt yehmáahn chāt dímjūng dá-móhngkàuh.
LÀUH GWOK SÌHNG: Gám, néih sīngkèih-luhk géidímjūng cháai-dāanchē a?
JACK: Ngóh sīngkèih-luhk hahjau sei dím bun cháai-dāanchē.
LÀUH GWOK SÌHNG: Sīngkèih-yaht nē? Sīngkèih-yaht néih géidímjūng wúih tek-bōa?
JACK: Sīngkèih-yaht ngóh seuhngjau gáu dím bun wúih tek-bō.

LÀUH GWOK SÌHNG: Jack, what time will you be playing tennis on Monday?
JACK: I will be playing at 7 p.m. Monday evening.
LÀUH GWOK SÌHNG: So what time will you go biking on Saturday?
JACK: I will go biking at 4:30 on Saturday afternoon.

| LÀUH GWOK SÌHNG: | And how about Sunday? What time will you be playing soccer? |
| JACK: | I will be playing soccer at 9:30 in the morning on Sunday. |

## Vocabulary

**Reading the clock** (CD1; 43–45)

Below is a list of the hours of the day. Try reading out each item aloud. If you have the audio for this book, you can model your pronunciation on the recording.

| yāt dímjūng | 1 o'clock | chāt dímjūng | 7 o'clock |
| léuhng dímjūng | 2 o'clock | baat dímjūng | 8 o'clock |
| sāam dímjūng | 3 o'clock | gáu dímjūng | 9 o'clock |
| sei dímjūng | 4 o'clock | sahp dímjūng | 10 o'clock |
| ńgh dímjūng | 5 o'clock | sahp-yāt dímjūng | 11 o'clock |
| luhk dímjūng | 6 o'clock | sahp-yih dímjūng | 12 o'clock |

Note that in speech the **jūng** "clock or hour" in **dímjūng** is often omitted, hence **yāt dím** is 1 o'clock and **léuhng dím** is 2 o'clock, etc. Notice that **léuhng** is used for "two."

To specify more precisely the time of day, one can add the following expressions:

| seuhngjau | in the morning |
| hahjau | in the afternoon |
| yehmáahn | in the evening/at night |
| bunyeh | after midnight |

Thus,

| seuhngjau chāt dímjūng | 7 a.m. |
| hahjau léuhng dímjūng | 2 p.m. |
| yehmáahn gáu dímjūng | 9 p.m. |
| bunyeh sāam dímjūng | 3 a.m. |

In Cantonese, the expression for the time of day always comes *before* the expression for the hour, e.g. **seuhngjau chāt dímjūng** and not *chāt dímjūng seuhngjau. To indicate the minutes, one uses **fān**, as below:

# Unit 4: Telling the time

| | |
|---|---|
| léuhng dím sahp fān | ten minutes past two |
| sāam dím yih-sahp fān | twenty minutes past three |
| sei dím sei-sahp baat fān | forty-eight minutes past four |

Note that when the minutes are indicated we only say **dím**, never **dímjūng**, thus **léuhng dím sahp fān** and never ***léuhng dímjūng sahp fān**.

Like English, Cantonese has special expressions for the half-hour and the quarter-hour, as below:

| | |
|---|---|
| léuhng dím bun | half past two |
| sāam dím bun | half past three |
| sei dím yāt go gwāt/sei dím sāam | a quarter past four |
| ńgh dím sāam go gwāt/ńgh dím gáu | a quarter to six (lit. "three quarters past five") |

Note that **gwāt** "a quarter of an hour" must take the classifier **go**. Note too that the use of **gwāt** is becoming increasingly uncommon among younger speakers in Hong Kong.

In Cantonese, there is one particular way of counting the minutes, not used in Mandarin Chinese. We divide up an hour into twelve five-minute units and we call each such unit a **jih**. **Jih**, like **gwāt**, must take the classifier **go**. Thus, **yāt go jih, léuhng go jih**. Below are some examples:

| | |
|---|---|
| chāt dím yāt go jih | five past seven |
| chāt dím léuhng go jih | ten past seven |
| chāt dím sāam go jih | a quarter past seven |
| chāt dím sei go jih | twenty past seven |

The **jih** in Cantonese refers to the numbers on the clock face. Thus, if it is, say, twenty minutes past two o'clock, the minute-hand of the clock will be pointing at the *fourth* number on the clock, which is the number 4 on the clock face, and hence **léuhng dím *sei* go jih**. Very often, in colloquial speech, **go jih** is omitted, and so:

| | |
|---|---|
| baat dím chāt | eight thirty-five |
| baat dím baat | eight forty |
| baat dím gáu | a quarter to nine |

Note that while **go jih** can be omitted, **fān** (for "minutes") cannot. Consequently, **baat dím chāt** can only mean thirty-five minutes past eight, *not* seven minutes past eight.

## Quick practice 1

Match the times in the left-hand column below with the Cantonese phrases in the right-hand column.

(a) 9:50 a.m.     seuhngjau sahp dím sei
(b) 11:35 a.m.    hahjau ńgh dím sahp-yāt
(c) 10:20 a.m.    hahjau sāam dím baat
(d) 5:55 p.m.     seuhngjau gáu dím sahp
(e) 6:25 p.m.     hahjau luhk dím ńgh
(f) 3:40 p.m.     seuhngjau chāt dím bun
(g) 7:30 a.m.     seuhngjau sahp-yāt dím chāt

## Quick practice 2

Look at the times on the digital clocks and then tell the time in **go jih**. First write out the answer and then read it aloud. The first one has been done for you.

(a)      **luhk dím chāt go jih**

(b)

(c)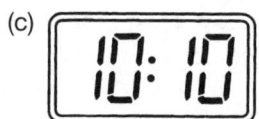

(d)

(e)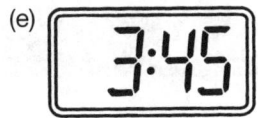

## Idioms and structures

The items in the list below appear in the same order as they do in the dialogues above. The *italicized* items are *new* items. In the notes, numbers in brackets refer to the expressions listed below.

1 **yìhgā** now
2 **géidímjūng a?** what time?
3 **yiu** must/have to
4 **ngóh yiu** *jáu la* I have to *leave*
5 **heui** go

### Géi (2)

**Géi** is an interrogative form in Cantonese, which means "what" or "how." In Unit 2 we learned that **géidō chín** is literally *and* functionally "how much money?" Here, **géidímjūng** is literally "what point of the clock?" and functionally means "what time?"

### Obligation (3)

**Yiu** is used here as a modal to express obligation, as in **Ngóh yiu jáu la** "I have to leave." This is to be distinguished from the use of **yiu** as a main verb, which means "want," as in Unit 2: **Ngóh jauh yiu yāt bohng lā** lit. "Then I want one pound."

### La (4)

**La** is a sentence-final particle in Cantonese to indicate changed status. In Dialogue 1 above, Emily uses **la** with **Ngóh yiu jáu** to indicate she is leaving instead of staying.

## Vocabulary

### Daily routine

Below are some vocabulary items referring to daily routine. Try reading each item aloud. If you have the audio of this book, model your pronunciation on the recording.

| | | | |
|---|---|---|---|
| héi-sān | to get up | fong-gūng | to leave work |
| sihk-jóuchāan | to have breakfast | sihk-máahnfaahn | to have dinner |
| fāan-gūng | to go to work | fan-gaau | to sleep |
| sihk-ngaan | to have lunch | | |

Note that **sihk-jóuchāan**, **sihk-ngaan**, and **sihk-máahnfaahn** are verb-object constructions formed with the verb **sihk** "to eat" and an object denoting a meal, **jóuchāan** for "breakfast," **ngaan** for "lunch" and **máahnfaahn** for "dinner."

### More time expressions

| | |
|---|---|
| gāmyaht | today |
| tīngyaht | tomorrow |
| chàhmyaht | yesterday |
| gāmmáahn | this evening/tonight |
| tīngmáahn | tomorrow evening/tomorrow night |
| chàhmmáahn | yesterday evening/last night |

Note that many Cantonese speakers say **kàhmmáahn** instead of **chàhmmáahn**. This is a kind of free variation, where neither pronunciation is more correct than the other.

## Exercise 1 Telling the time

You are in the street. Someone comes up to you and asks, "**Yìhgā géidímjūng a?**" Reply according to the times given below. Remember you have several options as to how to tell the time. Write your answers first and then try reading them aloud. (The first one has been done for you as an example.)

(a) 12:45 p.m.  Yìhgā (haih) sahp-yih dím gáu.
Yìhgā (haih) sahp-yih dím sei-sahp ńgh fān.
Yìhgā (haih) sahp-yih dím sāam go gwāt.

Unit 4: *Telling the time*

(b) 3:35 p.m.
(c) 9:18 a.m.
(d) 11:52 a.m.
(e) 5:15 p.m.

## Types of television program

| | |
|---|---|
| sānmán | news |
| tīnhei bougou | weather report |
| dihnsihkehk | TV drama |
| dihnyíng | movie/film |
| géiluhkpín | documentary |
| táiyuhk | sports |
| choimáh | horse-racing |

## Dialogue 3

**(CD1; 46)**

John is talking to Richard about their daily routine.

(a) What time does Richard get up in the morning?
(b) What time does Richard go to bed?
(c) What about John?

JOHN: Richard, néih tūngsèuhng géidímjūng héi-sān a?
RICHARD: Ngóh tūngsèuhng seuhngjau chāt dím sāam héi-sān.
JOHN: Gám néih yehmáahn géidímjūng fan-gaau a?
RICHARD: Ngóh yehmáahn tūngsèuhng sahp-yāt dím bun fan-gaau. Néih nē, John?
JOHN: Ngóh seuhngjau baat dím bun héi-sān. Yehmáahn daaihyeuk sahp-yih dím fan-gaau.

JOHN: Richard, what time will you get up tomorrow morning?
RICHARD: I will get up at 7:15 (tomorrow morning).
JOHN: So what time will you go to sleep (tonight)?
RICHARD: I usually go to sleep at 11:30 in the evening. How about you, John?
JOHN: I get up at 8:30 in the morning and go to sleep around 12:00 in the evening.

## Dialogue 4

**(CD1; 48)**
Carmen is talking to her friend Mary on the phone. Mary has a TV guide and Carmen is asking her about tonight's programs.

(a) What time is the evening TV movie?
(b) At what times is the daily news on?
(c) What time is the weather report?

CARMEN: Mary, néih gāmmáahn géidímjūng tái dihnsih a?
MARY: Gāmmáahn gáu dím bun yáuh hei tái.
CARMEN: Gám, géidímjūng yáuh sānmán tái a?
MARY: Gāmmáahn luhk dím bun tùhng sahp-yāt dím jūng dōu yáuh sānmán tái.
CARMEN: Gám, tīnhei bougou nē? Géidímjūng yáuh dāk tái a?
MARY: Tīnhei bougou hái chāt dím bun jouh.

CARMEN: Mary, what time will you watch television tonight?
MARY: There is a movie on at 9:30 tonight.
CARMEN: Then what time is the news on?
MARY: The news is on at both 6:30 and 11:00 p.m.
CARMEN: And what about the weather report? What time is that on?
MARY: The weather report is on at 7:30.

## Dialogue 5

**(CD1; 49)**
John is talking to Jack on the phone. Jack is telling him about the sports programs being shown on TV over the next two evenings.

(a) When is tennis shown on TV?
(b) When is soccer shown?
(c) What about horse-racing?

JOHN: Jack, gāmmáahn tùhng tīngmáahn dihnsih yáuh mātyeh hóutái a?
JACK: Gāmmáahn luhk dím yáuh móhngkàuh tái. Yìhnhauh baat dím bun yáuh jūkkàuh tái.
JOHN: Ngóh mh jūngyi tái móhngkàuh tùhng jūkkàuh. Gāmmáahn yáuh móuh choimáh tái a?

Unit 4: *Telling the time*

JACK: Gāmmáahn dihnsih móuh choimáh tái. Bātgwo tīngmáahn yáuh.
JOHN: Tīngmáahn géidímjūng yáuh dāk tái a?
JACK: Tīngmáahn gáu dím chāt yáuh dāk tái.

JOHN: Jack, is there anything good on TV tonight and tomorrow night?
JACK: There is tennis on tonight at 6:00. Afterwards at 8:30 there is soccer.
JOHN: I don't care for either tennis or soccer. Is there any horse-racing on tonight?
JACK: There is not horse-racing on tonight, but there is tomorrow night.
JOHN: When is the horse-racing on tomorrow night?
JACK: Horse-racing is on tomorrow night at 9:35.

## Idioms and structures

The items in the list below appear in the same order as they do in the dialogues above. The *italicized* items are *new* items. In the notes, numbers in brackets refer to the expressions listed below.

| | |
|---|---|
| 1 *tūngsèuhng* | usually |
| 2 **gāmmáahn géidímjūng yáuh hei tái a?** | At what time is the movie on tonight? |
| 3 **Géidímjūng yáuh *dāk* tái a?** | At what time *can* it be seen? |
| 4 *hái* **chāt dím bun *jouh*** | shows *at* half past seven |
| 5 *hóutái* | interesting (lit. "good to watch") |
| 6 *yìhnhauh* | then, later on, afterwards |
| 7 **Gāmmáahn *yáuh móuh* choimáh tái a?** | Is there any horse-racing on tonight? |

### Existential yáuh (2)

**Yáuh** is used existentially here, i.e., to indicate that something exists. (See Unit 3 for the uses of **yáuh**.) *Yáuh* **hei tái** means literally "There is a movie to see."

## Possibility (3)

**Dāk** is a verbal particle, which is used to indicate possibility or permission. For example, in Dialogue 4, in **Géidímjūng yáuh *dāk* tái a?**, *dāk* follows the existential verb **yáuh** and precedes the main verb **tái**, and the consequent expression **yáuh *dāk* tái** means "can be seen."

## Point of time (4)

Here **hái** is a time marker used as a preposition, meaning "at (a certain time)." Thus, **Tīnhei bougou *hái* chāt dím bun jouh** means "The weather report is shown at half past seven."

## Jouh (4)

**Jouh** is a verb with a wide range of meanings. Here it is not used with its most common meaning, "to do." Instead, it refers to a TV program or a movie being on. Thus, **Tīnhei bougou hái chāt dím bun *jouh*** means "The weather report is shown at half past seven," while **Nī chēut hei hái Palace Theater *jouh*** means "This movie is on at the Palace Theater" (**chēut** being the classifier for **hei**). Note that the word order of such sentences differs in Cantonese and English. In Cantonese, the time expression comes *before* the verb, hence **Tīnhei bougou hái chāt dímjūng *jouh***. In English, the time expression comes *after* the verb, as in "The weather report is (shown) at 7 o'clock."

## Yáuh móuh (7)

A choice-type question with the existential verb **yáuh** is formed from the positive verb **yáuh** and its negative counterpart **móuh**. (Note that **yáuh** is an exception to regular verbs in that it never takes the negative marker **m-**.) This choice-interrogative, **yáuh móuh**, is complemented by the particle **a**, in the function of sentence-question. Hence the question **Gāmmáahn *yáuh móuh* choimáh tái a?** "Is there horse-racing on tonight?"

## Exercise 2 Comprehension

Read the following questions. Then go back to Dialogues 3, 4, and 5 to find the answers.

Unit 4: *Telling the time*

(a) According to Dialogue 3, who sleeps longer every night?

    (i) John

    (ii) Richard

(b) According to Dialogue 4, how many times is the TV news shown in the evening?

    (i) once

    (ii) twice

    (iii) three times

(c) According to Dialogue 5, what kind of program does John like watching?

    (i) news

    (ii) soccer

    (iii) tennis

    (iv) horse-racing

(d) According to Dialogue 5, what kinds of program does Jack enjoy watching?

    (i) news and weather

    (ii) tennis and soccer

    (iii) horse-racing

## Exercise 3 Daily routine

The table shows the daily routines of John, Carmen, and Richard. Write your own routine in the fourth column. Then write sentences to describe each person's routine, including your own. After that, read the sentences aloud. (A few sentences have been written for you as examples.)

|  | John | Carmen | Richard | You |
|---|---|---|---|---|
| **héi-sān** | 8:00 | 7:30 | 7:15 | |
| **fāan-gūng** | 9:30 | 9:00 | 9:00 | |
| **sihk-ngaan** | 1:00 | 12:30 | 1:00 | |
| **fong-gūng** | 6:00 | 5:15 | 5:30 | |
| **sihk-máahnfaahn** | 8:00 | 8:00 | 7:00 | |
| **fan-gaau** | 12:00 | 1:00 | 11:30 | |

(a) *John*
   John seuhngjau baat dímjūng héi-sān, gáu dím bun fāan-gūng. Kéuih hahjau yāt dímjūng sihk-ngaan, yìhnhauh luhk dím fong-gūng ....

(b) *Carmen*

(c) *Richard*

(d) *You*
   Ngóh ... héi-sān ...

## Exercise 4 What's on TV tonight?

Referring to the TV guide here, answer all the questions by first writing out the answers and then reading them aloud.

| | |
|---|---|
| 7:05 p.m. | News |
| 7:25 p.m. | Weather report |
| 7:30 p.m. | TV drama |
| 8:30 p.m. | Documentary |
| 9:30 p.m. | TV movie |
| 11:45 p.m. | Late news |
| 12:10 a.m. | Weather report |
| 12:15 a.m. | Soccer |

(a) Gāmmáahn géidímjūng yáuh sānmán tái a?

(b) Gāmmáahn géidímjūng yáuh tīnhéi bougou tái a?

(c) Ngóh jūngyi tái géiluhkpín. Gāmmáahn yáuh móuh géiluhkpín tái a? Géidímjūng yáuh dāk tái a?

(d) Gāmmáahn gáu dím bun yáuh mātyéh tái a?

(e) Gāmmáahn géidímjūng yáuh móhngkàuh tái a?

## Recognizing Chinese characters

When telling the time in colloquial Cantonese, the expression **dímjūng** is used to refer to "o'clock." However, in written Chinese, a different expression

時

# Unit 4: *Telling the time*

(pronounced as **sìh** in Cantonese) is used instead. Thus,

一時

is "one o'clock,"

二時

is "two o'clock," and

三時

is "three o'clock." The Chinese word for "minute," namely

分

(**fān**), on the other hand, is shared by spoken Mandarin and colloquial Cantonese, as is the word for the "half-hour,"

半

(**bun**). The written Chinese word for the "quarter-hour,"

刻

(pronounced **hāak** in Cantonese), however, is also a completely different expression from **gwāt**, which is used exclusively in colloquial Cantonese.

一刻

is "a quarter of an hour" and

三刻

is "three-quarters of an hour." Below are some examples of times written in Chinese characters:

| | |
|---|---|
| 四時 | 4 o'clock |
| 五時十分 | 5:10 |
| 六時半 | 6:30 |
| 七時一刻 | 7:15 |
| 八時三刻 | 8:45 |

The Chinese word for "morning" is written as

上午

(pronounced **seuhngńgh** in Cantonese), and is different from the most common colloquial Cantonese term of **seuhngjau**, though both share **seuhng**, which means "the upper part." Similarly, the Chinese word for "afternoon" is written as

下午

(pronounced **hahńgh** in Cantonese), as opposed to **hahjau** in colloquial Cantonese, **hah** meaning "the lower part."

## Communicative activities

1 Ask your partner about his or her daily routine. What time do you get up? What time do you have breakfast? What time do you go to work? Switch roles and repeat.
2 Look up a TV guide (電視表 **dihnsih bíu**) on the Internet and see if you can find out what time the news and other programs are on in Hong Kong.

## Cultural point

China has a long history of technology and one of the earliest known clocks in the world, the water clock, is attributed to China. The oldest reference dates the use of the water clock in China to the 6th century B.C.E. In the second century C.E. the eminent Chinese astronomer Zhang Heng (78–139) created a mobile water-driven globe, which revolved in correspondence with the movements of celestial bodies. (Reference: Needham, Joseph (2000). *Science & Civilisation in China*. IV:2: *Mechanical Engineering*. Cambridge University Press.)

# Unit Five
# Ngoihbíu

Physical appearances

In Unit 5 you will learn about:

- describing people's age and physical appearance
- pointing out people and objects
- terms for family members
- possessive forms

## Dialogue 1

**(CD1; 52)**
John is on the phone arranging to meet CHAN Syut Wai, whom he has never met before. They need to find out about each other's appearance so that they can recognize each other when they meet.

(a) What does John look like?
(b) What does CHAN Syut Wai look like?

| | |
|---|---|
| CHAN SYUT WAI: | Chíng mahn néih haih dímyéung ga? |
| JOHN: | Ngóh daai ngáahngéng, géi gōu. |
| CHAN SYUT WAI: | Gám, néih fèih dihng sau a? |
| JOHN: | Ngóh mhaih hóu fèih, mhaih hóu sau. Gám, néih nē? Néih haih dímyéung ga? |
| CHAN SYUT WAI: | Ngóh haih yāt go dyún tàuhfaat ge néuihjái, sau-sáu-déi, mhaih géi gōu. |
| JOHN: | Gám néih yáuh móuh daai ngáahngéng a? |
| CHAN SYUT WAI: | Móuh, ngóh móuh daai ngáahngéng. |

| | |
|---|---|
| CHAN SYUT WAI: | May I ask what you look like? |
| JOHN: | I wear glasses and am fairly tall. |
| CHAN SYUT WAI: | So are you fat or thin? |
| JOHN: | I am not too fat or too thin. How about you, what do you look like? |
| CHAN SYUT WAI: | I am a woman with short hair, fairly thin and not too tall. |
| JOHN: | And do you wear glasses? |
| CHAN SYUT WAI: | No, I don't (wear glasses). |

## Dialogue 2

**(CD1; 54)**
John and Carmen are at a gathering of the Cantonese Students' Club. Carmen is pointing out Mr. Tong, her Cantonese teacher, to John.

(a) What does Mr. Tong, Carmen's Cantonese teacher, look like?
(b) What does Mrs. Lam, John's Cantonese teacher, look like?

Unit 5: *Physical appearances*

| | |
|---|---|
| JOHN: | Carmen, bīngo haih Tòhng lóuhsī a? |
| CARMEN: | Nē! Gó bīn hóu gōu, sau-sáu-déi, daai ngáahngéng gó go jauh haih Tòhng lóuhsī laak. |
| JOHN: | Gó bīn gōu-gōu-sau-sau, daai ngáahngéng, dyún tàuhfaat, géi lengjái gó go jauh haih Tòhng lóuhsī àh? |
| CARMEN: | Haih laak. Gám, néih go Gwóngdūngwá lóuhsī Làhm táai nē? Kéuih hái bīndouh a? |
| JOHN: | Nē! Gó bīn chèuhng tàuhfaat, móuh daai ngáahngéng, géi leng gó go jauh haih Làhm táai laak. |
| CARMEN: | Haih-mh-haih ngái-ngái-déi gó go a? |
| JOHN: | Haih laak. |
| CARMEN: | Kéuih hóu hauhsāang wo. |
| JOHN: | Haih a. Kéuih yih-sahp chāt seui ja. |

| | |
|---|---|
| JOHN: | Carmen, which is Teacher Tong? |
| CARMEN: | Look over there! Teacher Tong is the tall, thin one wearing glasses. |
| JOHN: | That good-looking tall and thin man with short hair wearing glasses is Teacher Tong? |
| CARMEN: | Yes. So, where is your Cantonese teacher, Mrs. Lam? |
| JOHN: | Over there! Mrs. Lam is the pretty woman with long hair and no glasses. |
| CARMEN: | Is she the fairly short one? |
| JOHN: | Right. |
| CARMEN: | She looks quite young. |
| JOHN: | Yes, she is only 27 years old. |

## Vocabulary

**(CD1; 55)**

### Physical appearances

Below are some words and expressions for describing people's physical appearances. Try reading each item aloud. If you have the audio recording for this book, model your pronunciation on the recordings.

| | | | |
|---|---|---|---|
| gōu | tall | lóuh | old |
| ngái | short | hauhsāang | young |
| gōudaaih | big | daai ngáahngéng | wears glasses |
| ngáisai | small | móuh daai ngáahngéng | does not wear glasses |
| fèih | fat | | |
| sau | thin | yáuh wùhsōu | has a moustache/beard |
| chèuhng tàuhfaat | long-haired | | |
| dyún tàuhfaat | short-haired | móuh wùhsōu | does not have a moustache/beard |
| leng | pretty | | |
| lengjái | handsome | | |

This list gives the adjectives or adjective phrases in pairs of opposite meanings. However, words such as **gōu** "tall" and **ngái** "short" represent two poles between which are intermediate points for various degrees of height. Below is a list of expressions for describing different perceptions of height:

| | |
|---|---|
| hóu gōu | very tall |
| géi gōu/gōu-gōu-déi | quite tall |
| mhaih géi gōu/màh-má-déi gōu | not too tall |
| géi ngái/ngái-ngái-déi | quite short |
| hóu ngái | very short |

### Reduplicated adjective + déi

The pattern "adjective + reduplicated adjective + **déi**," such as **gōu-gōu-déi**, is common in colloquial Cantonese. However, there is a rule to observe when forming such a pattern. The reduplicated adjective always undergoes a tone change and takes on the *high rising tone*. Thus, **géi sau** can be expressed as **sau-*sáu*-déi**, **géi fèih** as **fèih-*féi*-déi**, and **géi lóuh** as **lóuh-*lóu*-déi**. However, when the adjective is on a high level tone (e.g. **gōu**) or high rising tone (e.g. **ngái**), the tone of the reduplicated adjective remains unchanged, e.g. **gōu-gōu-déi**, **ngái-ngái-déi**.

Adjective phrases such as **daai ngáahngéng** vs. **móuh daai ngáahngéng** and **yáuh wùhsōu** vs. **móuh wùhsōu** belong to another category in that they represent "either-or" situations without any intermediate possibilities. Thus someone can only be **daai ngáahn-géng** or **móuh daai ngáahngéng** but never *****géi daai ngáahngéng**.

## Idioms and structures

The items in the list below appear in the same order as they do in the dialogues above. The *italicized* items are *new* items. In the notes, numbers in brackets refer to the expressions listed below.

1 *néih haih dímyéung ga?* — What do you look like?
2 *néih fèih dihng sau a?* — Are you fat or thin?
3 **Ngóh haih yāt go *dyún tàuhfaat* ge *néuihjái*.** — I am a short-haired woman.
4 **néih yáuh móuh daai ngáahngéng a?** — Do you wear glasses?
5 ***Nē!*** — Look over there!
6 *gó bīn* — over there
7 *gó go* — that person
8 ***Tòhng lóuhsī*** — my teacher Mr. Tong
9 **gó go *jauh haih* Tòhng lóuhsī *laak*** — *that is* my teacher Mr. Tong
10 **gó bīn ... gó go *jauh haih* Tòhng lóuhsī *àh?*** — *so,* the ... one over there *is* Mr. Tong (lit. "Teacher Tong")
11 ***Haih laak.*** — That's right./Right./Yes.
12 *néih go* **Gwóngdūngwá lóuhsī** — *your* Cantonese teacher
13 **Làhm táai** — Mrs. Lam
14 **Kéuih hóu hauhsāang *wo.*** — She looks very young.
15 **Kéuih *yih-sahp chāt seui ja.*** — She's *only 27 years old.*

(CD1; 56)

### Asking about physical appearance (1, 2, 4)

There are several ways to ask about somebody's appearance. The first way is to ask a general question:

| Kéuih (haih) dímyéung ga? | What does he/she look like? |

Note that to ask what somebody looks like, the particle **ga**, and not **a**, is used. The question **Kéuih dímyéung a?** has a different meaning, that of "How is he/she?," asking about feelings rather than appearance.

Instead of asking a general question, you can ask about a particular physical feature. There are two ways of doing this. The first way is to use the *unmarked* form of a pair of opposite attributes (for instance, "tall" is used in the pair of "tall vs. short") and form a choice-type question:

| Kéuih gōu-mh-gōu a? | Is he/she tall? |
| Kéuih fèih-mh-fèih a? | Is he/she fat? |

The second way is to form an "either/or" question with the two opposing attributes by using the word **dihng** "or" in between:

| Kéuih gōu dihng ngái a? | Is he/she tall or short? |
| Kéuih fèih dihng sau a? | Is he/she fat or thin? |

To ask about "glasses vs. no glasses" or "moustache/beard vs. no moustache/beard," a choice-type question using the existential verbs **yáuh** and **móuh** is used:

| Kéuih yáuh móuh daai ngáahngéng a? | Does he/she wear glasses? |
| Kéuih yáuh móuh wùhsōu a? | Does he have a beard/moustache? |

## Describing physical appearance (3)

There are two ways to form sentences to describe somebody's physical appearance. The first way is to use the adjectives *predicatively*, i.e. without a noun:

| Kéuih hóu gōu. | He is very tall. |
| Kéuih gōu-gōu-sau-sau. | He is tall and thin. |
| Kéuih màh-má-déi gōu. | He's not very tall. |

The second way is to use the adjectives *attributively*, that is, before the nouns they modify:

| | |
|---|---|
| Kéuih haih yāt go hóu gōu ge nàahmjái. | He is a very tall boy. |
| Kéuih haih yāt go gōu-gōu-sau-sau ge nàahmjái. | He is a tall, thin boy. |
| Kéuih haih yāt go màh-má-déi gōu ge nàahmjái. | He is not a very tall boy. |

There are several things to bear in mind when using the adjectives *attributively*. First of all, the verb **haih** is needed. Secondly, a noun phrase is formed with a numeral (in this case, **yāt**), a classifier (in this case, **go**), and a noun (in this case, **nàahmjái**). Lastly, there is a special particle **ge** which must be used after the adjective, hence **hóu gōu ge**, **gōu-gōu-sau-sau ge** and **màh-má-déi gōu ge**.

**Nàahmjái** can be translated into English as either "man" or "boy," depending on the context. It is used to refer to boys in their teens or young men in their twenties or thirties. The female counterpart of this is **néuihjái**. To refer to a more mature-looking man, the word **nàahmyán** is used. The female counterpart for **nàahmyán** is **néuihyán**.

## Exercise 1 Your family members

Now introduce your own family by first saying how many family members you have, and then describing what each of them looks like.

**Ngóh yáuh ... go ngūkkéiyàhn. Kéuihdeih haih ...**

## Interjective nē (5)

**Nē** is used here as an interjection to indicate that someone should look in a particular direction for a particular target. It is totally different in meaning from the **nē** used as a final particle.

## Adverbial phrase of place (6)

**Gó bīn** is an adverbial phrase of place that refers to people or objects not immediately close to the speaker, and can be translated into English as "over there." The corresponding adverbial phrase of place for referring to people or objects which are close to the speaker is **nī bīn**, which means "over here."

## Demonstrative pronoun (7)

**Gó go** is a demonstrative pronoun used to refer to a person or object not near to the speaker, and can be translated into English as "that." **Gó go** is made up of two parts, namely the determiner **gó** and the classifier **go**. Hence, it can only refer to nouns that can take the classifier **go**. For example, *gó go* **yàhn** "that person" and *gó go* **cháang** "that orange" are fine but *gó go hei is not. The corresponding demonstrative pronoun for referring to people or objects close to the speaker is **nī go**, which has the specifier **nī** and means "this."

## Addressing people by title (8)

**Lóuhsī** is a respectful word meaning "teacher." In Cantonese it can be used as a title after the surname of the teacher. Thus, a teacher whose surname is **Tòhng** would be addressed as **Tòhng lóuhsī**. The same applies to some professions that enjoy a high social status. For example, the word for "lawyer" is **leuhtsī**, and the word for "doctor" is **yīsāng**; thus a lawyer whose surname is **Tòhng** is addressed as **Tòhng leuhtsī**, and a doctor named **Tòhng** is addressed as **Tòhng yīsāng**.

## Emphasis (9)

In **gó go jauh haih Tòhng lóuhsī laak**, both the adverb **jauh**, which means "precisely," and the final particle **laak**, which is often used to indicate changed status, are used to give emphasis to **gó go haih Tòhng lóuhsī** "That is Mr. Tong."

## Question with àh (10)

**Gó go jauh haih Tòhng lóuhsī àh?** is a question which is not asking for new information, but simply acknowledges what has been said and asks for confirmation. **Gó go jauh haih Tòhng lóuhsī** is a repetition of the original statement and the final particle **àh** turns it into a question.

## Genitive pronoun (12)

Here **néih go** is used as a genitive (possessive) phrase to mean "your" and so **néih go Gwóngdūngwá lóuhsī** means "your Cantonese teacher." Notice that the genitive phrase **néih go** is made up of the pronoun **néih** "you" and the classifier **go**. By the same token, "my mango" would be **ngóh go mōnggwó**, and "his book" would be **kéuih bún syū**, **bún** being the classifier for books.

## Addressing married women (13)

In Cantonese, we address a married woman by using the word **taai-táai** *after* her husband's surname. Thus, "Mrs. Lam" is **Làhm taai-táai**, which in colloquial speech is often shortened into **Làhm táai**. Note, though, that if one asked a married woman's name in the formal way, **gwai sing** (see Unit 1), it would be common for her to give her maiden name as that remains her surname after marriage. In order to be addressed socially as Mrs. Lam, a woman with the name WONG Ming Fong (married to a man surnamed Lam), might say **Ngóh sing Wòhng, Ngóh sīngsāang sing Làhm** "My surname is Wong, but my husband's surname is Lam."

## Final particle wo (14)

**Wo** is a final particle to express emphatic recognition of a mildly surprising fact; in the case of the sentence **Kéuih hóu hauhsāang wo** the unexpected observation is how young Mrs. Lam looks.

## Expressing age (15)

**Seui** means "years of age," and so **yih-sahp chāt seui** is "twenty-seven years old." Below are some examples of different ages:

| | |
|---|---|
| yāt seui | one year old |
| léuhng seui | two years old |
| sāam seui | three years old |
| sahp seui | ten years old |
| yih-sahp seui | twenty years old |
| yih-sahp ńgh seui | twenty-five years old |
| sāam-sahp seui | thirty years old |

As the numbers under a hundred are so commonly used in colloquial speech, the two-syllable words such as **yih-sahp, sāam-sahp, sei-sahp** are often contracted in natural speech to form new shorter sounds. For example, **yih-sahp** is contracted into the single syllable **y'ah** (the apostrophe denotes the elision); thus, **y'ah seui** is "20 years old" and **y'ah yāt seui** is "21 years old." **Sāam-sahp** is contracted as **sā'ah** and so **sā'ah seui** is "30 years old" and **sā'ah chāt seui** is "37 years old." Here is a list of such contracted forms:

| | | |
|---|---|---|
| y'ah seui | yih-sahp seui | twenty years old |
| sā'ah seui | sāam-sahp seui | thirty years old |
| sei'ah seui | sei-sahp seui | forty years old |
| ńgh'ah seui | ńgh-sahp seui | fifty years old |
| luhk'ah seui | luhk-sahp seui | sixty years old |
| chāt'ah seui | chāt-sahp seui | seventy years old |
| baat'ah seui | baat-sahp seui | eighty years old |
| gáu'ah seui | gáu-sahp seui | ninety years old |

To ask somebody's age, you say: **Néih géidō seui a?** (lit. "You how many years old?") or alternatively, **Néih géidaih?** (lit. "You how big?") The former is typical when the expected response is smaller, say 1–18 years. The latter can be used with any expected age, but is especially appropriate for those past adolescence.

## Exercise 2 Contracted forms of numbers

Read the following contracted forms of numbers and then write the numbers in English. The first one has been done for you as an example. (A more beneficial way of doing this exercise is to listen to the audio recording and write down the numbers.)

(a) y'ah sei seui            24 years old

(b) ńgh'ah yih seui

(c) sā'ah baat seui

(d) chāt'ah yāt seui

(e) gáu'ah luhk seui

(f) sei'ah gáu seui

## Final particle ja (15)

**Jā** is a final particle which adds the meaning of "only." **Jā** itself is a contraction of the final particle **jē** "only" and **ā** "emphatic marker." For example, **Kéuih yih-sahp chāt seui ja** means "She's *only* 27," while **Ngóh yáuh sahp mān ja** means "I have *only* ten dollars."

## Vocabulary

### Kinship terms

Chinese kinship terms are much more specific and complex than English ones. Below is a list of the most common ones. Try reading each aloud, and listen to them if you have the audio recordings.

| | | | |
|---|---|---|---|
| bàh-bā | father | jèih-jē/gājē | elder sister |
| màh-mā | mother | (mùih-)múi | younger sister |
| gòh-gō/daaihlóu | elder brother | jái | son |
| dàih-dái/sailóu | younger brother | néui | daughter |

Notice that the first six are all reduplicated words, but the same character is pronounced on two different tones, though all six terms begin with a *low falling tone*. The alternatives for "elder brother," "younger brother," and "elder sister" do not follow the same pattern. **Daaihlóu** literally means "big boy," **daaih** meaning "big," **sailóu** literally means "small boy," **sai** meaning "small," and **gājē** literally means "big sister at home," as **gā** by itself means "home."

## Dialogue 3

**(CD1; 58)**

John is looking at Emily's family photo. Emily is telling him about the members of her family.

(a) How old are Emily's parents?
(b) How old is Emily's brother?
(c) How old is Emily's sister?

EMILY: Nī géi go jauh haih ngóh dī ngūkkéiyàhn laak.
JOHN: Nī go haih-mh-haih néih bàh-bā a?

EMILY: Haih laak. Nī go jauh haih ngóh bàh-bā laak. Gaaklèih nī go haih ngóh màh-mā. Ngóh bàh-bā tùhng ngóh màh-mā dōu haih sei-sahp gáu seui.
JOHN: Kéuihdeih sei-sahp gáu seui làh? Kéuihdeih go yéung hóu hauhsāang wo.
EMILY: Haih a. Nē! Gaaklèih gó léuhng go jauh haih ngóh go sailóu tùhng ngóh go mùih-múi laak. Ngóh sailóu gamnín sahp-yih seui. Ngóh go múi gamnín sahp-yat seui.

---

EMILY: These are my family members.
JOHN: Is this one your father?
EMILY: Yes, this is my father. Next (to him) is my mother. My father and mother are both 49 years old.
JOHN: So they are 49? They appear so young!
EMILY: Yes (they do). Look! Next to the two of them are my younger brother and my younger sister. My younger brother is 12 years old and my younger sister is 11 years old.

##  Idioms and structures

The items in the list below appear in the same order as they do in the dialogue above. The *italicized* items are *new* items. In the notes, numbers in brackets refer to the expressions listed below.

| 1 | *Nī géi go* | these (several people) |
| 2 | *ngūkkéiyàhn* | family members |
| 3 | *ngóh dī* ngūkkéiyàhn | *my* family members |
| 4 | *ngóh* bàh-bā | *my* father |
| 5 | *gaaklèih* | by the side/next to |
| 6 | Kéuihdeih sei-sahp gáu seui *làh?* | So they are 49? (showing surprise) |
| 7 | Kéuihdeih go *yéung* | Their appearance/they appear |
| 8 | *gāmnín* | this year |

## Demonstrative pronoun with classifier (1)

**Nī géi go** is the demonstrative pronoun **nī go** with the numeral **géi** (several) in between, meaning "these (several people)." Remember that **go** is a classifier for some nouns only, and other demonstrative pronouns with different classifiers are needed for certain nouns. In **Nī géi go jauh haih ngóh dī ngūkkéiyàhn laak** the noun that **nī géi go** refers to is **yàhn** (people), which takes the classifier **go**.

## Modification of plurals (3)

Although Cantonese nouns themselves are not marked for number, there are other ways to express the plural. Note that the marker **dī** *precedes* the noun it affects. The **dī** in **ngóh dī ngūkkéiyàhn** is a marker of modification for plural nouns. It combines with **ngóh** to form the modifier **ngóh dī** to indicate possession. (Remember **néih go Gwóngdūngwá lóuhsī**, above.) Thus, **ngóh dī ngūkkéiyàhn** means "my family members." Similarly, **ngóh dī syū** means "my books."

## Possession with family members (4)

**Ngóh bàh-bā** means "my father." It is a shortened form of **ngóh go bàh-bā**, where the classifier **go** is used. This kind of deletion ordinarily only takes place with nouns pertaining to close family relationships, such as **néih màh-mā**, and not with other nouns, hence **ngóh bún syū** cannot be replaced by *****ngóh syū**.

## Final particle làh (6)

**Làh** is a final particle used to form questions showing surprise. Here, the question **Kéuihdeih sei-sahp gáu seui *làh*?** is a response to **Ngóh bàh-bā tùhng ngóh màh-mā dōu haih sei-sahp gáu seui**. The proposition that both parents are forty-nine is repeated and the anticipated answer is a confirmatory **Haih a**.

## Exercise 3 John's college friends

The dialogue below is between John and Carmen. They are looking at a photograph of John's college friends. John is telling Carmen his friends' names. Read the dialogue or, preferably, listen to the audio recording, and then label the picture with the correct names. Also, write their nationalities in brackets under their names.

CARMEN: John, nī go yáuh wùhsōu ge haih bīngo a?
JOHN: Nī go yáuh wùhsōu, daai ngáahngéng ge haih Michael. Kéuih haih Méihgwok yàhn.
CARMEN: Gám, nī go gōu-gōu-sau-sau, chèuhng tàuhfaat ge néuihjái nē? Kéuih giu mātyeh méng a?
JOHN: Nī go gōu-gōu-sau-sau ge néuihjái haih Christine. Kéuih haih Faatgwok yàhn.
CARMEN: Gaaklèih nī go daai ngáahngéng ge néuihjái yauh haih bīngo a? Kéuih hóu leng wo.
JOHN: Haih a. Judy géi leng ga. Haih Yīnggwok yàhn.
CARMEN: Nī go ngái-ngái-déi, móuh daai ngáahngéng ge nàahmjái haih bīngo a? Kéuih haih-mh-haih Jūnggwok yàhn a?
JOHN: Haih a. Kéuih haih Jūnggwok yàhn. Kéuih giujouh Léih Mìhng.

---

CARMEN: John, who is the one with the moustache?
JOHN: The one with the moustache and glasses is Michael. He is American.
CARMEN: And what about the tall, thin girl with long hair?
JOHN: The tall, thin girl is Christine. She is French.
CARMEN: And who is the girl next to her wearing glasses? She is really pretty!
JOHN: Yes, Judy is quite pretty! (She) is English.
CARMEN: Who is the shorter boy without glasses? Is he Chinese?
JOHN: Yes, he is Chinese. His name is LI Ming.

Unit 5: *Physical appearances*

## Exercise 4 Teddy's family

Refer to the picture of Teddy's family and answer the questions. The first answer has been given for you as an example.

(a) **Teddy yáuh géidō go ngūkkéiyàhn a?**
Teddy yáuh sei go ngūkkéiyàhn. Kéuih bàh-bā giu Martin. Kéuih màh-mā giu Pam. Kéuih yáuh yāt go gājē, giujouh Clara. Kéuih yáuh yāt go sailóu, giujouh Jimmy.
(b) Martin gāmnín géidō seui a? Kéuih dímyéung ga?
Martin gāmnín ... seui. Kéuih daai ngáahngéng ...
(c) Pam géidō seui a? Kéuih gōu dihng ngái, fèih dihng sau a?
(d) Clara nē? Kéuih dímyéung ga? Kéuih leng-mh-leng ga?
(e) Jimmy gāmnín géidō seui a? Kéuih dímyéung ga?

## Recognizing Chinese characters

Below are the kinship terms relating to members of the family, written in Chinese characters.

| | |
|---|---|
| 爸爸 | father |
| 媽媽 | mother |
| 哥哥 | elder brother |
| 弟弟 | younger brother |
| 姊姊 | elder sister |
| 妹妹 | younger sister |

## Communicative activities

1 Interview a partner about his or her family. Find out how many members are in the immediate family. Do members of the extended family live with your friend?
2 Describe in detail the physical appearance of a friend or family member. If you have a study partner or a Cantonese friend, try describing someone to him or her while the partner tries to sketch the person.

Unit 5: *Physical appearances*

## Cultural points

1 When describing one's family it is usual to go from oldest to youngest and male to female, but listing yourself last: for instance, saying who is in one's family as: **bàh-bā, màhmā, jèhjē, tùhng ngóh**. "Father, mother, (older) sister, and myself."

2 Chinese people tend to refer to unrelated friends or even acquaintances by the family term that would fit that person's age relationship. For example, if you are a female in your late teens or twenties, children of friends might well refer to you as 姊姊 **jèhjē** or "older sister." Likewise, a male in his forties may be called 叔叔 **sūksuk** or "uncle" and a female of the same age may be called 阿姨 **a-yī** or "aunt."

3 Westerners are often taken aback by how directly the Chinese refer to aspects of physical appearance. A Chinese friend or even casual acquaintance might mention that you are fat or that your nose is quite large. Such directness is not always intended as rude, but is often just a matter-of-fact comment on how you look. It is best not to make too much of it.

# Unit Six
# Gachìhn
Prices

In Unit 6 you will learn about:

- larger numbers
- comparing
- using **-jó** for completion of action
- how to indicate the superlative

Unit 6: *Prices*

## Dialogue 1

**(CD1; 60)**

John and Carmen have been invited to dinner at Mrs. Lam's home. They are admiring the furniture in Mrs. Lam's flat.

(a) How much did Mrs. Lam's sofa cost?
(b) How much did Mrs. Lam's dining table and dining chairs cost?
(c) How much did Mrs. Lam's coffee table cost?

| | |
|---|---|
| CARMEN: | Làhmtáai, néih ngūkkéi dī gāsī hóu leng wo. |
| MRS. LAM: | Dōjeh. Ngóh dōu hóu jūngyi ngóh ngūkkéi dī gāsī ga. |
| CARMEN: | Nī jēung sōfá yiu géidō chín a? |
| MRS. LAM: | Nī jēung sōfá máaih-jó yāt-maahn yih-chīn ńgh-baak mān. |
| CARMEN: | Gám, nī jēung chāantói nē? |
| MRS. LAM: | Nī jēung chāantói máaih-jó chāt-chīn mān. Dī chāanyí jauh baat-baak mān yāt jēung. |
| JOHN: | Ngóh jeui jūngyi nī jēung chàhgēi. Yiu géidō chín a? |
| MRS. LAM: | Nī jēung chàhgēi yiu sei-chīn luhk-baak mān. |

## Dialogue 2

**(CD1; 62)**

John and Carmen are chatting to Jack, the sportsman.

(a) According to Jack, about how much does a decent tennis racket cost?
(b) About how much does a good pair of running shoes cost?
(c) About how much does a good bicycle cost?

| | |
|---|---|
| JOHN: | Jack, ngóh séung máaih yāt faai hóu ge móhngkàuh-páak. Daaihyeuk yiu géidō chín a? |
| JACK: | Yāt faai géi hóu ge móhngkàuhpáak daaihyeuk yiu yāt-chīn mān lā. |
| JOHN: | Gám, yāt deui hóu ge páaubouhhàaih nē? Yiu géidō chín a? |
| JACK: | Yāt deui páaubouhhàaih daaihyeuk yiu ńgh-baak mān. |
| CARMEN: | Ngóh séung máaih yāt ga dāanchē. Yiu géidō chín a? |
| JACK: | Yāt ga hóu ge dāanchē daaihyeuk yiu baat-chīn mān. |

## Vocabulary

**(CD1; 64)**
## Furniture

Below is a list of some items of furniture. The Cantonese word for "furniture," namely **gāsī**, is, like its English counterpart, a collective and "a piece of furniture" needs the classifier **gihn**, hence **yāt gihn gāsī**. The classifier for specific furniture items such as tables and chairs is **jēung**, hence **yāt jēung sōfá**, **yāt jēung chāantói**. The classifier for other furniture items is often **go**, as in **yāt go syūgá**.

| | |
|---|---|
| yāt jēung sōfá | a sofa |
| yāt jēung chāantói | a dining table |
| yāt jēung chāanyí | a dining chair |
| yāt jēung chàhgēi | a coffee table |
| yāt jēung ōnlohkyí | an easy chair |
| yāt go syūgá | a bookcase |

### Dining chair and coffee table

**Chāandang** is sometimes used instead of **chāanyí** to refer to "dining chairs." To refer to an ordinary chair, probably **dang** is more commonly used in colloquial speech than **yí**, which is used in spoken Mandarin and written Chinese.

A coffee table is referred to as **chàhgēi** (lit. "tea table") in Cantonese, as Chinese people drink *tea* at the same kind of short, four-legged table usually put in front of a sofa which Westerners drink *coffee* at and call a "coffee table."

## Amounts of money

In Unit 2 we introduced the numbers 1 to 100 and we noted that "dollar" is **mān** in Cantonese. In this unit we will talk about larger amounts of money, up to one million. Below is a list of expressions for different amounts of money. Try reading out each item aloud. If you have the audio material for this book, model your pronunciation on those recordings.

## Unit 6: Prices

| | |
|---|---|
| yāt mān | $1 |
| sahp mān | $10 |
| yāt-baak mān | $100 |
| yāt-chīn mān | $1,000 |
| yāt-maahn mān | $10,000 |
| sahp-maahn mān | $100,000 |
| yāt-baakmaahn mān | $1,000,000 |

The table below shows the Cantonese terms and English terms assigned to the digits up to a million.

| baakmaahn | sahpmaahn | maahn | chīn | baak | sahp | go |
|---|---|---|---|---|---|---|
| million | hundred thousand | ten thousand | thousand | hundred | ten | unit |

To state a particular number, one reads from the leftmost digit to the right, as in English. The figures in the second table are spelt out below.

| baakmaahn | sahpmaahn | maahn | chīn | baak | sahp | go |
|---|---|---|---|---|---|---|
| | | | | | 8 | 9 |
| | | | | 1 | 2 | 3 |
| | | | 6 | 5 | 4 | 3 |
| | | 5 | 6 | 7 | 8 | 9 |
| 3 | | 3 | 0 | 0 | 0 | 0 |
| | | | | 2 | 7 | 0 |

**baat-sahp gáu**
**yāt-baak yih-sahp sāam**
**luhk-chīn ńgh-baak sei-sahp sāam**
**ńgh-maahn luhk-chīn chāt-baak baat-sahp gáu**
**sāam-sahp sāam maahn**
**yih-baak chāt-sahp maahn**

## Quick practice 1

Translate the sums of money into Cantonese. The first one has been done for you as an example.

(a) $147     yāt-baak sei-sahp chāt mān
(b) $256
(c) $1,789
(d) $5,620
(e) $15,000
(f) $37,500
(g) $937,000
(h) $562,100
(i) $1,520,000
(j) $4,689,000

Note that when there are zeros in the middle of a figure, like $194,022, the word **lìhng** is used to link up the two parts. Thus, $194,022 is read as **sahp-gáu maahn sei chīn lìhng yih-sahp yih mān**.

## Quick practice 2

Translate the following figures into Cantonese. The first one has been done for you as an example.

(a) $203     yih-baak lìhng sāam mān
(b) $1,030
(c) $27,005
(d) $500,400
(e) $1,900,800

### Uncertain amounts of money (CD1; 65)

Sometimes when the speaker is not certain about the exact amount of money, then the Cantonese word **géi** is used as a "wild card" to refer to the uncertain part. For example, **géi mān** is "several dollars," and **géi-baak mān** is "a few hundred dollars." On the other hand, **sahp-géi mān** means "ten dollars odd," while **baak-géi mān** means "a hundred odd dollars" or "around a hundred dollars." Below is a list showing how the word **géi** functions in such uncertain contexts:

# Unit 6: Prices

| | |
|---|---|
| géi mān | $? |
| sahp-géi mān | $1? |
| géi-sahp mān | $?0 |
| baak-géi mān | $1?? |
| géi-baak mān | $?00 |
| chīn-géi mān | $1,??? |
| géi-chīn mān | $?,000 |
| maahn-géi mān | $1?,??? |
| géi-maahn mān | $?0,000 |
| sahp-géi maahn mān | $1??,??? |
| géi-sahp maahn mān | $?00,000 |
| baak-géi maahn mān | $1,???,??? |
| géi-baak maahn mān | $?,000,000 |

**Several**

While the Cantonese word **géi** can be translated into either "several," as in **géichīn mān** ("several thousand dollars"), or "odd," as in **baakgéi mān** ("a hundred dollars odd"), there is apparently no equivalent in English for **géisahp mān**, which literally means "several ten dollars."

## Quick practice 3

Translate each of the "uncertain" figures below into Cantonese, using the word **géi**. The first one has been done for you as an example.

(a) $32?     **sāam-baak yih-sahp géi mān**
(b) $5??
(c) $4,2??
(d) $36,???
(e) $1??,???
(f) $92?,???
(g) $1,2??,???
(h) $4,???,???

## Idioms and structures (CD1; 66)

The items in the list below appear in the same order as they do in the dialogues above. The *italicized* items are *new* items. In the notes, numbers in brackets refer to the expressions listed below.

1 Nī jēung sōfá yiu géidō chín a? — How much did this sofa cost?
2 *máaih-jó* — *bought*
3 Nī jēung sōfá máaih-jó yāt-maahn yih-chīn ńgh-baak mān — I bought this sofa for $12,500.
4 baat-baak mān yāt jēung — $800 each
5 yāt faai hóu ge móhngkàuh-páak — a decent tennis racket
6 yāt *deui páaubouhhàaih* — a *pair* of *running shoes*
7 yāt *ga* dāanchē — a bicycle (**ga** is the classifier for vehicles)

### The verb yiu (1)

The verb **yiu** by itself means "need" or "require." For example, **Dá móhngkàuh** *yiu* **géidō go yàhn a?** is "How many people does it take to play a game of tennis?" In the context of prices, **géidō chín** is used. For example, **Dá yāt chi móhngkàuh** *yiu géidō chín* **a?** is "How much does it cost to play a game of tennis?"

### The aspect marker -jó for completion of action (2)

Cantonese verbs do not change in the way English verbs do ("buys, bought, buying") to show past, present, future, and so on. However, certain aspects of the verb—whether it is a completed action or an action in progress, for example—are shown by attaching a particle (an aspect marker) to the end of the verb.

**Máaih** is a verb that means "buy," and **-jó** is an aspect marker that indicates completion of an action. Thus, **Nī jēung sōfá ngóh máaih-***jó* **yāt-maahn yih-chīn ńgh-baak mān** translates into "This sofa was bought for $12,500." Similarly, **Ngóh máaih-***jó* **yāt dā pìhnggwó** translates into "I have bought a dozen apples."

Unit 6: *Prices* 101

The aspect marker **-jó** is a bound form: it cannot exist by itself or be separated from the verb, hence the hyphen before **jó**. In the case of a verb-object construction, **-jó** will come between the verb and the object, as in **Kéuih heui-jó léuihhàhng** (he/she has gone traveling).

## Exercise 1 At the travel agent's

John and Carmen plan to go for a ten-day holiday, but have not decided where to go. They are now at the travel agent's, asking the prices of holidays to different destinations. The travel agent is called Grace.

Read the dialogue, then complete the table that follows.

GRACE: Néihdeih séung heui bīndouh léuihhàhng a?
CARMEN: Ngóhdeih séung heui Yahtbún léuihhàhng. Heui Yahtbún yiu géidō chín a?
GRACE: Heui Yahtbún sahp yaht daaihyeuk yiu yāt-maahn yih-chīn mān.
CARMEN: Gam gwai àh? Gám, heui Hahwāiyìh nē? Heui Hahwāiyìh yiu géidō chín a?
GRACE: Heui Hahwāiyìh dōu haih yiu yāt-maahn yih-chīn mān.
JOHN: Hóu gwai wo. Gám, heui bīndouh pèhng-dī a?
GRACE: Heui Hòhngwok lā. Heui Hòhngwok daaihyeuk baat-chīn ńgh-baak mān jēk.
JOHN: Baat-chīn ńgh-baak mān dōu haih gwai wo. Gám, heui bīndouh jeui pèhng a?
GRACE: Heui Fēileuhtbān lā. Heui Fēileuhtbān yiu sei-chīn mān jēk.

| Destination | Price of holiday |
|---|---|
| Japan | |
| Hawaii | |
| Korea | |
| the Philippines | |

## Dialogue 3

**(CD1; 67)**

BAAK Yu Ping is talking to his colleague Kathy, who has recently arrived in Hong Kong from the U.S. and wants to find out about the postal rates in Hong Kong.

(a) How much does it cost to post a local letter?
(b) How much does it cost to send a postcard or an air-mail letter to the U.S.?
(c) How much does it cost to send a letter to the U.S. by surface mail?

| | |
|---|---|
| KATHY: | BAAK Yu Ping, hái Hēunggóng gei-seun pèhng-mh-pèhng a? |
| BAAK YU PING: | Hái Hēunggóng gei-seun hóu pèhng. |
| KATHY: | Gám, gei yāt fūng seun yiu géidō chín a? |
| BAAK YU PING: | Gei yāt fūng bún góng seun yiu go sei jēk. |
| KATHY: | Hóu pèhng wo. Gám, gei yāt jēung mìhngseunpín heui Méihgwok yiu géidō chín a? |
| BAAK YU PING: | Gei mìhngseunpín heui Méihgwok yiu léuhng go sei. Gei seun heui Méihgwok dōu haih sāam mān jēk. |
| KATHY: | Gám, gei pìhngyàuh seun nē? Gei pìhngyàuh seun géidō chín a? |
| BAAK YU PING: | Gei pìhngyàuh seun pèhng-dī, léuhng mān jēk. |

## Idioms and structures (CD1; 66)

The items in the list below appear in the same order as they do in the dialogue above. The *italicized* items are *new* items. In the notes, numbers in brackets refer to the expressions listed below.

1 ***gei-seun***                   to send something by post

2 ***Gei yāt fūng bún góng seun yiu go sei jēk.***    Sending a local letter costs only $1.40.

3 ***gei ... heui Méihgwok***      to send ... to the U.S.

## The verb-object construction gei-seun (1)

**Gei-seun** is a verb-object construction in which **gei** means "to send by post," while **seun** refers to any postal item(s). Thus, **Ngóh yiu gei-seun** means "I have to get something posted" while **Ngóh yiu gei yāt fūng seun** means "I have to post a letter," with **seun** meaning literally "a letter."

## Jēk (2)

**Jēk** is a sentence-final particle which indicates "no more than" or "only," here emphasizing the cheapness of the rate.

## Adjectives for comparing prices

The following three adjectives are probably the most commonly used in comparing prices:

| | |
|---|---|
| **pèhng** | cheap |
| **gwai** | expensive |
| **dái** | good value |

When we compare the prices of two items, we use one of the two bound particles of comparison, namely **-gwo** and **-dī**, depending on the structure.

**-gwo** is used when both items for comparison are mentioned:

**Nī faai móhngkàuhpáak gwai-*gwo* gó faai (móhngkàuhpáak).**
This tennis racket is more expensive than that (tennis racket).

**Nī ga dāanchē dái-*gwo* gó ga (dāanchē).**
This bicycle is better value than that (bicycle).

However, when only one item is mentioned, **-di** is used:

**Nī faai móhngkàuhpáak gwai-*dī*.**
This tennis racket is more expensive.

**Nī ga dāanchē dái-*dī*.**
This bicycle is better value.

When three or more items are compared, the superlative **jeui** is often used, as follows:

**Nī deui páaubouhhàaih *jeui* pèhng.**
This pair of running shoes is the cheapest.

**Nī jēung chāantói *jeui* gwai.**
This dining table is the most expensive.

Often—when the context is clear—adjectives have an inherently comparative sense. For example, asking who is the tallest in a group, one can simply say **bīngo gōu?** Or for which is the better of two, one can simply say **bīngo hóu?**

## Vocabulary

### Small units of money

In Cantonese, a smaller unit of money than the dollar (**mān**) is **hòuhjí**, which is a "ten-cent unit." Thus, "ten cents" is **yāt hòuhjí**, "twenty cents" is **léuhng hòuhjí**, and "ninety cents" is **gáu hòuhjí**. When both dollars and cents are mentioned, we put the dollars before the cents. For example, "three dollars and forty cents" is **sāam mān sei hòuhjí**, and "five dollars and seventy cents" is **ńgh mān chāt hòuhjí**. However, in colloquial speech, most people would use a shorter form by dropping the **hòuhjí** at the end and using **go** instead of **mān** in between the two numbers. In this way, "three dollars forty" becomes **sāam go sei**, and "five dollars seventy" becomes **ńgh go chāt**. Below are a few more examples:

| | | | | |
|---|---|---|---|---|
| chāt go luhk | $7.60 | | sāam go yih | $3.20 |
| baat go yāt | $8.10 | | sei go bun | $4.50 |
| gáu go sei | $9.40 | | go chāt | $1.70 |
| sahp-yih go sāam | $12.30 | | | |

Note that $3.20 can be read as **sāam mān léuhng hòuhjí** or **sāam go yih**, but not *****sāam go léuhng**. (This is because when we say **léuhng hòuhjí** we are counting the number of **hòuhjí**'s there are, hence we use **léuhng**; but when we say **sāam go yih** we are reading out the number 2 from the figure $3.20, and hence **yih** is used.) However, $4.50 is read as **sei mān ńgh hòuhjí** or **sei go bun**, **bun** meaning "half (a dollar)," but not as *****sei go ńgh**. $1.70 can be read as **yāt mān chāt hòuhjí** or **go chāt**, the **yāt** being dropped for the latter. Similarly, $1.80 is read as **go baat**.

Unit 6: *Prices*

## Quick practice 4

Translate each of the following amounts into Cantonese, using the short colloquial form. The first one has been done for you as an example.

(a) $5.90  **ńgh go gáu**
(b) $9.10
(c) $5.50
(d) $8.20
(e) $1.40
(f) $0.60

### Postage

Below is a list of different mail items. Pay special attention to the classifiers used—**fūng** for letters, **jēung** for postcards.

| | |
|---|---|
| **yāt fūng seun** | a letter |
| **yāt fūng búngóng seun** | a local letter |
| **yāt fūng hūngyàuh seun** | an air-mail letter |
| **yāt fūng pìhngyàuh seun** | a surface mail letter |
| **yāt jēung mìhngseunpín** | a postcard |

> **Búngóng**
>
> The Cantonese word in Hong Kong for "local letter," **búngóng**, is made up of two forms, **bún**, which means "local," and **góng**, which is the second half of the name **Heūnggóng** (Hong Kong).

## Exercise 2 Buying fruit

Carmen is buying some fruit at Ah-WONG's fruit-stall. Read the dialogue between Carmen and Ah-WONG then complete the table with the information about how much of each fruit Carmen has bought and how much she has paid.

CARMEN:   Dī cháang dím maaih a?
AH-WONG:  Dī cháang léuhng go bun yāt go.
CARMEN:   Ngóh yiu ńgh go cháang.

| | |
|---|---|
| AH-WONG: | Ńgh go cháang, sahp-yih go bun lā. |
| CARMEN: | Ngóh juhng yiu dī pìhnggwó. |
| AH-WONG: | Pìhnggwó go chāt yāt go. |
| CARMEN: | Ngóh yiu sei go. |
| AH-WONG: | Sei go pìhnggwó, luhk go baat lā. |
| CARMEN: | Yáuh móuh sāigwā a? |
| AH-WONG: | Yáuh a. Dī sāigwā hóu leng a. |
| CARMEN: | Sāigwā géidō chín yāt bohng a? |
| AH-WONG: | Sāigwā go sei yāt bohng ... Nī go jeui leng laak ... sahp bohng ... sahp-sei mān lā. |
| CARMEN: | Júngguhng géidō chín a? |
| AH-WONG: | Dī cháang sahp-yih go bun, pìhnggwó luhk go baat, sāigwā sahp-sei mān. Júngguhng sāam-sahp sāam go sāam lā. |
| CARMEN: | Nīdouh sāam-sahp sāam go sāam. Mgōi. |
| AH-WONG: | Dōjeh. |

| Fruit | Amount | Price |
|---|---|---|
| | | |
| | | Total: |

## Exercise 3 At the furniture shop

You are a salesperson in a furniture shop. A customer comes in and asks for the prices of various pieces of furniture. Answer the questions by referring to the price-list. The first item has been done for you as an example.

| | |
|---|---|
| sofa | $7,800 |
| coffee table | $1,400 |
| easy chair | $1,050 |
| dining table | $8,250 |
| dining chair | $910 |
| bookcase | $2,100 |

(a) **Nī go syūgá géidō chín a?**
   *Nī go syūgá yih-chīn yāt-baak mān.*

(b) Gám, nī jēung chāantói nē? Maaih géidō chín a?

(c) Dī chāanyí géidō chín yāt jēung a?
(d) Gó jēung sōfá yauh géidō chín a?
(e) Nī jēung ōnlohkyí yauh géidō chín a?

## Exercise 4 Carmen's classmates

Refer to the picture of Carmen's classmates, and answer the questions about their physical appearance. The first one has been done for you as an example.

(a) **Bīngo néuihjái jeui gōu a?**
 *Diana jeui gōu.*
(b) Bīngo nàahmjái jeui ngái a?
(c) Bīngo néuihjái jeui sau a?
(d) Bīngo nàahmjái jeui fèih a?
(e) Sally dihng Elsie fèih-dī a?
(f) William dihng Raul sau-dī a?
(g) Bīngo néuihjái yáuh daai ngáahngéng a?
(h) Bīngo nàahmjái yáuh wùhsōu a?

## Exercise 5 Which apples?

Four kinds of apples are sold in the supermarket. (See the picture.) They come from four different countries, namely Australia, the U.S., Japan, and China. Compare their prices and then answer the questions. The first has been done for you as an example.

(a) **Oujāu pìhnggwó dím maaih a?**
**Oujāu pìhnggwó sahp mān sāam go.**
(b) Méihgwok pìhnggwó géidō chín yāt go a?
(c) Jūnggwok pìhnggwó dím maaih a?
(d) Yahtbún pìhnggwó nē? Géidō chín yāt go a?
(e) Bīndī pìhnggwó jeui pèhng a?
(f) Bīndī pìhnggwó jeui gwai a?
(g) Oujāu pìhnggwó tùhng Méihgwok pìhnggwó bīndī pèhng-dī a?
(h) Bīndī pìhnggwó jeui dái a?

## Exercise 6 Comparisons

Translate the following sentences into Cantonese, using the comparative particles **-gwo** and **dī** and the superlative **jeui** as appropriate. The first has been done for you as an example.

Unit 6: *Prices* 109

(a) John is taller than Carmen.
 **John gōu-gwo Carmen.**
(b) Carmen is thinner than Emily.
(c) This coffee table is better value than that one.
(d) That dining chair is prettier.
(e) My tennis racket is more expensive.
(f) This sofa is the cheapest.
(g) Carmen's bicycle is the best value.

## Recognizing Chinese characters

| 十 | ten |
| 百 | hundred |
| 千 | thousand |
| 萬 | ten thousand |
| 十萬 | hundred thousand |
| 百萬 | million |

Thus, "two hundred thousand" is

二十萬,

元 being the Chinese character for "dollars," "three hundred dollars" is

三百元,

"four thousand dollars" is

四千元,

"fifty thousand dollars" is

五萬元,

and "sixty-seven thousand dollars" is

六萬七千元.

## Communicative activities

1. Take turns discussing some of your recent purchases. What did you buy, how much did it cost?
2. Imagine you need to furnish a new apartment or flat. With a partner, role-play a trip to a furniture store. Tell the sales clerk what you are looking for and ask about prices. Assume a budget of HK$30,000.

## Cultural point

### Hong Kong currency

The basic unit of currency in Hong Kong is the Hong Kong dollar. The Hong Kong dollar has been historically pegged to the U.S. dollar at about HK$7.75 to U.S.$1. Some bank notes are shown below. Note that there are special numbers for currency and accounting in Chinese in place of the simpler Chinese numbers, which can be easily altered. For example, instead of 二十 **yihsahp** "twenty," one sees instead 貳拾. Such numerals were formerly used in markets as well, but have largely given way to Arabic numerals.

# Unit 6: *Prices*

# Unit Seven
# Fāan-gūng
Commuting

In Unit 7 you will learn about:

- describing means of transportation
- discussing how long journeys take
- expressing necessity

Unit 7: *Commuting*

## Dialogue 1

**(CD1; 69)**

John and Carmen are chatting to Emily.

(a) How does Carmen go to work? And how long does it take?
(b) How does John go to work? How long does it take?
(c) How about Emily? What means of transportation does she use to go to work? And how long does it take her?

| | |
|---|---|
| EMILY: | Carmen, néih jīujóu dímyéung fāan-gūng a? |
| CARMEN: | Ngóh jīujóu dōsou daap-deihtit fāan-gūng. |
| EMILY: | Gám, daap-deihtit yiu géinoih a? |
| CARMEN: | Yiu daaihyeuk gáu go jih. |
| EMILY: | Yiu gáu go jih gam noih àh? |
| CARMEN: | Haih a. |
| EMILY: | Gám, néih nē, John? Néih daap mātyéh chē fāan-gūng a? |
| JOHN: | Ngóh jā-chē fāan-gūng. |
| EMILY: | Gám, yiu jā géinoih chē a? |
| JOHN: | Yiu jā daaihyeuk y'ah ńgh fānjūng chē. Gám, néih nē, Emily? Néih yauh dímyéung fāan-gūng a? |
| EMILY: | Ngóh msái daap-chē. Ngóh hàahng-louh fāan-gūng. Daaihyeuk hàahng bun go jūngtàuh jauh dāk laak. |
| CARMEN: | Gám, dōu géi faai wo! |

## Dialogue 2

**(CD1; 71)**

HO Syut Hwa and Jack are talking about how each of them goes to work.

(a) How does Jack go to work? How long does it take?
(b) How does HO Syut Hwa go to work? How long does it take?

| | |
|---|---|
| HO SYUT HWA: | Jack, néih jyuh hái bīndouh a? |
| JACK: | Ngóh jyuh hái lèihdóu. |
| HO SYUT HWA: | Gám, néih haih-mh-haih yiu daap-syùhn fāan-gūng a? |
| JACK: | Haih a. |

HO SYUT HWA: Gám, yiu daap géinoih syùhn a?
JACK: Yiu daap yāt go jūngtàuh léuhng go jih. Gám, néih nē, HO Syut Hwa? Néih dím fāan-gūng a?
HO SYUT HWA: Ngóh dōsou daap-dīksí fāan-gūng. Daaihyeuk daap léuhng go jih dīksí jauh dāk laak.

## Vocabulary

### Means of transportation

Below is a list of expressions about taking different means of transportation. Note that each of them is a verb-object construction, composed of the verb **daap**, which means "to take a ride on," and a particular means of transportation. Try reading out each item aloud. If you have the audio material for this book, model your pronunciation on the recording.

| | |
|---|---|
| **daap-deihtit** | to take the subway (in Hong Kong, MTR or Mass Transit Railway) |
| **daap-fóchē** | to take a train |
| **daap-bāsí** | to take a bus |
| **daap-síubā** | to take a minibus |
| **daap-dihnchē** | to take a streetcar |
| **daap-dīksí** | to take a taxi |
| **daap-syùhn** | to take a ferry |
| **daap-fēigēi** | to take a plane |

"To drive," on the other hand, is **jā-chē**, which literally means "drive-(a)-car." "To walk" is **hàahng-louh**, which literally means "walk-(along the)-road."

### Duration of time

Below are ways in which duration of time is expressed in Cantonese. Some items require the classifier **go** while others do not. Try reading each item aloud, or model your pronunciation on the audio recording if you have it.

# Unit 7: Commuting

| | |
|---|---|
| yāt fānjūng | 1 minute |
| yāt go jūngtàuh | 1 hour |
| yāt yaht | 1 day |
| yāt go láihbaai/sīngkèih | 1 week |
| yāt go yuht | 1 month |
| yāt nìhn | 1 year |

Note that special attention needs to be paid to the pronunciation of **yāt yaht** "one day" as there is only *tonal difference* between **yāt** and **yaht**.

As discussed in Unit 4, **jih** is used to refer to five-minute spans, and it takes the classifier **go**. For example:

| | |
|---|---|
| yāt go jih | 5 minutes |
| léuhng go jih | 10 minutes |
| sāam go jih | 15 minutes |

## Idioms and structures

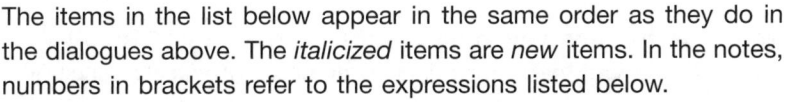

The items in the list below appear in the same order as they do in the dialogues above. The *italicized* items are *new* items. In the notes, numbers in brackets refer to the expressions listed below.

| | | |
|---|---|---|
| 1 | *jīujóu* | *in the early morning* |
| 2 | néih jīujóu *dímyéung* fāan-gūng a? | *how do you get to work* in the morning? |
| 3 | *dōsou* | *mostly/usually* |
| 4 | daap-deihtit *yiu géinoih* a? | How long *does it take* to go by subway? |
| 5 | Yiu gáu go jih *gam noih* àh? | Does it really take *as long as* 45 minutes? |
| 6 | gam noih | so long (time) |
| 7 | Néih *daap mātyéh chē* fāan-gūng a? | *What means of transportation do you take* to go to work? |
| 8 | *yiu jā géinoih* chē *a?* | *How long does it take by car?* |
| 9 | Ngóh *msái* daap-chē | I *don't need to* take any means of transportation. |

| | |
|---|---|
| 10 **Daaihyeuk hàahng bun go jūngtàuh jauh *dāk* laak.** | I walk for half an hour and that's all it takes. |
| 11 **Gám, dōu géi *faai* wo!** | That's pretty *quick*! |
| 12 **Néih *jyuh* hái bīndouh a?** | Where do you *live*? |
| 13 **Ngóh jyuh hái *lèihdóu*.** | I live here. |
| 14 **Yiu daap yāt go jūngtàuh léuhng go jih.** | It takes one hour ten minutes. |

## Means of transportation (2, 7)

There are two ways of asking somebody what means of transportation they use, say, to commute to work. The first way is to use the question word **dímyéung**, sometimes reduced to **dìm**:

| | |
|---|---|
| **Néih dímyéung fāan-gūng a?** | How do you get to work? |

Another way is to form a question with the question-word **mātyéh**:

| | |
|---|---|
| **Néih daap mātyéh chē fāan-gūng a?** | What means of transportation do you take to go to work? |

Note that the word **chē** in the expression **daap mātyéh chē** does not mean "private car," but refers to all kinds of vehicles, including buses, streetcars, etc.

To say what means of transportation you use to commute to work, you mention the means of transportation *before* the verb **fāan-gūng**:

| | |
|---|---|
| **Ngóh daap-dihnchē fāan-gūng.** | I go to work by streetcar. |
| **Ngóh gòh-gō daap-syùhn fāan-gūng.** | My elder brother goes to work by ferry. |
| **Ngóh mùih-múi hàahng-louh fāan-gūng.** | My younger sister walks to work. |

## Asking and saying how long (4, 8)

To ask about the time taken to do something, for example to go to work, the question word **géinoih** "how long?" is used. Two kinds of structure are possible. The first uses the verb **yiu** "require" immediately before **géinoih**:

# Unit 7: Commuting

**Néih jā-chē fāan-gūng *yiu géinoih* a?**
How long does it take you to drive to work?

**Néih hàahng-louh fāan-gūng *yiu géinoih* a?**
How long does it take you to walk to work?

In the second structure, **yiu** is used as a modal preceding the verb, while the question-word **géinoih** is inserted between the verb and the object in the verb-object construction:

**Néih fāan-gūng *yiu* jā *géinoih* chē a?**
How long do you have to drive to go to work?

**Néih fāan-gūng *yiu* hàahng *géinoih* louh a?**
How long do you have to walk to go to work?

Similarly, two kinds of structure are employed in saying how long it takes to commute to work. The first structure is to use **yiu** as the main verb as follows:

**Ngóh jā-chē fāan-gūng yiu ńgh go jih.**
It takes me 25 minutes to drive to work.

**Ngóh hàahng-louh fāan-gūng yiu bun go jūngtàuh.**
It takes me half an hour to go to work on foot.

The second structure uses **yiu** as a modal, followed by a *split verb-object construction*:

**Ngóh fāan-gūng yiu jā ńgh go jih chē.**
I have to drive for 25 minutes to go to work.

**Ngóh fāan-gūng yiu hàahng bun go jūngtàuh louh.**
I have to walk for half an hour to go to work.

## Exercise 1 Durations of time

Translate the following times into Cantonese. Some can have more than one possible answer. The first one is done for you as an example.

(a) 20 minutes    **yih-sahp fānjūng** or **sei go jih**
(b) 36 minutes
(c) 45 minutes
(d) 55 minutes

(e) 1 hour 50 minutes
(f) 2 hours 7 minutes

## Question with àh to express surprise (5)

Here the question with **àh** expresses surprise, or in this case, Emily's shock at hearing how long it takes Carmen to commute to work, hence the comment **gám noih àh?**

## Msái (9)

**Msái**, which means "do(es) not need to," is the opposite of **yiu**, which means "need(s) to." It is important to remember that **sái** is always used with **m-** to mean the negative while **yiu** "need" is always used in the positive. Hence, ***Ngóh sái daap-chē** is wrong and so, in this context, is **Ngóh myiu daap-chē**. To form a choice-type question to ask about necessity, **sái**, rather than **yiu**, is used, hence **Néih sái-mh-sái daap-chē fāan-gūng a?** but not ***Néih yiu-mh-yiu daap-chē fāan-gūng a?**

## Halves (10)

**Bun** is used to refer to "halves" of time units, as follows:

| | |
|---|---|
| **bun fānjūng** | half a minute |
| **bun go jūngtàuh** | half an hour |
| **bun yaht** | half a day |
| **bun go láihbaai/sīngkèih** | half a week |
| **bun go yuht** | half a month |
| **bun nìhn** | half a year |

Special attention has to be paid to the position of **bun** in expressions involving a whole number plus a half. For time durations that do not take the classifier **go**, **bun** comes right after the time unit, for example, "five and a half days" is **ńgh yaht *bun***. For time durations that do require the classifier **go**, **bun** comes after **go** rather than the time unit. Thus, "three and a half hours" is **sāam go *bun* jūngtàuh**, and not ***sāam go jūngtàuh bun**. Below is a list showing how the "halves" are expressed:

| | |
|---|---|
| yāt fān bun jūng | 1½ minutes |
| yāt go bun jūngtàuh | 1½ hours |
| yāt yaht bun | 1½ days |
| yāt go bun láihbaai/sīngkèih | 1½ weeks |
| yāt go bun yuht | 1½ months |
| yāt nìhn bun | 1½ years |

Note that when the figure is 1½, the word **yāt** is often omitted. Thus 1½ minutes can become **fān bun jūng**, 1½ hours can become **go bun jūngtàuh**, and 1½ days can become **yaht bun**, and so on. Another possible omission is the **tàuh** in **jūngtàuh**, and so 1½ hours can simply be expressed as **go bun jūng**.

## Dāk (10)

**Dāk** is an adjective which means "OK" or "all right," indicating successful achievement of a goal. When the expression **jauh dāk laak** is used as the comment of a topic-comment construction it emphasizes the relative ease with which something is done.

## Faai (11)

The adjective **faai** has two meanings. The first meaning is "at a *fast speed*," and the opposite is **maahn**, which means "slow." But in this context **faai** refers to the "*short time* it takes," and is the opposite of **noih**, as in the expression **géinoih**, discussed above.

## Lèihdóu (13)

In Hong Kong, there are a number of outlying islands (**Lèihdóu**), which are linked to Hong Kong Island, the commercial center of the territory, by ferry, the most important being Lantau Island, Cheung Chau, Peng Chau, and Lamma Island.

## **Durations of time** (14)

When a duration consists of both hours and minutes, the hours (the larger unit) come before the minutes (the smaller unit), as in English:

| | |
|---|---|
| léuhng go jūngtàuh sei go jih | 2 hours 20 minutes |
| sei go jūngtàuh ńgh-sahp fānjūng | 4 hours 50 minutes |

With units of time larger than the hour, the word **lìhng**, which can be translated as "and," is used to join the larger unit and the smaller one. For example:

| | |
|---|---|
| sei go láihbaai lìhng sāam yaht | 4 weeks and 3 days |
| sāam nìhn lìhng baat go yuht | 3 years and 8 months |

## Vocabulary

### Stations, terminals, and stops

Cantonese does not distinguish between stations, terminals, and stops, and all are called **jaahm** in Cantonese. However, sometimes **júngjaahm** refers to bus terminals and tram terminals when precise specification is called for or when those places serve as main locations. Below is a list of places where one boards vehicles and ferries.

| | |
|---|---|
| deihtitjaahm | subway (MTR) station |
| fóchējaahm | rail station |
| bāsí júngjaahm | bus terminal |
| bāsíjaahm | bus stop |
| dihnchē júngjaahm | streetcar terminal |
| dihnchējaahm | streetcar stop |
| máhtàuh | ferry pier |

### Describing a sequence of actions

When a journey involves more than one means of transportation, a detailed step-by-step description of the itinerary might use the following expressions:

| | |
|---|---|
| sáusīn | first of all |
| yìhnhauh/gānjyuh | and then, later on |
| joi | and again |
| jeui hauh | finally |

Unit 7: *Commuting*

## Exercise 2 Traveling to work

Three people are describing their journeys to work. Read the texts and then use the information to draw a diagram. Jane's part has been done for you as an example.

JANE: Ngóh jīujóu chāt dímjūng chēut-mùhnháu, sáusīn hàahng léuhng go jih louh heui fóchējaahm, yìhnhauh daap sei-sahp fānjūng fóchē, gānjyuh hàahng yāt go jih louh jauh fāan dou gūngsī laak.
HOME → walk (10 minutes) → train (40 minutes) → walk (5 minutes) → OFFICE

JIM: Ngóh yiu daap-syùhn fāan-gūng. Ngóh chāt dímjūng chēut-mùhnháu, hàahng sahp-ńgh fānjūng louh heui máhtàuh, gānjyuh daap ńgh-sahp fānjūng syùhn, joi hàahng sahp fānjūng louh jauh fāan dou gūngsī laak. Júngguhng yiu yāt go jūngtàuh sāam go jih.
HOME → ... OFFICE

BILL: Ngóh jīujóu baat dím bun chēut-mùhnháu, hàahng yāt go jih louh heui bāsíjaahm, yìhnhauh daap sāam go jih bāsí heui deihtitjaahm, gānjyuh daap bun go jūngtàuh deihtit jauh fāan dou gūngsī laak. Júngguhng daaihyeuk ńgh-sahp fānjūng lā.
HOME → ... OFFICE

## Dialogue 3

**(CD1; 73)**

Richard is telling John how he travels to work.

(a) How many kinds of transportation does Richard have to take to commute to work?
(b) How long is his walk to the MTR station?
(c) How long is his MTR ride?
(d) How long is his bus ride?
(e) How long does it take Richard to go from home to work?

JOHN: Richard, néih fāan-gūng sái-mh-sái daap-chē a?
RICHARD: Yiu a. Ngóh fāan-gūng yiu daap deihtit tùhng bāsí.
JOHN: Gám, yiu géinoih a?

RICHARD: Ngóh jīujóu baat dímjūng chēut-mùhnháu, sáusīn hàahng léuhng go jih louh heui deihtitjaahm, yìhnhauh daap bun go jūngtàuh deihtit, gānjyuh daap sei go jih bāsí, daaihyeuk gáu dímjūng jauh fāan dou gūngsī laak.
JOHN: Gám, júngguhng yiu géinoih a?
RICHARD: Yàuh ngūkkéi fāan dou gūngsī júngguhng yiu daaihyeuk yāt go jūngtàuh lā.

## Dialogue 4

**(CD1; 75)**

Mrs. Wong teaches in the same school as Mrs. Lam. She is asking Mrs. Lam how she travels to work in the morning.

(a) Altogether how long does it take Mrs. Lam to go to her school?
(b) How long is her walk to the rail station?
(c) How long is her train ride?
(d) How long is her MTR ride?
(e) How long is her walk to the school?

MRS. WONG: Làhm táai, néih jīujóu dímyéung fāan-hohk a?
MRS. LAM: Ngóh jyuh dāk yúhn, yiu yāt go jūngtàuh sīnji fāan dou hohkhaauh. Ngóh sáusīn hàahng léuhng go jih louh heui fóchējaahm, yìhnhauh daap ńgh go jih fóchē, yìhnhauh jyun deihtit, daap sei go jih deihtit, joi hàahng léuhng go jih louh sīnji fāan dou hohkhaauh.
MRS. WONG: Gám, jān haih yiu sèhng go jūngtàuh wo!

##  Idioms and structures

The items in the list below appear in the same order as they do in the dialogues above. The *italicized* items are *new* items. In the notes, numbers in brackets refer to the expressions listed below.

| | | |
|---|---|---|
| 1 | **Yiu a.** | Yes, I do (need to). |
| 2 | ***chēut-mùhnháu*** | *leave home* (lit. *"go out the door"*) |
| 3 | **hàahng *léuhng go jih louh*** | *subway station* |
| 4 | **daaihyeuk gáu dímjūng jauh *fāan dou* gūngsī laak** | I *arrive* at work about 9 a.m. |

| | |
|---|---|
| 5 **jūngguhng** | altogether |
| 6 *yàuh* **ngūkkéi fāan dou gūngsī** | *from* home to the office |
| 7 **fāan-hohk** | go to school |
| 8 **Ngóh** *jyuh dāk yúhn*. | I *live far away (from school)*. |
| 9 **yìhnhauh** *jyun* **deihtit** | and then I *transfer to* the subway |
| 10 **joi hàahng léuhng go jih louh** *sīnji* **fāan dou hohkhaauh** | and (I) walk for another ten minutes *and only then* do I arrive at the school |
| 11 *sèhng* **go jūngtàuh** | a *whole* hour |
| 12 **Gám,** *jānhaih* **yiu sèhng go jūngtàuh wo!** | So it *really does* take a whole hour! |

## Expressing necessity (1)

Here **Yiu a** is a short response to the question **néih fāan-gūng sái-mh-sái daap-chē a?**, meaning "Yes, I need to (commute to work)." A long response would be **Ngóh fāan-gūng yiu daap-chē a**. Once again, note that a negative response would be **Msái**, which means "No, I don't need to (commute to work)," and not **Myiu**, in which **yiu** is not used as a modal of necessity but as a verb meaning "want to."

## Destinations (3, 4)

In a sentence which describes action or motion, the destination always comes at the end, introduced by the word **heui**:

**Ngóh hàahng yih-sahp fāanjūng louh** *heui deihtitjaahm*.
I walk for twenty minutes to the subway station.

**Heui** is the word used to introduce a destination: for example, **Ngóh séung gei-seun** *heui Méihgwok* "I want to send some mail to the U.S." However, for "going to the office" and "going to school" we use **fāan**, which literally means "return," hence **fāan gūngsī** and **fāan hohkhaauh**. A more predictable use is, of course, **fāan ngūkkéi** "to go home."

**Ngóh jā baat go jih chē** *fāan gūngsī*.
I drive for 40 minutes to go to my office.

**Ngóh daap yāt go jūngtàuh syùhn *fāan hohkhaauh*.**
I take a one-hour ferry ride to go to my school.

## Dou (4, 6, 10)

**Dou** is a particle used between a verb of motion and a noun denoting a destination. **Fāan *dou* gūngsī** indicates the "successful" arrival at the office. Similar expressions are **fāan *dou* hohkhaauh** "arrive at the school," **fāan *dou* ngūkkéi** "arrive home," **heui *dou* deihtitjaahm** "arrive at the subway station," and **heui *dou* máhtàuh** "arrive at the pier."

## Fāan-hohk (7)

**Fāan-gūng** is a verb-object construction which means "to go to work." **Fāan-hohk**, on the other hand, means "to go to school," but it applies to both students, who "go to school to learn," and teachers, who "go to school to teach."

## Dāk (8)

The particle **dāk** is used between a verb and an adjective to indicate the result of an action. **Ngóh jyuh *dāk* yuhn** is "I live far away," while **Ngóh jyuh dāk káhn** means "I live near." Similar expressions are **Kéuih páau dāk faai** "He/She runs fast" and **Néih jouh dāk hóu hóu** "You've done a good job."

## Sīnji (10)

**Sīnji** is an adverb often used with the modal **yiu** to emphasize the fact that a condition has to be satisfied to accomplish something. When used in a question, it stresses the "How long does it take you?" part of the question. When used in a statement, it stresses the effort made to accomplish something, and bears the opposite connotation to that of **jauh dāk laak**, discussed earlier in this unit. A comparison of the sentences below will illustrate the contrast.

> **Ngóh *yiu* jā yāt go jūngtàuh chē *sīnji* fāan dou gūngsī.**
> It takes me a whole hour to drive to work.

> **Ngóh jā-chē fāan-gūng ńgh go jih *jauh dāk laak*.**
> It takes me *only* 25 minutes to drive to work.

## Sèhng (11)

**Sèhng go jūngtàuh** is an emphatic way of saying "an hour," and goes together well with the word **sīnji**, as the sentence **yiu sèhng go jūngtàuh sīnji fāandou hohkhaauh** "it takes a whole hour to get to my school" shows. Similar expressions are **sèhng yaht** "a whole day," **sèhng go láihbaai** "a whole week," **sèhng go yuht** "a whole month," and **sèhng nìhn** "a whole year."

## Exercise 3 Durations of time

Translate the following time durations into Cantonese, paying special attention to instances where the word **lìhng** has to be used. The first one has been done for you as an example.

(a) 38 minutes            **sāam-sahp baat fānjūng**

(b) 5 hours 55 minutes

(c) 6 days

(d) 1 week and 4 days

(e) 3 months

(f) 2 years and 11 months

## Exercise 4 Durations of time

Translate the following time durations into Cantonese, using the word **bun** if applicable, and paying special attention to its position. The first one has been done for you as an example.

(a) 30 minutes            **bun go jūngtàuh**

(b) 2 hours 30 minutes

(c) 4½ hours

(d) 5½ days

(e) 9½ weeks

(f) 7½ months

(g) 5 years and 6 months

## Exercise 5 How you go to work

Now describe how you travel to work and then write out the description in Cantonese.

HOME → ... WORK
*Description*:
**Ngóh ... chēut-mùhnháu ...**

## Exercise 6 The optimist and the moaner

Some people take a long time to commute to work, depending on where they live and where their office is, while others take much shorter times. At the same time, some people are born optimists and accept things cheerfully while others moan about everything. In this exercise, each item provides information about how two people commute to work in exactly the same way and take the same amount of time but describe their journeys in different styles.

Follow the example and write out what each person says.

(a) A ½-hour bus ride, the optimist:
   **Ngóh daap bun go jūngtàuh bāsí *jauh* fāan dou gūngsī *laak*.**

(b) A ½-hour bus ride, the moaner:
   **Ngóh yiu daap bun go jūngtàuh bāsí *sīnji* fāan dou gūngsī *a*.**

(c) A 20-minute walk, the optimist.

(d) A 20-minute walk, the moaner.

(e) A 50-minute train ride and a 15-minute walk, the optimist.

(f) A 50-minute train ride and a 15-minute walk, the moaner.

## Exercise 7 Going to Guangzhou

Imagine you work for a travel agency, and specialize in organizing trips between Hong Kong and Guangzhou. Some potential customers are at your office asking for information. Answer their questions by referring to the price-list. The first one is done for you as an example.

*Price-list of trips between Hong Kong and Guangzhou for the year 2009*

|          | Price              | Duration         |
|----------|--------------------|------------------|
| by air   | HK$1,210           | 30 minutes       |
| by train | HK$190             | 2 hrs 45 minutes |
| by ferry | HK$147 (to Nansha) | 1 hr 20 minutes  |
| by bus   | HK$80              | 3 hrs            |

Note: Prices and time durations are the same for both HK → GZ and GZ → HK.

## Conversation 1:

CUSTOMER: Chíng mahn yàuh Hēunggóng heui Gwóngjāu dímyéung jeui faai a?
YOU: Yàuh Hēunggóng heui Gwóngjāu daap-fēigēi jeui faai.
CUSTOMER: Gám, daap-fēigēi yiu géidō chín a?
YOU: (i)
CUSTOMER: Gám, yiu daap géinoih a?
YOU: (ii)
CUSTOMER: Gám, daap-syùhn nē? Daap-syùhn yauh géidō chín a?
YOU: (iii)
CUSTOMER: Daap-syùhn yiu daap géinoih a?
YOU: (iv)
CUSTOMER: Hóu, mgōi saai.

## Conversation 2:

CUSTOMER: Chíng mahn Hēunggóng heui Gwóngjāu daap-fóchē dihng daap-bāsí pèhng-dī a?
YOU: (i)
CUSTOMER: Gám, daap-fóchē yiu géinoih a? Daap-bāsí yauh yiu géinoih a?
YOU: (ii)
CUSTOMER: Gám, daap-syùhn nē? Daap-syùhn yauh dím a?
YOU: (iii)
CUSTOMER: Hóu, mgōi saai néih.

## Conversation 3:

CUSTOMER: Chíng mahn heui Gwóngjāu dímyéung jeui dái a?
YOU:

# Recognizing Chinese characters

| | |
|---|---|
| 地鐵站 | subway station |
| 火車站 | rail station |
| 巴士站 | bus stop |
| 的士站 | taxi rank |
| 飛機場 | airport |

This list of Chinese characters shows places where different means of public transport can be taken. The word

站

(**jaahm**) is used in all items except the airport (**fēigē ichèuhng**), with

場

(**chèuhng**) meaning literally "field," though sometimes the word 飛 **fēi** is omitted and 飛機場 **fēigēichèuhng** becomes 機場 **gēichèuhng**.

## Communicative activities

1 Ask a Cantonese-speaking acquaintance how he or she gets to work. Include the means of transportation and how long it takes to get there. How long does it take in all?
2 Imagine that you have invited your friend over to your new place for dinner. Describe in Cantonese how to get to your home. How long will each section of the trip take?

## Cultural point

Hong Kong is one of the most densely populated cities in the world and has a world-class transportation system to serve it that includes a network of subway trains, surface trains, double-decker buses, taxis, minivans, and ferry boats. The subway system (MTR) is among the most efficient and extensive in the world. The light rail and the KCR (Kowloon Canton Railway) both tie in to the MTR system. Its first line was opened in 1979 and the system now has 10 lines and 150 stations, including 68 light rail stops. Below is a map of the system. See if you can recognize any characters on the map.

# Unit 7: Commuting

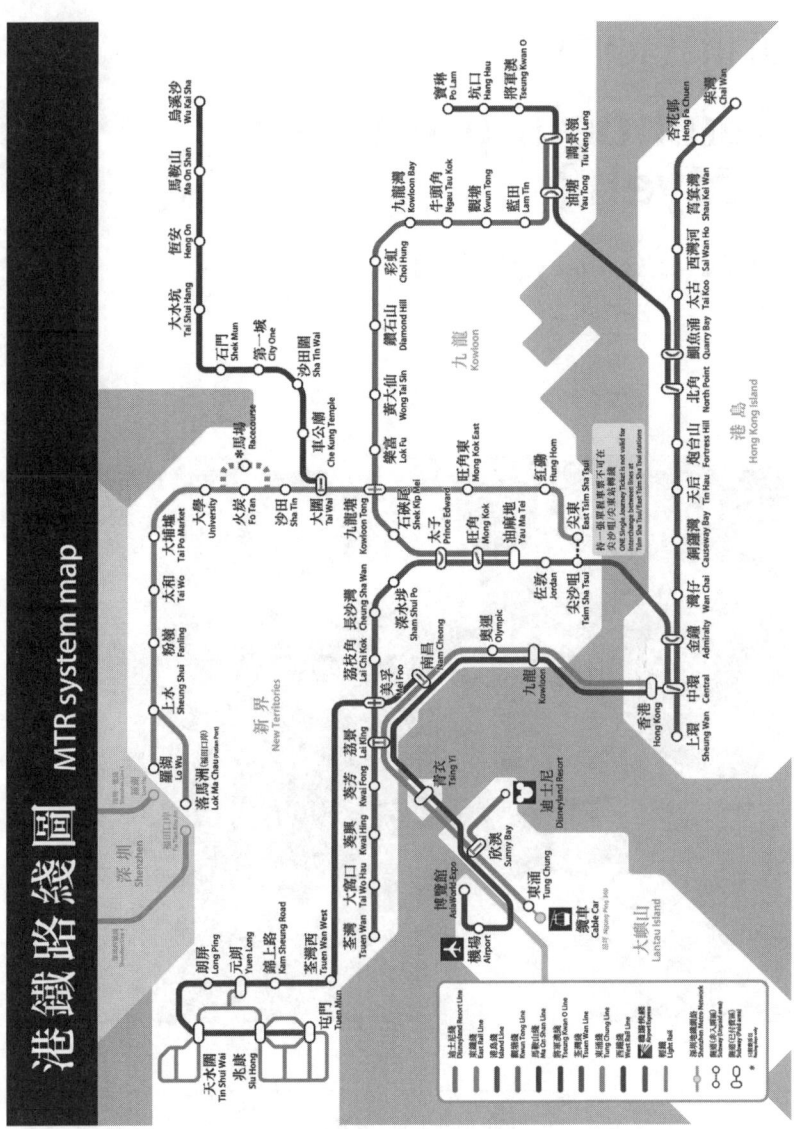

# Unit Eight
## Kéuihdeih jouh-gán mātyéh?
What are they doing?

### In Unit 8 you will learn about:

- discussing what people are doing and where
- using **-gán** to show action in progress
- more uses of **-jó** for completed actions

Unit 8: *What are they doing?*

## Dialogue 1

**(CD2; 1)**
John and Carmen have been invited to Mrs. Lam's home for dinner. They are having a chat in her sitting room before dinner.

(a) How many rooms are there in Mrs. Lam's flat? What are they?
(b) How many people live in the flat? Who are they?
(c) How old are Mrs. Lam's two children?

| | |
|---|---|
| JOHN: | Làhm táai, néih gāan ngūk hóu daaih wo. |
| MRS. LAM: | Haih a. Nī gāan ngūk syun géi daaih ga la. |
| JOHN: | Gám, júngguhng yáuh géidō gāan fóng a? |
| MRS. LAM: | Júngguhng yáuh léuhng go tēng tùhng sei gāan fóng: yāt go haaktēng, yāt go faahntēng, sāam gāan seuihfóng, tùhng yāt gāan syūfóng. Lihngngoih yáuh yāt go chyùhfóng, léuhng go chisó, tùhng yāt go gūngyàhnfóng. |
| CARMEN: | Gám, néihdeih ngūkkéi júngguhng yáuh géidō yàhn a? |
| MRS. LAM: | Júngguhng luhk go yàhn. Ngóh tùhng ngóh sīnsāang lā, ngóh bàh-bā tùhng ngóh màh-mā lā, juhng yáuh ngóh go jái Kenny tùhng ngóh go néui Angel. |
| CARMEN: | Kenny tùhng Angel yáuh géi daaih a? |
| MRS. LAM: | Kenny gāmnín baat seui, Angel jauh chāt seui. |

## Vocabulary

In Hong Kong most people live in rather small flats in high-rise residential blocks. Only the wealthy can afford to live in detached houses or mansions. However, there is no distinction between flats, houses, and mansions in Cantonese. They are all referred to as **ngūk**, which takes the classifier **gāan**, hence "a flat" is **yāt gāan ngūk**, "my flat" is **ngóh gāan ngūk**, and "your flat" is **néih gāan ngūk**.

The typical Hong Kong flat consists of a sitting room, a dining room, two to three bedrooms, a kitchen, and toilet/bathroom. Gardens and garages are luxuries found only in the houses of the wealthy, though a servant's room is not uncommon in some of the bigger flats. Below is a list of Cantonese words related to different parts of a flat. All of these take **go** as the classifier, though the items ending in **fóng** can also take **gāan** as their classifier. Try reading out each item aloud. If you have the audio for this book, you can model your pronunciation on the recording.

**(CD2; 5)**

| | |
|---|---|
| yāt go haaktēng | a sitting room |
| yāt go faahntēng | a dining room |
| yāt go chisó | a toilet |
| yāt go fāyún | a garden |
| yāt go chēfòhng | a garage |
| yāt go/gāan seuihfóng | a bedroom |
| yāt go/gāan syūfóng | a study |
| yāt go/gāan haakfóng | a guest room |
| yāt go/gāan chyùhfóng | a kitchen |
| yāt go/gāan yuhksāt | a bathroom |
| yāt go/gāan gūngyàhnfóng | a servant's room |

---

### Rooms

Most of the words for rooms end in **fóng**, which translates satisfactorily into the English word "room." But Cantonese distinguishes between **tēng** and **fóng**, in that **tēng** refers to bigger rooms often used for entertaining guests. This is a function of the sitting room and the dining room, hence the terms **haaktēng** (lit. "guest room") and **faahntēng** (lit. "meal room"). Also, the word **chyùhfóng** "kitchen" has the alternative pronunciation of **chèuihfóng**. In fact, the two pronunciations are both common, and can be regarded as free variations. The **fòhng** in **chēfòhng** "garage" refers to the same Chinese word as the **fóng** in **seuihfóng** or **syūfóng**, but it takes the *low falling tone* when combined with **chē**, hence **chēfòhng**.

---

## Idioms and structures (CD2; 6)

The items in the list below appear in the same order as they do in the dialogue above. The *italicized* items are *new* items. In the notes, numbers in brackets refer to the expressions listed below.

Unit 8: *What are they doing?*

1 **Nī gāan ngūk syun géi daaih ga la.**    *I suppose* it's quite a large flat.
2 **Lihngngoih ...**    *In addition, ...*
3 **néihdeih ngūkkéi**    *your family*
4 **ngóh sīnsāang**    *my husband*
5 **Ngóh tùhng ngóh sīnsāang lā ...**    *There's* me and my husband ...
6 **Kenny tùhng Angel yáuh géi daaih a?**    *How old* are Kenny and Angel?

## Syun (1)

**Syun** is a word used before the comment in a topic-comment sentence to indicate concession, as if saying in English: "Well, I suppose you can say that." A more literal translation is "... can be regarded as ...." The mood is often reinforced by the use of the double particle **ga la** at the end of the sentence, as in **Kéuih syun géi gōu ga la**, which translates into "He can be regarded as tall" or "You can say he's rather tall."

## The possessive néihdeih (3)

Here **néihdeih** is used as a possessive adjective, and so **néihdeih ngūkkéi** is "your family." Again, the classifier **go** is omitted because close family relationships are being referred to. (See Unit 5, p. 84.)

## Sīnsāang (4)

The noun **sīnsāang** has several meanings. It is a polite way of addressing a man (see Unit 1). It also means "teacher" (both male and female) as well as "husband." The distinction between **sīnsāang** meaning "teacher" and meaning "husband" lies in the presence of the classifier **go**. In the former use, this noun is most likely to be qualified by the subject taught and the classifier **go** is used, as in **Kéuih haih ngóh go Yīngmán sīnsāang** "He is my English teacher." In the latter, as with all intimate family relationships, **go** is omitted and so **Kéuih haih ngóh sīnsāang** has to be "He is my husband." The Cantonese word for "wife" is **taai-táai**, and "my wife" is **ngóh taai-táai**.

## The particle lā (5)

One function of the particle **lā** is listing a number of items of the same nature. In Dialogue 1, Mrs. Lam is listing the people in her family. Another example would be: **Ngóh yáuh hóu dō sihou: yàuh-séui lā, dá-móhngkàuh lā, tek-jūkkàuh lā, tùhng cháai-dāanchē** "I have many hobbies: swimming, playing tennis, playing soccer, and cycling."

## Asking about age (6)

In Unit 5 we introduced the question **Néih géidō seui a?** to ask somebody's age. Another way of asking someone's age is **Kéuih yáuh géi daaih a?**, which literally means "How big is he/she?" The former is typical when the expected age is younger.

## Vocabulary

### Completed actions (CD2; 5)

In Unit 6, we learned that the bound particle **-jó** is used with a verb to indicate the completion of an action. For example, **Kéuih máaih-jó yāt ga chē** is "He has bought a car." Below are some more expressions, all beginning with **heui-jó**, some followed by a word denoting a place and some by a word denoting an action. The first expression **heui-jó gāai**, however, means simply "has gone out" but does not specify where or why.

| | |
|---|---|
| heui-jó gāai | has/have gone out |
| heui-jó tòuhsyūgún | has/have gone to the library |
| heui-jó gāaisíh | has/have gone to the market |
| heui-jó hóitāan | has/have gone to the beach |
| heui-jó wihngchìh | has/have gone to the swimming pool |
| heui-jó tái-hei | has/have gone to watch a movie |
| heui-jó yám-bējáu | has/have gone for a beer |
| heui-jó dá-móhngkàuh | has/have gone to play tennis |
| heui-jó yàuh-séui | has/have gone swimming |
| heui-jó tái-jūkkàuh | has/have gone to watch football |
| heui-jó tēng-yāmngohkwúi | has/have gone to a concert |

Unit 8: *What are they doing?*

Very often both the "where" and the "why" are mentioned in a statement. In such a case the "where" always comes before the "why":

> **Ngóh taai-táai heui-jó gāaisíh máaih sāanggwó.**
> My wife has gone to the market to buy fruit.
>
> **Kéuih gòh-gō heui-jó hóitāan yàuh-séui.**
> His brother has gone to the beach to swim.

In certain instances the word **fāan**, which literally means "return," is used instead of **heui**. The best examples are **fāan ngūkkéi** "to go home," **fāan hohkhaauh** "to go to school," and **fāan gūngsī** "to go to the office." (See Unit 7, pp. 123–4.) They are fixed expressions and it would be wrong to replace **fāan** by **heui**, regardless of where the speaker is. In other words, both "He has gone home" (said by, say, a colleague in the office on the phone) and "He has come home" (said by, say, one member of the family to another at home) would translate into **Kéuih fāan-jó ngūkkéi**. Below are two more examples:

> **Kéuih fāan-jó hohkhaauh dá-móhngkàuh.**
> He/She has gone to his/her school to play tennis.
>
> **Kéuih fāan-jó gūngsī hōi-wúi.**
> He/She has gone to the office for a meeting.

To ask where somebody has gone, however, **heui-jó** is used (and never **fāan-jó**), together with the question-word **bīndouh**, as follows:

> **Kéuih heui-jó bīndouh a?**
> Where has he/she gone?

## Dialogue 2

**(CD2; 3)**
John and Carmen are still chatting with Mrs. Lam in the sitting room before dinner.

(a) Where is Mrs. Lam's husband?
(b) Where is Mrs. Lam's father?
(c) Where is Mrs. Lam's mother?

(d) Where has Kenny gone?
(e) Where has Angel gone?

| | |
|---|---|
| JOHN: | Làhm táai, néih sīnsāang hái bīndouh a? |
| MRS. LAM: | Ngóh sīnsāang juhng hái gūngsī. Kéuih yìhgā hōi-gán wúi. Kéuih daaihyeuk chāt dímjūng jauh fāan lèih ga laak. |
| JOHN: | Gám, néih bàh-bā tùhng màh-mā nē? |
| MRS. LAM: | Ngóh màh-mā hái chyùhfóng jyū-gán faahn. Ngóh bàh-bā jauh hái kéuih gāan fóng tái-gán dihnsih. |
| CARMEN: | Gám, Kenny tùhng Angel nē? |
| MRS. LAM: | Kenny heui-jó yàuh-séui. Angel fāan-jó hohkhaauh. |
| CARMEN: | Kenny heui-jó bīndouh yàuh-séui a? |
| MRS. LAM: | Kéuih heui-jó wihngchìh yàuh-séui. |
| JOHN: | Gám, Angel fāan hohkhaauh jouh mātyéh a? |
| MRS. LAM: | Angel fāan-jó hohkhaauh cheung-gō. Kéuihdeih daaihyeuk luhk dím bun jauh fāan lèih ga laak. |

## Idioms and structures (CD2; 6)

The items in the list below appear in the same order as they do in the dialogue above. The *italicized* items are *new* items. In the notes, numbers in brackets refer to the expressions listed below.

1 **néih sīnsāang hái bīndouh a?**  Where is your husband?

2 **Ngóh sīnsāang *juhng* hái gūngsī.**  My husband is *still* at his office.

3 **Kéuih yìhgā *hōi-gán wúi*.**  He is *having a meeting*.

4 **Keuih daaihyeuk chāt dímjūng jauh fāan lèih *ga laak*.**  *I'm sure* (he) will be back at seven.

5 **Ngóh màh-mā hái chyùhfóng jyú-gán faahn.**  My mother is in the kitchen cooking.

### Asking and stating where somebody is      (1)

As discussed in Unit 3, **hái** is a locative marker, which can be either *verbal* or *prepositional*. In the question **Néih sīnsāang *hái* bīndouh a?** "Where is your husband?," **hái** is used as a verb and the enquiry is about a *state* rather than an action.

## Progressive action (CD2; 6) (3)

In Cantonese, we use the aspect marker **-gán** with a verb to describe an action which is in the process of taking place. Thus, **Kéuih dá-*gán* móhngkàuh** is "He/She is playing tennis," and **Ngóh tēng-*gán* yāmngohk** is "I am listening to music." Below are some more examples of "actions in progress."

| | |
|---|---|
| **tái-gán dihnsih** | watching television |
| **jyú-gán faahn** | cooking |
| **chūng-gán lèuhng** | taking a bath/shower |
| **dūhk-gán syū** | studying |
| **fan-gán gaau** | sleeping |
| **góng-gán dihnwá** | talking on the phone |

To ask what somebody is doing at a particular time, we use the verb **jouh** with the aspect marker **-gán**, as follows:

**Kéuih (yìhgā) jouh-gán mātyéh a?**
What is he/she doing (now)?

## Exercise 1 Action in progress

Answer the questions with the cue word provided, using **-gán** for action in progress. The first one has been done for you as an example.

(a) **John jouh-gán mātyéh a?**     **yàuh-séui**
    **John yàuh-gán seui.**

(b) **HO Syut Hwa jouh-gán mātyéh a?**     **jyú-faahn**

(c) **CHAN Syut Wai jouh-gán mātyéh a?**     **cheung-gō**

(d) **Jimmy jouh-gán mātyéh a?**     **dá-làahmkàuh**

(e) **Wendy jouh-gán mātyéh a?**     **tái-dihnsih**

## Ga laak (4)

**Ga laak** is a combination of two sentence-final particles used to express *reassurance*.

## Stating whereabouts and action (5)

Very often, in a statement, information is given about both where somebody is and what he or she is doing there:

**Ngóh mùih-múi hái syūfóng tái-gán syū.**
My younger sister is reading in the study.

There are two ways of interpreting the statement, depending on the emphasis. If it is a response to the question **Néih mùih-múi hái bīndouh a?** "Where is your younger sister?," then the emphasis of the statement is on **hái syūfóng**, while **tái-gán syū** provides supplementary information about what she is doing, and in such cases the function of **hái** remains that of a verb.

On the other hand, if **hái syūfóng** is *known* information and the statement is a response to the question **Néih mùih-múi hái syūfóng jouh-gán mātyéh a?** "What is your younger sister doing in the study?," then the emphasis is shifted from the state of where someone is to the *action* that is taking place, such as **tái-gán syū**, and at the same time the function of **hái** changes from that of a verb to that of a preposition. Bear in mind, though, that regardless of where the emphasis of the statement lies, the prepositional phrase indicating location, such as **hái syūfóng**, *always precedes* the verb phrase (**tái-gán syū**).

## Exercise 2 Comprehension

Read Dialogue 2 again, or if you have the audio for this book, listen to the recording again, and then answer the following questions.
    During Mrs. Lam's conversation with John and Carmen,

(a) What is Mr. Lam doing?
(b) What is Mrs. Lam's father doing?
(c) What is Mrs. Lam's mother doing?
(d) What is Kenny doing?
(e) What is Angel doing?

## Exercise 3 Actions in progress vs. habitual actions

Remember that **-gán** is used only when referring to actions currently taking place, not when referring to habitual actions or likes and dislikes. Translate the English sentences into Cantonese, focusing on the use of the verb. The first one has been done for you as an example.

(a) He is reading in his study.
    *Answer:* **Kéuih hái syūfóng tái-gán syū.**

Unit 8: *What are they doing?*

(b) I go to work by MTR.
(c) She enjoys watching movies.
(d) I play tennis every Tuesday.
(e) My mother is sleeping.
(f) My father likes listening to music.
(g) My wife enjoys cooking.
(h) My older sister is playing games.

## Exercise 4 My house

(a) The Chans live in a flat on the sixth floor of a residential block. Referring to the picture below, complete Mr. Chan's description of his flat.

   MR. CHAN:  **Ngóhdeih gāan ngūk yáuh yāt go haaktēng, yāt go faahntēng, ...**

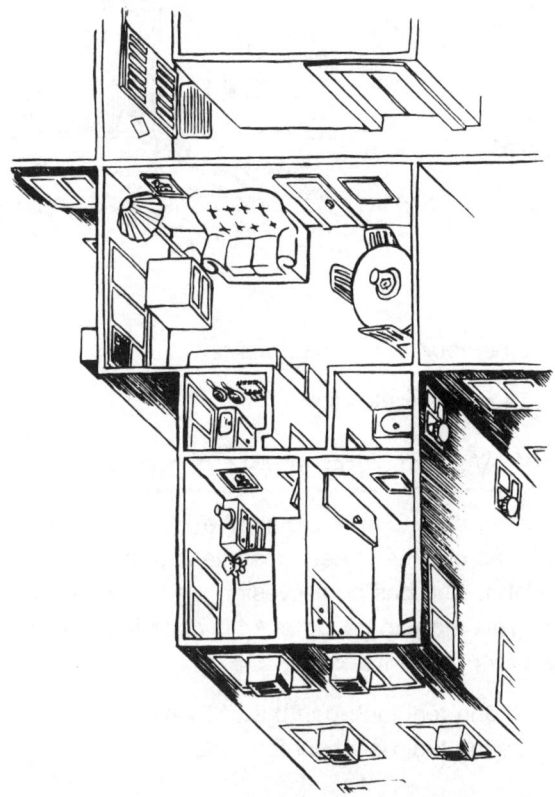

(b) The Poons are one of the few rich families in Hong Kong who can afford to live in a garden house. Referring to the picture below, complete Mr. Poon's description of his house.

MR. POON: **Ngóhdeih gāan ngūk yáuh yāt go haaktēng ...**

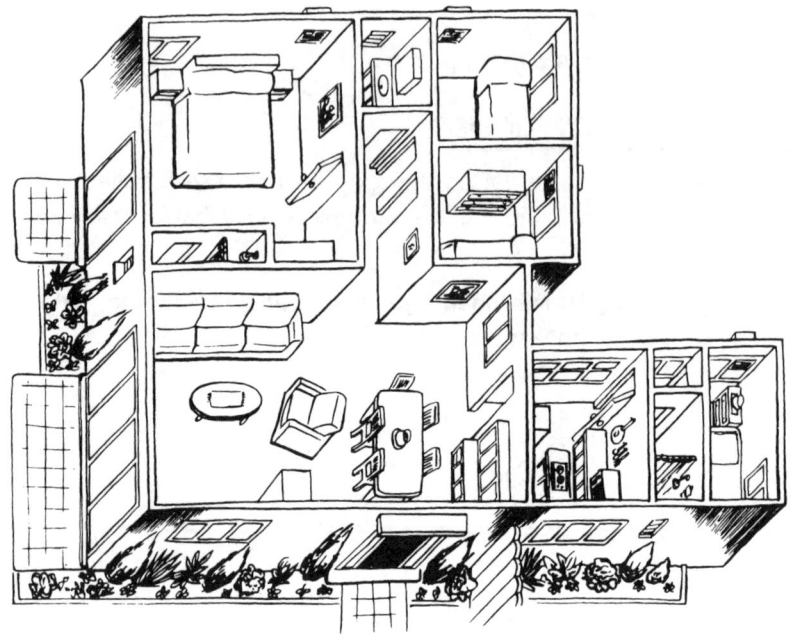

(c) Now describe your own house or flat.

YOU: **Ngóh gāan ngūk yáuh ....**

## Exercise 5 What are they doing?

The Wongs are a nosy couple. They like watching the activities of their neighbors across the street. This evening they are watching the Chans. Mr. Wong, who has poor eyesight, is asking what Mrs. Wong sees. Referring to the picture on p. 141, complete the conversation between Mr. Wong and Mrs. Wong.

MR. WONG: Chàhn táai jouh-gán mātyéh a?
MRS. WONG: Chàhn táai hái chyùhfóng sái-gán wún.

Unit 8: *What are they doing?*

MR. WONG: Gám, Chàhn sīnsāang nē?
MRS. WONG: (a) Chàhn sīnsāang hái faahntēng ...
MR. WONG: Gám, kéuihdeih go jái jouh-gán mātyéh a?
MRS. WONG: (b) Kéuih hái haaktēng ...
MR. WONG: Kéuihdeih go néui nē?
MRS. WONG: (c) Kéuih ...

## Exercise 6 Where have they gone?

It is Sunday. John rings Mrs. Lam, and her father answers the phone. He tells John that the whole family have gone out for different activities with various friends, and patiently tells John where each one has gone. Referring to the information below, complete the conversation between John and Mrs. Lam's father.

Mr. Lam: to watch a football match
Mrs. Lam: shopping
Kenny: to play tennis
Angel: to a concert

| JOHN: | Làhm táai heui-jó bīndouh a? |
|---|---|
| MRS. LAM'S FATHER: | (a) Kéuih heui-jó ... |
| JOHN: | Gám, Làhm sīnsāang nē? |
| MRS. LAM'S FATHER: | (b) Kéuih ... |
| JOHN: | Kenny yauh heui-jó bīndouh a? |
| MRS. LAM'S FATHER: | (c) Kenny ... |
| JOHN: | Gám, Angel nē? |
| MRS. LAM'S FATHER: | (d) |

## Recognizing Chinese characters

| 客廳 | sitting room |
|---|---|
| 飯廳 | dining room |
| 睡房 | bedroom |
| 書房 | study |
| 客房 | guest room |
| 厨房 | kitchen |
| 厠所 | toilet |
| 浴室 | bathroom |
| 工人房 | servant's room |

## Communicative activities

1 Ask your partner about things he or she has done recently. (For example, have you been swimming? If so, when and where?)
2 Ask your partner to describe the place where he or she lives. Is it large? How many rooms are there? What sorts of rooms are there?

## Cultural point

Cantonese has many ways to greet people. We have learned the formal **Néih hóu**, but commonly people greet by stating the obvious, such as **fāangong a**? "So (you) are going to work (then)?" or even **sihkfaahn a?** "So (you) are eating (then)?" The appropriate response then is to affirm that you are doing what the person mentions or sometimes correct their perception. These kinds of exchanges are simply conventional ways to acknowledge someone, just as in English asking how someone is does not really constitute a question but a salutation.

# Unit Nine
# Bōng ngóh jouh dī yéh
Can you help me?

### In Unit 9 you will learn about:

- asking people to do things
- responding to requests
- using **meih** for actions still to be taken
- using **yùhn** to discuss when actions are completed

Unit 9: *Can you help me?*

## Dialogue 1

**(CD2; 7)**

Mrs. Lam is busy with housework, and wants her children to help.

(a) What does Mrs. Lam want help with?
(b) Which of her two children is able to help?

| | |
|---|---|
| MRS. LAM: | Angel, dī sāam meih sái. Néih hó-mh-hóyíh tùhng ngóh sái-sāam a? |
| ANGEL: | Mdāk a, māmìh. Ngóh yiu heui yàuh-séui a. |
| MRS. LAM: | Gám, Kenny nē? Néih tùhng ngóh sái-sāam dāk-mh-dāk a? |
| KENNY: | Dāk, móuh mahntàih. |

## Dialogue 2

**(CD2; 9)**

It is eight in the evening. The Lams have just finished dinner.
Mrs. Lam is distributing the housework to the members of her family.

(a) Who is going to clear the table?
(b) Who is going to wash up?
(c) Who is going to empty the trash bin?

| | |
|---|---|
| MRS. LAM: | Kenny, néih bōngsáu jāp-tói dāk-mh-dāk? |
| KENNY: | Háu ak. |
| MRS. LAM: | Gám, Angel, mgōi néih sái-wún ā. |
| ANGEL: | Dāk, ngóh sái-wún lā. |
| MRS. LAM: | Gám, George, néih hó-mh-hóyíh dóu-laahpsaap a? |
| MR. LAM: | Hóyíh. |

## Vocabulary

### Housework (CD2; 11)

Below is a list of household tasks. Try reading out each item aloud. If you have the audio for this book, you can model your pronunciation on the recording.

| | |
|---|---|
| jāp-chòhng | to make the bed |
| jyú-faahn | to cook |
| jāp-tói | to clear the table |
| sái-wún | to wash the dishes/wash up |
| dóu-laahpsaap | to empty the trash bin |
| máaih-yéh | to go shopping |
| máaih-sung | to buy food (for meals) |
| sái-sāam | to wash the clothes |
| lohng-sāam | to hang the clothes out |
| tong-sāam | to iron the clothes |
| sou-deih | to sweep the floor |
| kāp-chàhn | to vacuum-clean |
| maat-chēung | to clean the windows |

The examples of housework in the list above are all expressed in *verb-object constructions*, and are thus hyphenated. Most of the translations in the right-hand column are literal translations of the verb and the object. Exceptions include **jyú-faahn**, which literally means "cook-rice," **dóu-laahpsaap**, which literally means "pour-rubbish," **máaih-yéh**, which literally means "buy-things," and **kāp-chàhn**, which literally means "suck-dust." **Jyú-faahn** is used when it is assumed that a Chinese meal is being prepared, but if the cooking is apparently not Chinese, the more general term of **jyú-yéhsihk** (lit. "cook-food") can be used. Similarly, **sái-wún** (lit. "wash-bowls") is used if the meal is Chinese, and bowls are used instead of plates; another expression, **sái-díp** (lit. "wash-plates"), can be used if the meal is apparently Western.

> ### Máaih-sung
> In the construction **máaih-sung**, the object **sung** refers specifically to raw food (meat and vegetables) which one buys in the traditional Chinese wet market to cook for lunch or dinner. It does not include food one usually buys in a supermarket such as cereals, cheese, cake, ice cream, etc. It has no exact equivalent in English.

Unit 9: *Can you help me?*

## Idioms and structures (CD2; 15)

The items in the list below appear in the same order as they do in the dialogues above. The *italicized* items are *new* items. In the notes, numbers in brackets refer to the expressions listed below.

| | | |
|---|---|---|
| 1 | dī sāam *meih sái* | the clothes *have yet to be washed* |
| 2 | **Néih** *hó-mh-hóyíh* tùhng ngóh sái-sāam a? | Can you wash the clothes for me? |
| 3 | **Mā** | Mom |
| 4 | **Néih** tùhng ngóh sái-sāam *dāk-mh-dāk* a? | Can you wash the clothes for me? |
| 5 | **Néih** *bōngsáu* jāp-tói dāk-mh-dāk a? | Can you *help* to clear the table? |
| 6 | **Dāk,** ngóh sái-wún *lā.* | OK, I'll wash the dishes. |

### Meih to refer to action not yet taken  (1)

Here **meih** indicates action that is not yet taken. Thus, **dī sāam *meih sái*** means "the clothes have yet to be washed." Similarly, **dī chēung *meih* maat** means "the windows have yet to be cleaned," and **dī laapsaap *meih* dóu** means "the bin is yet to be emptied."

### Asking a favor and responding to the request  (2, 4, 5, 6)

There are four ways of asking a favor, as follows:

(a) By using the modal **hóyíh** in a choice-type question:

   **Néih hó-mh-hóyíh tùhng ngóh sái-wún a?**
   Can you wash the dishes for me?

   Note that in a choice-type question, only the first syllable of a two-syllable word is repeated, thus **hó-mh-hóyíh** but not *\*hóyíh-mh-hóyíh*. **Tùhng ngóh** means "for me" but note that, unlike English "for me," it comes *before* the verb.

(b) By using the question-phrase **dāk-mh-dāk**, plus the particle **a** at the end of the sentence:

**Néih tùhng ngóh sái-wún dāk-mh-dāk a?**
Is it all right if I ask you to wash the dishes for me? (Or more literally, "Wash the dishes for me, all right?")

(c) By using **Mgōi néih** ("Please" or "Would you please ...") at the beginning of a sentence with an optional **ā** at the end:

**Mgōi néih tùhng ngóh sái-wún (ā).**
Please wash the dishes for me.

(d) An alternative to using **Mgōi** is to use **Màhfàahn**. This form is more common when you are asking a favor of someone of similar or greater age and position:

**Màhfàahn néih tùhng ngóh sái-wún ā.**
Can I trouble you to wash the dishes for me?

The most direct responses to the question in (a) are:

| | **Hóyíh.** | Yes, I can. |
|---|---|---|
| or | **Mhóyíh.** | No, I can't. |

The most direct responses to the question in (b) are:

| | **Dāk.** | Yes, it's all right. |
|---|---|---|
| or | **Mdāk.** | No, it's not all right. |

Two universal positive responses to (a), (b), (c) and (d) are:

| **Dāk, móuh mahntàih.** | Yes, no problem. |
|---|---|
| **Hóu aak.** | OK. |

A universal negative response to (a), (b), (c) and (d) is:

| **Mdāk a.** | I'm afraid I can't help. |
|---|---|

Note that the sentence-final particle **a** in **Mdāk a** helps express regret at not being able to help. You can use the expression **Deuimjyuh** to complement **Mdāk a** to sound more apologetic, for instance, *Mdāk a, deui mjyuh*, ngóh mhóyíh tùhng néih sái-wún a.

# Lā (6)

The sentence-final particle **lā** used here helps to convey cheerful acceptance of the task.

| | |
|---|---|
| ANGEL: | Hóu lā. Ngóh tùhng néih tong lā. |
| MRS. LAM: | Mgōi, Angel. Juhng yáuh, deihhá hóu wūjōu, bīngo hóyíh tùhng ngóh sou-deih a? |
| MR. LAM: | Ngóh tùhng néih sou-deih lā. |
| MRS. LAM: | Mgōi saai, George. Gám, Kenny, néih géidímjūng tái-yùhn jūkkàuh a? |
| KENNY: | Juhng yáuh sāam go jih jauh tái yùhn la. |
| MRS. LAM: | Gám, néih tái yùhn jūkkàuh tùhng ngóh maat-jó dī chēung dāk-mh-dāk a? |
| KENNY: | Dāk, móuh mahntàih. |

## Idioms and structures (CD2; 15)

The items in the list below appear in the same order as they do in the dialogues above. The *italicized* items are *new* items. In the notes, numbers in brackets refer to the expressions listed below.

1  **Ngóh séung wán yàhn tùhng ngóh dá géi fūng seun. Bīngo dākhàahn a?** — I am looking for someone to type several letters for me. Who is free?

2  **Yáuh móuh yàhn hóyíh tùhng ngóh yíngyan a?** — Is there anyone who can help me do some photocopying?

3  **Ngóh *bōng* néih yíngyan lā.** — I'll *help* you to do the photocopying.

4  ***Mgōi saai.*** — Thank you so much.

5  ***Msái mgōi.*** — You are welcome./Not at all. (A conventional response to **mgōi**, which literally means "There's no need to thank me.")

6  **Bīngo hóyíh tùhng ngóh tong-jó dī sāam a?** — Who can help me *get the clothes ironed*?

7  **Juhng yáuh ...** — And also ...

8  ***deihhá* hóu *wūjōu*** — *the floor* is *dirty*

9  **Néih géidímjūng tái-yùhn jūkkàuh a?** — When will you *finish watching* soccer?

10  **Juhng yáuh sāam go jih jauh tái yùhn laak.** — Fifteen more minutes to go, and then I'll finish watching (soccer).

## Asking for a volunteer to help (1, 2)

One way to ask for a volunteer to help get something done is to say what you want done and then ask who is free:

**Ngóh séung wán yàhn tùhng ngóh dá géi fūng seun. Bīngo dākhàahn a?**
I am looking for someone to type several letters for me. Who is free?

**Wán** in the phrase **wán yàhn** is a verb which means "to look for." **Yàhn**, on the other hand, is a noun of an indefinite nature in this context, and can thus be translated into either "someone" or "people." The modal verb **séung** used before the phrase can be translated into "want to" or "wish to."

Another way to ask around for a volunteer is to use the question word **bīngo** "who" with the modal **hóyíh**, as below:

**Bīngo hóyíh tùhng ngóh dá géi fūng seun a?**
Who can help me type a few letters?

A third way to make an open request for a favor is to use the question phrase **Yáuh móuh yàhn** "Is there anybody?" with the modal **hóyíh** to form a question, as follows:

**Yáuh móuh yàhn hóyíh tùhng ngóh dá-jih a?**
Is there anyone who can do some typing for me?

## The verbal particle saai (4)

The particle **saai** is used with a verb and conveys the meaning of "completely." Thus, **mgōi** *saai* is an emphatic form of "thank you" for a favor, while **dōjeh** *saai* is an emphatic form of "thank you" for a gift.

## Anticipating completion of action (6)

Unit 6 introduced the use of the aspect marker **-jó** to refer to completed action. Sometimes when we ask people to do a favor we can use the aspect marker **-jó** with the verb to indicate anticipation of some action being completed soon. This use is not unlike the notion of "getting something done" in English. Below are two examples:

**Néih hó-mh-hóyíh tùhng ngóh dóu-jó dī laahpsaap a?**
Could you get the trash bin emptied for me, please?

**Bīngo hóyíh tùhng ngóh gei-jó dī seun a?**
Can somebody get these letters posted for me, please?

## Hóu (8)

**Hóu** in **deihhà *hóu* wūjōu** functions as an adverb meaning "very," to qualify the adjective **wūjōu** when it is stressed (i.e. when the tone and segment is fully pronounced). But when it is *not* stressed, **hóu** in colloquial Cantonese does not carry the meaning of "very." So *hóu* **wūjōu** simply means "dirty" rather than "very dirty."

## The verbal particle yùhn (9)

**Yùhn** is a particle used after a verb to indicate finishing an action. It is different from the aspect marker **-jó** in that it is used to specify the finishing time of an action in progress. The question in Dialogue 4: **néih géidímjūng tái-*yùhn* jūkkàuh a?** asks when Kenny will finish watching soccer, as he is watching while his mother is talking to him. Similarly, if you telephoned your friend and found that he was having dinner, then you could ask: **Néih géidímjūng sihk *yùhn* faahn a?** "When will you finish eating your dinner?" If you telephoned your friend for a chat in the evening, you might start the conversation by asking: **Néih sihk-jó faahn meih a?** "Have you eaten your dinner?" This habit of asking whether somebody has had a meal, by the way, is a social norm among Cantonese speakers, and can be compared to English people talking about the weather as an opener to a conversation.

## Juhng yáuh ... jauh (10)

**Juhng yáuh** in this context means "there is still," with **yáuh** in its existential use, while **jauh** is used to mean "and then," leading on to the consequence of a condition. Thus, ***juhng yáuh* sāam go jih *jauh* tái yùhn jūkkàuh laak** literally means "There are fifteen more minutes to go and then I'll finish watching soccer."

## Exercise 2 Mr. Nice Guy

Nick is a very nice person and never says no to a favor asked. You want Nick to do three things for you: type two letters, borrow three books from the library, and buy a train ticket. Complete the conversation with polite requests for favors.

YOU: Nick, néih dāk-mh-dākhàahn tùhng ngóh jouh géi yeuhng yéh a?
NICK: Dāk, móuh mahntàih.
YOU: (a) Néih hó-mh-hóyíh bōng ngóh ...
NICK: Hóyíh.
YOU: (b) Gám, ...
NICK: (c)
YOU: (d)
NICK: (e)
YOU: Mgōi saai, Nick.
NICK: (f)

## Exercise 3 The selfish family

The members of the Chow family are very selfish, and seldom offer to help with housework. This is another typical evening when Mrs. Chow is appealing in vain to her family for help. Everyone claims that he or she is busy doing something else. Referring to the picture, complete the conversation.

MRS. CHOW: Bīngo dākhàahn bōng ngóh sái-wún a?
JANE: Ngóh mdākhàahn a, mā. Ngóh cheung-gán gō a.
MRS. CHOW: Gám, néih nē, Kelvin?
KELVIN: (a) Ngóh dōu mdākhàahn a. Ngóh ...
MRS. CHOW: Jane tùhng Kelvin dōu mdākhàahn. Gám, néih bōng ngóh sái-wún dāk-mh-dāk a, bàh-bā?
MR. CHOW: (b) Deui mjyuh ...

# Unit 9: *Can you help me?*

# Recognizing Chinese characters

| | |
|---|---|
| 煮飯 | to cook meals |
| 洗碗 | to wash bowls |
| 買餸 | to buy food for meals |
| 洗衣 | to wash the clothes |
| 掛衣 | to hang (the) clothes (out) |
| 燙衣服 | to iron the clothes |
| 掃地 | to sweep the floor |
| 吸塵 | to vacuum-clean |
| 抹窗 | to clean the windows |

Unit 9: **Bōng ngóh jouh dī yéh**

## Communicative activities

1 Find out from a Cantonese-speaking partner about who does what jobs around his or her home. Who makes the bed? Who washes the dishes? Who vacuums?
2 Suppose that you are trying to get out of doing work around the place where you live. With a partner take the role of the reluctant or lazy household member and say why you cannot do what he or she is asking you to do.

## Cultural point

Friendship and obligation are viewed in a distinctly different way in Chinese culture as compared with the West. Friendships often take longer to develop, but when they are established expected obligations are typically stronger. The Chinese sometimes see Western friendliness as superficial. When you are traveling to a faraway place, it is common for Chinese friends to ask you to take a package with you for one of their friends. Once you establish a relationship, favors are freely requested and given between friends.

# Unit Ten
# Hái bīndouh?
Where is it?

In Unit 10 you will learn about:

- discussing where an object is
- discussing where a building is
- using **dóu** to indicate succeeding in an action

Dialogue 1

**(CD2; 16)**
The Chans are an untidy family. The children, Sylvan and Sally, often leave things lying around in odd places. Their father Mr. Chan is not much better. Mrs. Chan is probably the only organized person in the house. At the moment Sally is about to go out, and is desperately trying to find her handbag and her gloves.

(a) Where is Sally's handbag?
(b) Where are her gloves?

| | |
|---|---|
| SALLY: | Māmìh, ngóh go sáudói mgin-jó a. Néih jī-mh-jī ngóh go sáudói hái bīndouh a? |
| MRS. CHAN: | Nē! Néih go sáudói hái sōfá seuhngmihn a. |
| SALLY: | Haih wo. Gám, ngóh deui sáumaht nē? Ngóh wán mdóu deui sáumaht a. |
| MRS. CHAN: | Néih deui sáumaht hái ōnlohkyí seuhngmihn a. Gin-mh-gin a? |
| SALLY: | Gin dóu la. Mgōi saai, māmìh. |

 Dialogue 2

**(CD2; 17)**
Mr. Chan is hunting around for his eyeglasses while his son Sylvan is frantically searching for his missing comb and socks.

(a) Where are Mr. Chan's eyeglasses?
(b) Where is Sylvan's comb?
(c) Where are Sylvan's socks?

| | |
|---|---|
| MR. CHAN: | Taai-táai a, ngóh wán mdóu ngóh go ngáahngéng a! |
| MRS. CHAN: | Nē! Néih go ngáahngéng mhaih hái chàhgēi seuhng-mihn lō! Gin-mh-gin a? |
| MR. CHAN: | Bīndouh a? … Gin dóu la. Hái chàhgēi seuhng-mihn ā ma. |
| SYLVAN: | Māmìh, néih yáuh móuh gin dóu ngóh bá sō a? Ngóh bá sō mgin-jó a. |
| MRS. CHAN: | Néih bá sō àh? Nē! Néih bá sō mhaih hái dihnsi-gēi seuhngmihn lō! |
| SYLVAN: | Haih wo. Gám, ngóh deui maht nē? Néih gin-mh-gin a? |

Unit 10: *Where is it?*

MRS. CHAN: Néih deui maht hái deihhá a. Nē, chāantói hahmihn a.
SYLVAN: Gin dóu la. Mgōi, māmìh.

## Vocabulary

### Personal belongings (CD2; 18)

Below are some things commonly found at home. They are presented with their assigned classifiers.

| | |
|---|---|
| yāt *go* sáudói | a handbag |
| yāt *go* ngàhnbāau | a purse |
| yāt *go/fu* ngáahngéng | a pair of eyeglasses |
| yāt *deui* maht | a pair of socks |
| yāt *deui* sáumaht | a pair of gloves |
| yāt *deui* tōháai | a pair of slippers |
| yāt *jek* maht/sáumaht/tōháai | a sock/glove/slipper |
| yāt *jī* bāt | a pen |
| yāt *bá* jē | an umbrella |
| yāt *bá* sō | a comb |
| yāt *go* séuibūi | a glass |
| yāt *go* chàhbūi | a cup |
| yāt *bouh* luhkyínggēi | a video-recorder |
| yāt *béng* luhkyíngdáai | a video-tape |
| yāt *jek* DVD-dín | a DVD |
| yāt *bouh* DVD-gēi | a DVD player |

### Classifiers

Apart from the most common classifier **go**, which is used for "roundish" objects and many other less obviously roundish ones such as people (**yāt go yàhn**) and eyeglasses (**yāt go ngáahngéng**), most classifiers are rationally determined. In the examples given above, **yāt deui** is literally "a pair," while **jek** is the classifier for single pieces of footwear or gloves. **Jī** is used for long, slender objects which are cylindrical in shape, for instance **yāt jī bāt** "a pen," while **bá** is used for long, slender objects that are not cylindrical, such as **yāt bá jē** "an umbrella" and **yāt bá sō** "a comb."

Idioms and structures

The items in the list below appear in the same order as they do in the dialogues above. The *italicized* items are *new* items. In the notes, numbers in brackets refer to the expressions listed below.

1 **mgin-jó** — has gone missing/is missing
2 **Néih jī-mh-jī ngóh go sáudói hái bīndouh a?** — Do you know where my handbag is?
3 **Néih go sáudói *hái sōfá seuhngmihn* a.** — Your handbag is *on the sofa*.
4 ***wán mdóu*** — cannot find
5 **Gin-mh-gin a?** — Do you see them?
6 **Gin dóu la.** — I can see them now.
7 **Néih go ngáahngéng *mhaih* hái chàhgēi seuhngmihn *lō?*** — *Aren't those* your glasses on the coffee table?
8 **Hái chàhgēi seuhngmihn ā ma.** — On the coffee table, *as you said.*
9 **néih *yáuh móuh gin dóu* ngóh bá sō a?** — Have *you seen* my comb?
10 **Néih bá sō *àh?*** — *Did you say* your comb?

## Mgin-jó (1)

The verb **gin** means "to see," and the verb **mgin** "to lose" is formed from it by adding the negative prefix **m-**. **Mgin** is very often used with the aspect marker **-jó**, which indicates completion of action, to form the expression **mgin-jó**. In its stative use, describing the state of something, **mgin-jó** would translate into English as "missing," as in **ngóh go sáudói *mgin-jó*** "My handbag is *missing*." In its verbal use, **mgin-jó** would translate into English as "has/have lost," as in **Ngóh mgin-jó ngóh go sáudói** "I have *lost* my handbag."

# Asking where something is (2)

To ask where something is, the question phrase **hái bīndouh** is used with the interrogative particle **a**. Note particularly the word order: the question phrase comes at the end of the sentence.

**Ngóh deui tōháai *hái bīndouh* a?**
Where are my slippers?

**Néih jī-mh-jī ngóh go sáudói *hái bīndouh* a?**
Do you know where my handbag is?

# Saying where an object is (3)

To indicate location in Cantonese, the verbal form of the word **hái** is used, together with an adverb of location. However, the use is different from the use of prepositions in English. To indicate location, English employs the following pattern:

| Noun A | Verb "to be" | Preposition | Noun B |
|---|---|---|---|
| The book | is | on | the coffee table. |

In Cantonese, the constituent parts come in a different order, as follows:

| Noun A | *hái* | Noun B | Adverb of location |
|---|---|---|---|
| **Bún syū** | **hái** | **jēung chàhgēi** | **seuhngmihn.** |
| The book | is | the coffee table | on top. |

Note that while the definite article "the" is used for a specified noun in English, Cantonese uses the determiner **gó** and an appropriate classifier for a specified noun, such as **gó bún syū** "the book," **gó jēung chàhgēi** "the coffee table." However, the determiner **gó** is often omitted, hence **Bún syū hái jēung chàhgēi seuhngmihn.**

Below is a list of common adverbs of location used in Cantonese. The familiar nouns **syū** "book," **chàhgēi** "coffee table," **sōfá** "sofa," **dihnsihgēi** "TV set," **syūgá** "bookshelves," and **ōnlohkyí** "easy chair" are used to form sentences to illustrate the use.

**Bún syū *hái* jēung chàhgēi *seuhngmihn*.**
The book *is on* the coffee table.

**Bún syū *hái* jēung chàhgēi *hahmihn*.**
The book *is under* the coffee table.

**Jēung chàhgēi** *hái* **jēung sōfá** *gaaklèih*.
The coffee table *is beside* the sofa.

**Go dihnsihgēi** *hái* **jēung sōfá** *chìhnmihn*.
The TV set *is in front of* the sofa.

**Go syūgá** *hái* **jēung sōfá** *hauhmihn*.
The bookshelves *are behind* the sofa.

To say Object A is between Object B and Object C, again the adverb of location comes at the end, as follows:

**Jēung sōfá** *hái* **jēung chàhgēi** *tùhng* **jēung ōnlohkyí** *jūnggāan*.
The sofa *is between* the coffee table *and* the easy chair.

To say something (say, the book) is on the floor, you can say:

**Bún syū** *hái deihhá seuhngmihn*.

or simply:

**Bún syū** *hái deihhá*.

## The verbal particle dóu (4, 6)

The verbal particle **dóu** is often used after a verb to indicate success in doing something. For example, the verb **wán** means "to look for" and **wán dóu** means "to be able to find." Hence **Ngóh wán dóu go sáudói la** is "I found the handbag." The negative form of **wán dóu** is formed by adding the negative prefix **m-** to **dóu** and the phrase becomes **wán mdóu**, which translates into "to fail to find." Thus, **Ngóh wán mdóu deui sáumaht** is "I cannot find the gloves." Later in Dialogue 1, **Gin dóu la** in response to the question **Gin-mh-gin a?** stresses the fact that one can now see something which one failed to see a minute before.

## Mhaih ... lō! (7)

The structure **mhaih ... lō!** gives positive emphasis. Although **mhaih** is negative by itself, the sentence-final particle **lō** turns the whole structure positive. This structure can be compared to the rhetorical question of "Aren't those your glasses lying on the coffee table?" Another example can be found later in Dialogue 2: **Néih bá sō mhaih hái dihnsihgēi seuhngmihn lō!** "Isn't that your comb on top of the television?"

## The double particle ā ma (8)

**ā ma** are two particles used together at the end of a statement which repeats another speaker's message to acknowledge it. In Dialogue 2, Mrs. Chan tells Mr. Chan his glasses are on the coffee table (**hái chàhgēi seuhngmihn**), and when Mr. Chan finally finds his glasses he acknowledges receipt of the message by saying **Hái chàhgēi seuhngmihn ā ma** "On the coffee table, as you said."

## Yáuh móuh ... dóu? (9)

The verb **gin** is very often used with the verbal particle **dóu** to mean "to have seen," with emphasis on someone having seen something in the immediate past. To form a choice-type question with **gin dóu**, the verbs **yáuh** and **móuh** are used. Hence **néih yáuh móuh gin dóu ngóh bá sō a?** "Have you seen my comb?"

## Question with àh (10)

Here the question with **àh** (see Unit 5, p. 84) acknowledges the first question, and buys time for a reply. In Dialogue 2, Sylvan asks the question **Néih yáuh móuh gin dóu ngóh bá sō a?**, and Mrs. Chan responds by saying **Néih bá sō àh?**, to give herself time to look around for the comb. Similarly, if the question was **Néih yáuh móuh gin dóu Sylvan bún syū a?**, then the response would be **Sylvan bún syū àh?**

## Vocabulary

### Shops (CD2; 19)

Below is a list of different shops. Try reading out each item aloud. If you have the audio for this book, model your pronunciation on the recording.

| | |
|---|---|
| màhngeuihdim | stationery shop |
| syūdim/syūgúk | bookstore |
| tòhnggwódim | sweet shop |
| fādim | flower shop |
| fuhkjōngdim | dress shop |

| | |
|---|---|
| **mihnbāaupóu** | bakery |
| **fēifaatpóu** | barber's shop |
| **hàaihpóu** | shoe shop |
| **dihnheipóu** | electrical appliance store |
| **yeuhkfòhng** | drugstore |
| **chīukāpsíhchèuhng** | supermarket |

> **Shop/store**
>
> Most of the items in the list above are compound nouns ending either in **dim** or **póu**, both of which mean "shop" or "store." For example, "sweets" is **tòhnggwó**, and a "sweet shop" is **tòhnggwódim**. Two exceptions are **yeuhkfòhng** "drugstore," in which **fòhng** (lit. "room") is used, and **chīukāpsíhchèuhng**, which is a literal translation of supermarket, with **chī ukāp** meaning "super" and **síhchèuhng** meaning "market." Another exception is the alternative term for "bookstore," **syūgúk**, in which **gúk** is used to refer to a large shop. All these shops use the classifier **gāan**, hence **yāt gāan mihnbāaupóu**, **yāt gāan dihnheipóu**, and so on.

## Dialogue 3

**(CD2; 20)**

Auntie Kate has come to visit the Chans from Canada, and is staying with them for a month. She is asking Sally where she can buy certain things.

(a) Where is the shoe shop that Sally recommends?
(b) How far away is it?
(c) Where is the dress shop that Sally recommends?

| | |
|---|---|
| AUNTIE KATE: | Sally, ngóh séung máaih deui hàaih. Néih jī-mh-jī bīndouh yáuh hàaihpóu a? |
| SALLY: | Ngóh jī hái deihtitjaahm deuimihn yáuh yāt gāan hàaihpóu. Gódouh dī hàaih géi leng ga. |
| AUNTIE KATE: | Gám, gāan hàaihpóu káhn-mh-káhn nīdouh ga? |

Unit 10: *Where is it?*

| | |
|---|---|
| SALLY: | Hóu káhn ja. Daaihyeuk hàahng léuhng go jih jauh dou la. |
| AUNTIE KATE: | Gám, nīdouh fuhgahn yáuh móuh fuhkjōngdim a? Ngóh juhng séung máaih géi gihn sāam. |
| SALLY: | Yáuh yāt gāan, jauh hái hàaihpóu chèhdeui-mihn. |
| AUNTIE KATE: | Gám, ngāam saai laak! |

## Dialogue 4

**(CD2; 21)**

Today Auntie Kate wants to see a movie, and asks Sylvan about the nearest movie theater.

(a) What is the name of the nearest movie theater?
(b) How long does it take to walk there?
(c) How long does it take to go by taxi?

| | |
|---|---|
| AUNTIE KATE: | Sylvan, ngóh séung heui tái chēut-hei. Lèih ngūkkéi jeui káhn gāan heiyún hái bīndouh a? |
| SYLVAN: | Lèih nīdouh jeui káhn gāan heiyún haih Capitol Cinema. Bātgwo dōu géi yúhn a, yiu hàahng daaihyeuk ńgh go jih sīnji douh a. |
| AUNTIE KATE: | Gám, daap dīksí yiu géinoih a? |
| SYLVAN: | Daap dīksí jauh hóu faai, léuhng go jih jauh heui douh laak. |

## Idioms and structures

The items in the list below appear in the same order as they do in the dialogues above. The *italicized* items are *new* items. In the notes, numbers in brackets refer to the expressions listed below.

| | | |
|---|---|---|
| 1 | **Néih jī-mh-jī *bīndouh* yáuh hàaihpóu a?** | Do you know *where I can find* a shoe store? |
| 2 | ***Hái deihtitjaahm deuimihn* yáuh yāt gāan hàaihpóu.** | *There's a shoe store opposite the subway station.* |
| 3 | **Ngóh juhng séung máaih *géi gihn sāam*.** | I also want to buy *some clothes*. |

4 **Gám**, *ngāam saai laak!* — That's great!
5 **Ngóh séung heui tái chēut**-hei. — I want to go see a movie. (**Chēut** is the classifier for **hei** or **dihnyīng**.)
6 *Lèih ngūkkéi jeui káhn* **gāan heiyún hái bīndouh a?** — Where is the nearest movie theater to your house?
7 **Bātgwo** *dōu* **géi** *yúhn* a. — Even so it's quite *far away*.
8 *Yiu* **hàahng daaihyeuk ńgh go jih** *sīnji* **douh a.** — It *takes* about 25 minutes to walk there.

## Location (1, 2)

To indicate the location of buildings, we use similar structures to those discussed earlier in this unit. Below are several examples using a movie theater (**heiyún**) and a supermarket (**chīukāpsíhchèuhng**) as two points of orientation.

**(Gāan) mihnbāaupóu** *hái* **(gāan) heiyún** *gaaklèih*.
The bakery *is beside* the movie theater.

**(Gāan) fādim** *hái* **(gāan) heiyún** *deuimihn*.
The flower shop *is opposite* the movie theater.

**(Gāan) syūdim** *hái* **(gāan) chī ukāp síhchèuhng** *chèhdeuimihn*.
The bookstore *is diagonally across from* the supermarket.

**(Gāan) yeuhkfòhng** *hái* **(gāan) fādim** *tùhng* **(gāan) hàaihpóu jūnggāan**.
The drugstore *is between* the flower shop *and* the shoe store.

**(Gāan) dihnheipóu** *hái* **(gāan) heiyúhn** *fuhgahn*.
The electrical appliance shop *is near* the movie theater.

To ask whether there is a certain kind of shop nearby, the existential verbs **yáuh** and **móuh** are used, as follows:

**Nīdouh fuhgahn** *yáuh móuh* **yeuhkfòhng a?**
Is there a drugstore nearby?

An alternative is to use the question word **bīndouh** "where":

**Fuhgahn** *bīndouh* **yáuh yeuhkfòhng a?**
Where can I find a drugstore around here?

To answer these questions, the information about the whereabouts is usually put at the beginning of the sentence:

**Hái heiyúhn deuimihn yáuh yāt gāan yeuhkfòhng.**
There is a drugstore opposite the movie theater.

## Exercise 1 Where is everything?

Translate into Cantonese the following statements about where things are. The first one has been done for you as an example.

(a) The book is on the easy chair.
   **Bún syū hái jēung ōnlohkyí seuhngmihn.**
(b) The umbrella is beside the sofa.
(c) The glasses are on the floor.
(d) The cup is on the bookshelves.
(e) The slippers are under the coffee table.
(f) The glass is on the TV set.
(g) The pen is between the glass and the cup.

## Géi gihn sāam (3)

**Sāam** in the phrase **géi gihn sāam** refers to items of clothing, and **gihn** is the classifier for **sāam**.

## Ngāam saai laak (4)

In the idiomatic expression **ngāam saai laak**, the word **ngāam** is a verb which means "to fit" while **saai** is a particle which means "completely," and the expression literally means "it fits perfectly well (with my plans)."

## Serial construction (5)

As discussed in previous units, in Cantonese two or more verbs can be used consecutively to express a series of actions. In this example the three verbs **séung** "to want to," **heui** "to go," and **tái** "to see" are used serially.

## Distances (6)

The Cantonese words for "near" and "far" are **káhn** and **yúhn** respectively, but structurally they are used slightly differently. The adjective **káhn** can be used alone, as below:

**Gāan mihnbāaupóu hóu *káhn*.**
The bakery is very near.

It can also be used *before* a point of reference:

**Gāan mihnbāaupóu hóu *káhn* ngūkkéi.**
The bakery is near home.

It can also be used with the word **lèih**, which functions like the English preposition "from," in which case **káhn** comes after the point of reference:

**Gāan mihnbāaupóu *lèih* ngūkkéi hóu *káhn*.**
The bakery is near home.

As for **yúhn**, it can be used either alone or with the word **lèih**, but it cannot be used before the point of reference. Below are two examples:

**Gāan fādim hóu *yúhn*.**
The flower shop is far away.

**Gāan fādim *lèih* ngūkkéi hóu *yúhn*.**
The flower shop is far from home.

To ask whether a shop is near or far away, the adjective **káhn** or **yúhn** is reduplicated in a choice-type question:

**Gāan fēifaatpóu *káhn-mh-káhn* nīdouh a?**
Is the barber's shop near here?

**Gāan tòhnggwódim lèih nīdouh *yúhn-mh-yúhn* a?**
Is the sweet shop far from here?

## Dōu (7)

Here the word **dōu** is used to mark the apparent contrast between the expression **jeui káhn gāan heiyún** "the nearest movie theater" and **géi yúhn** "quite *far away*." More explicitly, it means "Even if I say it's the nearest movie theater it is quite a long distance away."

# Unit 10: *Where is it?*

## Subjective distances (8)

To indicate how long it takes to go, say, on foot, to a certain destination, two kinds of pattern are used, depending on whether the speaker thinks it is near or far away:

> (Gāan) mihnbāaupóu hàahng ngh fānjūng *jauh* dou *laak*.
> It only takes five minutes to walk to the bakery.

> (Gāan) fādim *yiu* hàahng bun go jūngtàuh *sīnji* dou.
> It's half-an-hour's walk to go to the flower shop.

The use of the pattern **yiu ... sīnji** to indicate the considerable effort required to get a task accomplished and the use of the pattern **jauh ... lak** to emphasize the ease of doing something were discussed in Unit 7.

## Exercise 2 Where are the shops?

Richard has just moved into a new flat in a housing estate. Today, he wants to do some shopping, but as he is not very familiar with the nearby shops, he asks his neighbor Kathy to give him some directions. Read the dialogue between Richard and Kathy. Then help Richard to complete the sketch map so that he can find the shops easily.

RICHARD: Kathy, ngóh séung máaih géi bún syū. Néih jī-mh-jī fuhgahn bīndouh yáuh syūgúk a?

KATHY: Ngóh jīdou hái chīukāpsíhchèuhng gaaklèih, fādim deuimihn yáuh yāt gāan syūgúk. Gódouh géi dō syū maaih ga.

RICHARD: Gám, hái syūgúk fuhgahn yáuh móuh yeuhkfòhng a?

KATHY: Yáuh. Jauh hái syūgúk chèhdeuimihn, fādim gaaklèih jauh yáuh gāan yeuhkfòhng laak.

RICHARD: Ngóh juhng séung máaih dī dihnhei. Jeui káhn gāan dihnheipóu hái bīndouh a?

KATHY: Dihnheipóu àh? Jeui káhn gó gāan jauh haih hái heiyún chèhdeuimihn, hàaihpóu gaaklèih.

RICHARD: Gám, mihnbāaupóu nē? Bīndouh yáuh mihnbāaupóu a?

KATHY: Hái heiyún deuimihn, chīukāpsíhchèuhng gaaklèih mhaih yáuh mihnbāaupóu lō!

RICHARD: Hái chīukāpsíhchèuhng gaaklèih àh? Hóu lā. Juhng yáuh, fuhgahn yáuh móuh tòhnggwódim a? Ngóh séung máaih dī tòhnggwó.

KATHY: Yáuh. Hái heiyún tùhng fuhkjōngdim jūnggāan yáuh yāt gāan tòhnggwódim.
RICHARD: Gāan tòhnggwódim hái heiyún tùhng fuhkjōngdim jūnggāan. Hóu. Mgōi saai.

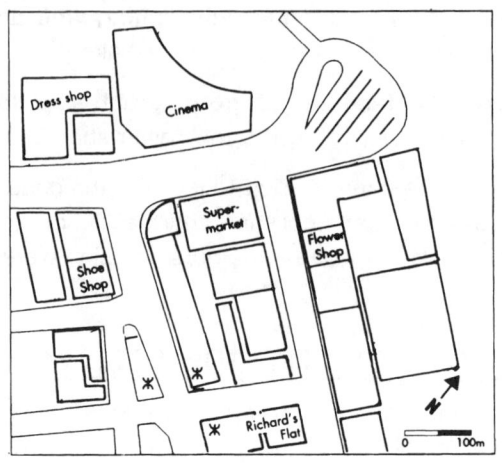

## Exercise 3 The scene of the crime

The Poons came home on Saturday evening to find that their house had been burgled and the usually orderly sitting room was in a mess. They telephoned the police, and Inspector Ko and his team arrived shortly after. Inspector Ko is examining the things scattered all over the sitting room and using his recorder to make a list of where different objects are found. Referring to the picture, complete Inspector Ko's monologue.

**Hái sōfá seuhngmihn yáuh yāt go sáudói, yāt jek maht ...**

Unit 10: *Where is it?*

## Exercise 4 The nearest shop

Your friend CHING Ping from Guangzhou is staying with you for a few weeks. Before he leaves, he wants to do some shopping. He is asking you to recommend some nearby shops where he can buy certain things. Referring to the map, complete the dialogue.

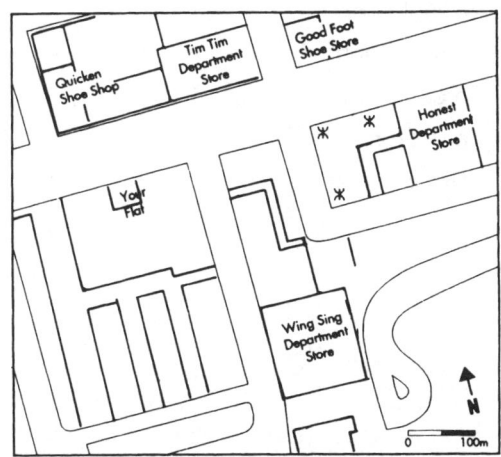

| CHING PING: | Ngóh séung máaih dī sāam. Nidouh fuhgahn yáuh móuh fuhkjōngdim a? |
|---|---|
| YOU: | Yáuh. Yáuh géi gāan, Tim Tim lā, Wing Sing la, tùhng Honest. |
| CHING PING: | Gám, bīn gāan jeui káhn a? |
| YOU: | (a) |
| CHING PING: | Gám, nī gāan haih-mh-haih jeui daaih a? |
| YOU: | (b) |
| CHING PING: | Gám, bīn gāan jeui daaih a? |
| YOU: | (c) |
| CHING PING: | Nī gāan yúhn-mh-yúhn a? |
| YOU: | (d) |
| CHING PING: | Ngóh juhng séung máaih yāt deui hàaih. Nīdouh fuhgahn yáuh móuh hàaihpóu a? |
| YOU: | (e) |
| CHING PING: | Gám, léuhng gāan bīn gāan káhn-dī a? |
| YOU: | (f) |
| CHING PING: | Yiu hàahng géi noih? |
| YOU: | (g) |

## Recognizing Chinese characters

| 文具店 | stationery shop |
|---|---|
| 書店 | bookstore |
| 糖果店 | sweet shop |
| 花店 | flower shop |
| 服裝店 | dress shop |
| 藥店(房) | drugstore |
| 超級市場 | supermarket |

## Communicative activities

1 Have a partner describe his or her neighborhood or another place of interest. Ask where places are in relation to each other.
2 Sketch out a room in your home and then describe the details of it to a partner. Your partner sketches it as you speak. When you have finished, compare your sketches.

## Cultural point

### Shops and shopping in Hong Kong

Hong Kong is among the most famous shopping destinations in the world. Its dense population and its place as a major import-export hub allow just about any kind of shop to exist. Hong Kong has it all: world class boutiques, upscale shopping centers, street markets, luxury goods markets, and cutting edge electronics. Traditionally, Hong Kong—like many Chinese cities—had districts specializing in certain kinds of goods. Some of these districts still exist. For example, Mongkok district is known for its electronics and cameras. The Jade Market is in the Yau Ma Tei district at Kansu and Battery streets. In these specialty districts, you see shop after shop selling similar products.

# Unit Eleven
# Giu yéh sihk
Ordering food

In Unit 11 you will learn about:

- ordering food and asking for the bill
- stating preferences

Unit 11: *Ordering food*

## Dialogue 1

**(CD2; 23)**
John is going to his Cantonese class, which begins at 6:15 p.m. It's now 6 p.m., and he is feeling hungry, so he stops by a noodle shop to get something to eat.

(a) What does John order?
(b) What does the waiter suggest that John order?
(c) How much does John pay for his food?

| | |
|---|---|
| WAITER: | Sīnsāang, sihk dī mātyéh a? |
| JOHN: | Mgōi néih yāt wún wàhntānmihn, tùhng yāt wún gahpdáijūk. |
| WAITER: | Hóu, yāt wún wàhntānmihn, yāt wún gahpdáijūk. Yiu-mh-yiu dihp yàuhchoi tīm a? Gāmyaht dī choisām hóuh leng wo. |
| JOHN: | Hóuh lā, yiu dihp yàuhchoi tīm lā. |

(*Some time later.*)

| | |
|---|---|
| JOHN: | Fógei, mgōi tái-sou. |
| WAITER: | Júngguhng y'ah baat mān. Chēutmihn béi lā. |

## Dialogue 2

**(CD2; 24)**
It's Sunday and the Lams have gone to their favorite tea-house for a **dímsām** lunch. They are being greeted by a waiter.

(a) What kinds of tea do the Lams order?
(b) What kinds of **dímsām** do they order?
(c) How much does the food cost?
(d) How much does Mr. Lam pay?

| | |
|---|---|
| WAITER: | Sīnsāang, géidō wái a? |
| MR. LAM: | Sei wái, mgōi. |
| WAITER: | Sei wái àh? Nīdouh lā. |
| MR. LAM: | Hóu, mgōi. |
| WAITER: | Yám mātyéh chàh a? |
| MRS. LAM: | Mgōi yāt wùh hēungpín, yāt wùh bóuléi ā. |

(*After a few minutes the waiter comes back with the teas.*)

| | |
|---|---|
| WAITER: | Yāt wùh hēungpín, yāt wùh bóuléi. Chíng mahn giu dī mātyéh dímsām a? |

| | |
|---|---|
| MRS. LAM: | Mgōi léuhng lùhng hāgáau, yāt lùhng sīumáai, tùhng léuhng lùhng chāsīubāau. |
| KENNY: | Yiu dō yāt dihp daahntāat. |
| ANGEL: | Tùhngmàaih yāt lùhng fángwó. |
| WAITER: | Hóu, léuhng lùhng hāgáau, yāt lùhng sīumáai, yāt lùhng fángwó, léuhng lùhng chāsīubāau, tùhng yāt dihp daahntāat. |

(Some time later the Lams are ready to go.)

| | |
|---|---|
| MR. LAM: | Fógei, mgōi màaih-dāan. |
| WAITER: | Hóu. |

(The waiter returns.)

| | |
|---|---|
| WAITER: | Dōjeh yāt-baak gáu-sahp yih mān. |
| MR. LAM: | Nī douh yih-baak mān. Msái jáau laak. |
| WAITER: | Dōjeh. |

## Vocabulary

### In a noodle shop (CD2; 25)

The Chinese restaurants in Hong Kong mainly serve Cantonese-style food, unless otherwise specified. Also commonly found in Hong Kong are small Cantonese-style noodle shops, where noodles, rice, and congee (a kind of rice porridge commonly eaten in south-east Asia) are served. In a noodle shop, food is ordered by the container, such as bowls and plates. Below is a list of common dishes served in a Cantonese-style noodle shop.

| | |
|---|---|
| yāt *wún* wàhntānmihn | a *bowl* of won-ton noodles |
| yāt *wún* yùhdáanmihn | a *bowl* of fish-ball noodles |
| yāt *wún* gahpdáijūk | a *bowl* of congee with mixed meat |
| yāt *wún* ngàuhyuhkjūk | a *bowl* of congee with beef |
| yāt *dihp* yàuhchoi | a *plate* of vegetables with oyster sauce |

### In a tea-house (CD2; 26)

One of the favorite pastimes of Cantonese people is to go to a tea-house in a large group for a hearty meal of **dímsām** (dumplings either steamed in bamboo baskets or fried and then served on a plate) always accompanied by a choice of Chinese teas. When Cantonese speakers say **heui yám-chàh**, which literally means "go-drink-tea," they mean having **dímsām** in a tea-house.

When people go to a tea-house, after sitting down at a table, they first order tea, and then they order **dímsām** either from **dímsām** trolleys or by placing an order through a waiter (**fógei**). Tea is ordered by the pot (**wùh**), and **dímsām** are ordered either by the bamboo basket (**lùhng**) or by the plate (**dihp**). Below is a list of some of the most popular Chinese teas and **dímsām** offered in a tea-house.

## Chinese teas

| | |
|---|---|
| yāt wùh *bóuléi* | a pot of *Pu-erh* (dark) tea |
| yāt wùh *hēungpín* | a pot of *jasmine* tea |
| yāt wùh *lùhngjéng* | a pot of *Lung-ching* (light) tea |

## Dímsam (CD2; 27)

| | |
|---|---|
| yāt lùhng *hāgáau* | a basket of steamed shrimp dumplings |
| yāt lùhng *sīumáai* | a basket of *steamed pork dumplings* |
| yāt lùhng *chāsīubāau* | a basket of *steamed barbecued-pork buns* |
| yāt lùhng *fángwó* | a basket of *steamed shrimp and bamboo-shoot dumplings* |
| yāt dihp *chēungyún* | a plate of *spring rolls* |
| yāt dihp *daahntāat* | a plate of *custard tarts* |

---

### Asking for the bill

After eating, you ask for the bill. There are two ways to ask for the bill in Cantonese, depending on the context. In a noodle shop, we usually say **Mgòi tái-sou!**, which literally means "Please see amount!," i.e. "Please check the amount that I have to pay." This is because in a small noodle shop the convention is for the waiter to call out an amount to notify the cashier what sum of money he will be receiving. The alternative expression **Mgōi màaih-dāan!** is used in a bigger eating place such as a restaurant or tea-house, where proper bills are issued by the cashier and brought to the table by the waiter—hence the word **dāan** "bill." This expression literally means "Please close (the) bill."

Idioms and structures

The items in the list below appear in the same order as they do in the dialogues above. The *italicized* items are *new* items. In the notes, numbers in brackets refer to the expressions listed below.

1 **Yiu-mh-yiu dihp yàuhchoi *tīm* a?** Do you want a plate of yàuchoi *as well*?
2 ***Chēutmihn béi* lā!** Please pay *at the front*.
3 **Yám mātyéh chàh a?** What tea would you like to drink?
4 **Yiu *dō* yāt dihp daahntāat.** A plate of custard tarts, *too*.
5 ***Tùhngmàaih yāt lùhng fángwó.*** *And* a basket of Fangwo.
6 ***Msái jáau* laak.** *Keep the change.*

### Suggesting something additional (1)

The word **tīm** means "in addition" and is used for suggesting an additional item. It is always put *at the end of a proposition*, hence **Yiu-mh-yiu dihp yàuhchoi tīm a?** and **yiu dihp yàuhchoi tīm lā**, but never \***ngóh tīm yiu yāt dihp yàuhchoi**.

### Chēutmihn (2)

**Chēutmihn** is another adverb of location: it means "outside," while the word for "inside" is **léuihmihn**. Here, in the context of the noodle shop, the waiter is asking the customer to "pay outside" because conventionally he does not bring the customer the bill. The customer has to go to the cashier, who usually sits at the entrance to the shop.

### Asking for something additional (4)

The word **dō** is used with a verb to suggest either an addition or an extension to the action concerned. For example, **Yiu *dō* yāt dihp daahntāat** means "(I) *also* want a plate of custard tarts," while **Ngóh séung dá *dō* bun go jūngtàuh móhngkàuh** means "I want to play tennis for half an hour *more*." Notice that **dō** is always positioned immediately after the verb.

To summarize, there are three ways to ask for an additional item, say, a plate of custard tarts. The difference is mostly a matter of style and emphasis.

**Ngóh séung yiu *dō* yāt dihp daahntāat.**
**Ngóh séung yiu (yāt) dihp daahntāat *tīm*.**
**Ngóh *juhng* séung yiu (yāt) dihp daahntāat.**

See Unit 9 (pp. 151 and 153) for **juhng** as "also."

## Msái jáau laak (6)

The idiom **Msái jáau laak** has exactly the same function as "Keep the change" in English, though they have different literal meanings. The verb **jáau** means "to give money back as change," and so **Msái jáau laak** more explicitly means "There is no need for you to give me the change."

# Vocabulary

### At a fast-food shop (CD2; 28)

Below is some of the food one might eat at a fast-food shop. Note the classifier used for each item.

#### Snacks

| | |
|---|---|
| yāt go *honbóubāau* | a *hamburger* |
| yāt go *jīsí honbóubāau* | a *cheeseburger* |
| yāt go *yùhláuhbāau* | a *fishburger* |
| yāt jek *yihtgáu* | a *hot-dog* |
| yāt bāau *syùhtíu* | a packet of *chips/French fries* |

#### Drinks

| | |
|---|---|
| yāt būi *chàh* | a cup of *tea* |
| yāt būi *gafē* | a cup of *coffee* |
| yāt būi *hólohk* | a cup of *cola* |
| yāt būi *cháangjāp* | a cup of *orange juice* |

As most fast-food shops are self-service, there is not much negotiation between the customer and the salesperson. One question, though, that the salesperson often asks the customer is: **Hái (nī) douh sihk dihng līk jáu a?** which means "Eat-in or take-away?"

## Exercise 1 Taking food orders

Imagine you work for a fast-food shop. Read or listen to the dialogue. Then note down the food items ordered.

| | |
|---|---|
| CUSTOMER: | Mgōi néih, ngóh séung yiu léuhng go honbóubāau, sāam go yihtgáu, tùhng léuhng bāau syùhtíu. |
| YOU: | Hóu. Léuhng go honbóubāau, sāam go yihtgáu, tùhng léuhng bāau syùhtíu. Syùhtíu yiu daaih dihng sai a? |
| CUSTOMER: | Yiu daaih ge. |
| YOU: | Gám, yiu-mh-yiu dī yéh yám tīm a? |
| CUSTOMER: | Yiu a. Yiu léuhng būi chàh, léuhng būi gafē, tùhng yāt būi cháangjāp. |
| YOU: | Dāk. Léuhng būi chàh, léuhng būi gafē, tùhng yāt būi cháangjāp. |
| CUSTOMER: | Haih laak. Mgōi. |

### Dialogue 3

**(CD2; 29)**

Carmen is on her way to her Cantonese lesson. She is hungry and stops by a fast-food shop.

(a) What does Carmen buy?
(b) Is she eating in or taking the food away?
(c) How much does the food cost?

| | |
|---|---|
| SALESPERSON: | Fūnyìhng gwōnglàhm. |
| CARMEN: | Mgòi béi yāt go jìsí honbóubāau, yāt bāau daaih syùhtíu, tùhng yāt būi sai hólohk. |
| SALESPERSON: | Hái douh sihk dihng līk jáu a? |
| CARMEN: | Līk jáu ga. |
| SALESPERSON: | Dòjeh yi sahp-chāt go bun. |
| CARMEN: | Nīdouh saām-sahp mān. |
| SALESPERSON: | Dòjeh. Jáau fāan léuhng go bun. |
| CARMEN: | Mgòi. |

## Dialogue 4

**(CD2; 30)**
Carmen is discussing with LEIH Man Chung the kinds of food they like.

(a) Which does Carmen prefer, Japanese food or Chinese food?
(b) Which does LEIH Man Chung prefer, Chinese food or French food?
(c) What is John's favorite food?

| | |
|---|---|
| LEIH MAN CHUNG: | Carmen, néih jūng-mh-jūngyi sihk Yahtbún choi a? |
| CARMEN: | Jūngyi a. Ngóh hóu jūngyi sihk Yahtbún choi ga. |
| LEIH MAN CHUNG: | Gám, néih haih-mh-haih jeui jūngyi sihk Yahtbún choi a? |
| CARMEN: | Mhaih wo. Ngóh dōu hóu jūngyi sihk Jūnggwok choi wo. |
| LEIH MAN CHUNG: | Gám, néih jūngyi bīn yeuhng dō-dī a? |
| CARMEN: | Yahtbún choi tùhng Jūnggwok choi, ngóh dōuhaih jūngyi Jūnggwok choi dō-dī. Néih nē, LEIH Man Chung? |
| LEIH MAN CHUNG: | Ngóh mjūngyi sihk Yahtbún choi. Ngóh jūngyi Faatgwok choi tùhng Jūnggwok choi. Bātgwo ngóh dōu haih jūngyi Faatgwok choi dō-gwo Jūnggwok choi. |
| CARMEN: | Gám néih tùhng John yāt yeuhng laak. John dōu haih jeui jūngyi sihk Faatgwok choi. |

## Idioms and structures

The items in the list below appear in the same order as they do in the dialogues above. The *italicized* items are *new* items. In the notes, numbers in brackets refer to the expressions listed below.

1 ***Fūnyìhng gwōnglàhm***     a formal and respectful way of saying "*Welcome.*"
2 **yāt bāau daaih syùhtíu**     one large French fries
3 **yāt būi sai hólohk**     one small cola

4  *Jáau fāan* léuhng go bun.   Your change is $2.50.
5  *Yahtbún choi tùhng Jūnggwok choi, ngóh dōuhaih jūngyi Jūnggwok choi dō-dī.*   I like Chinese food better than Japanese food.

## Adjectives of size (2)

**Daaih** is "large" in Cantonese while **sai** is "small." Notice here that **daaih** and **sai** are put immediately before **syùhtíu** and **hólohk** and not the containers **bāau** and **būi**.

## The verbal particle fāan (4)

The verbal particle **fāan** in *jáau fāan léuhng go bun* indicates that the action is "in response" to a previous action. Hence the expression more explicitly means "I am giving you HK$2.50 as change in response to your payment." Similarly, when returning a borrowed object to the owner, you say **Béi *fāan* néih** to indicate that it is a return action.

## Stating preferences (5)

In Cantonese, there is no exact equivalent to the expression "I prefer A to B." Below are sentences showing how preferences are expressed in Cantonese, using Chinese food (**Jūnggwok choi**) and Japanese food (**Yahtbún choi**) as examples.

> **Jūnggwok choi tùhng Yahtbún choi, ngóh *béigaau jūngyi* Jūnggwok choi.**
> (lit.) Chinese food and Japanese food, I comparatively like Chinese food.

> **Jūnggwok choi tùhng Yahtbún choi, ngóh *jūngyi* jūnggwok choi *dō-dī*.**
> (lit.) Chinese food and Japanese food, I like Chinese food more.

> **Ngóh *jūngyi* Jūnggwok choi *dō-gwo* Yahtbún choi.**
> (lit.) I like Chinese food more than Japanese food.

**Béigaau** functions like the English word "comparatively" and is put immediately before a verb or an adjective. For example, **Jūk tùhng**

Unit 11: *Ordering food*

**mihn, ngóh béigaau héifūn sihk jūk** means "I prefer eating congee to eating noodles"; while **Nī deui hàaih béigaau pèhng** is "This pair of shoes is comparatively cheap."

The distinction between the usage of **dō-dī** and **dō-gwo** is very similar to that described in the discussion about comparison of prices. (See Unit 6, p. 103.) When only the preferred item is mentioned in the clause of comparison, **dō-dī** is used, but when both compared items are mentioned, then **dō-gwo** is used, and is positioned *after* the preferred item and *before* the less preferred one. In other words, **dō-dī** always comes in a sentence-final position while **dō-gwo** never does. Below are examples, which both have roughly the same meaning: "I prefer watching soccer to watching horse-racing."

> **Tái jūkkàuh tùhng tái páaumáh, ngóh jūngyi tái jūkkàuh *dō-dī*.**
> **Ngóh jūngyi tái jūkkàuh *dō-gwo* tái páaumáh.**

## Exercise 2 Dream holidays

John, Carmen, and Richard are discussing their favorite places for a holiday. Read or listen to the dialogue. Afterwards, note each speaker's favorite or preferred places for a holiday.

JOHN: Richard, néih jeui jūngyi heui bīndouh léuihhàhng a?
RICHARD: Ngóh heui-gwo hóu dō gwokgā. Ngóh jeui jūngyi Fēileuihtbān tùhng Yandouh.
CARMEN: Gám, Fēileuihtbān tùhng Yandouh néih jūngyi bīndouh dō-dī a?
RICHARD: Ngóh béigaau jūngyi Yandouh. Néihdeih nē? Néihdeih jeui jūngyi heui bīndouh a?
CARMEN: Ngóh jeui jūngyi heui Jūnggwok. Yahtbún ngóh dō jūngyi. Bātgwo dōu haih jūngyi Jūnggwok dō-dī. Néih nē, John?
JOHN: Ngóh jauh jūngyi Yahtbún dō-gwo Jūnggwok laak. Ngóh gokdāk Yahtbún béigaau hóuwáan.

## Exercise 3 The noodle shop waiter

Ah-Wing works as a waiter in a noodle shop. As a customer leaves, it is customary for him to work out the total immediately so that the customer knows how much to pay. Complete the following conversations according to the price-list. The first conversation has been completed for you as an example.

*Price-list*:

| | |
|---|---|
| won-ton noodles | HK$9.00 a bowl |
| fish-ball noodles | HK$8.00 a bowl |
| congee with mixed meat | HK$11.00 a bowl |
| congee with beef | HK$10.00 a bowl |
| vegetables with oyster sauce | HK$6.00 a plate |

1 Two customers have just had two bowls of won-ton noodles and one bowl of congee with beef.

CUSTOMER: Mgōi tái-sou.
AH-WING: Hóu. Léuhng wún wàhntān mihn, sahp-baat mān. Yāt wún ngàuhyuhkjūk, sahp mān. Júngguhng y'ah-baat mān lā.
CUSTOMER: Nīdouh sā'ah mān.
AH-WING: Jáau fāan léuhng mān.
CUSTOMER: Mgōi.
AH-WING: Dōjeh.

2 Three customers have just finished three bowls of fish-ball noodles, two plates of vegetables, and one bowl of congee with mixed meat.

CUSTOMER: Mgōi tái-sou.
AH-WING: (a)
CUSTOMER: Nīdouh yāt-baak mān.
AH-WING: (b)
CUSTOMER: Mgōi saai.
AH-WING: (c)

3 Four customers have just eaten four bowls of won-ton noodles, two bowls of fish-ball noodles, three bowls of congee with beef, and two plates of vegetables.

CUSTOMER: Mgōi tái-sou.
AH-WING: (d)
CUSTOMER: Nīdouh ńgh-baak mān.
AH-WING: (e)
CUSTOMER: Mgōi.
AH-WING: (f)

Unit 11: *Ordering food* 185

## Exercise 4 Ordering **dímsām**

You enjoy having **dímsām** in a tea-house. Today you are taking some foreign friends to a tea-house. As you are the only one who speaks Cantonese, you have to order the tea and **dímsām**. Complete the conversation.

WAITER: Géidō wái a?
YOU: (a)
WAITER: Nīdouh lā.
YOU: (b)
WAITER: Yám mātyéh chàh a?
YOU: (c)
WAITER: Sihk dī mātyéh dímsām a?
YOU: (d)

## Exercise 5 Preferences

Translate each sentence from English into Cantonese by using any of the three structures discussed. The first one has been done for you as an example.

(a) I prefer touring Korea to touring the Philippines.
   **Ngóh jūngyi heui Hòhngwok léuihhàhng dō-gwo heui Fēileuhtbān léuihhàhng.**
   or **Hòhngwok tùhng Fēileuhtbān, ngóh jūngyi heui Hòhngwok léuihhàhng dō-dī.**
   or **Hòhngwok tùhng Fēileuhtbān, ngóh béigaau jūngyi heui Hòhngwok léuihhàhng.**

(b) My father likes going to the tea-house more than going to watch a movie.

(c) My elder brother prefers playing basketball to playing tennis.

(d) His mother likes listening to the radio more than watching television.

(e) My younger sister prefers learning French to learning German.

## Recognizing Chinese characters

| | |
|---|---|
| 普洱茶 | Pu-erh tea |
| 香片 | jasmine tea |
| 龍井 | Lung-ching tea |
| 點心 | **dímsām** |
| 蝦餃 | steamed shrimp dumplings |
| 燒賣 | steamed pork dumplings |
| 叉燒包 | steamed barbecued-pork buns |
| 粉果 | steamed shrimp and bamboo-shoot dumplings |
| 春捲 | spring rolls |
| 蛋撻 | custard tarts |

## Communicative activities

1 Simulate a dinner at a Chinese restaurant. With a partner, take turns playing the waiter and the customer. Switch roles and repeat.
2 Plan a trip to a Cantonese restaurant in your area where waiters are Cantonese speakers. Prepare a list of things you might want to try, then order in Cantonese from the waiters.

## Cultural point

The Cantonese tea-house is more than a type of restaurant. It is a kind of institution in Hong Kong and other places where Cantonese have settled. It is a lively gathering place with a culture of its own. Traditional tea-houses are often large multi-story restaurants filled with large round tables. It is common to have small, unrelated groups seated at the same table. The tables are served by carts pushed by vendors. Instead of having menus the vendors call out whatever it is that they have on their carts: shrimp dumplings, pork buns, or even fried squid. Many of these **dímsām** are specialties of Cantonese tea-houses.

# Unit 11: Ordering food

# Unit Twelve
# Tīnhei
The weather

In Unit 12 you will learn about:

- understanding broadcast weather forecasts
- talking about the weather
- making predictions
- giving advice
- dates
- festive greetings

Unit 12: *The weather*

## Dialogue 1

**(CD2; 32)**
Paul is telephoning his brother Peter long-distance from Hong Kong. Peter studies in New Zealand and they are talking about the weather in Hong Kong and in New Zealand. It is mid-June.

(a) What is the weather like in New Zealand?
(b) What about Hong Kong?

PAUL: Peter, Náusāilàahn yìhgā dī tīnhei dímyéung a?
PETER: Náusāilàahn yìhgā dōu géi dung a, heiwān daaihyeuk sahp douh, bātgwo hóu hóutīn. Gám, Hēunggóng nē?
PAUL: Hēunggóng yìhgā hóu yiht la, daaihyeuk sāam-sahp douh. Tīnhei hóu chìuhsāp, mhaih géi syūfuhk.

## Dialogue 2

**(CD2; 33)**
Here is a radio weather forecast for Hong Kong. It is winter.

(a) What will the weather be like tomorrow?
(b) Will it rain tomorrow?
(c) What are the predicted highest and lowest temperatures?

FORECASTER: Yuhchāak tīngyaht wúih chēui bāk fūng, tīnhei hòhnláahng, yáuh mèihyúh. Jeui gōu heiwān daaihyeuk sahp-ńgh douh, jeui dāi heiwān daaihyeuk sahp-yāt douh.

## Vocabulary

### Describing the weather (CD2; 34)

The list below gives the most common words used in Cantonese for describing the weather. Try reading them aloud. If you have the audio for this book, you can model your pronunciation on the recording.

| | | | |
|---|---|---|---|
| tīnhei | the weather | gōn | dry |
| yiht | hot | hóutīn | fine/sunny |
| dung | cold | yāmtīn | overcast |
| nyúhn | warm | mahtwàhn | cloudy |
| lèuhng | cool | daaihfūng | windy |
| sāp | humid | tòihfūng | typhoon |

## The weather forecast

The broadcast weather forecast is usually written in fairly formal Chinese and then read aloud. As a result, some rather bookish expressions are used. These expressions are usually two-syllable versions of their more colloquial counterparts. For example, **yiht** "hot" becomes **yìhmyiht** and **nyúhn** "warm" becomes **wānnyúhn**. The formal version of **dung** is **hòhnláahng**. Below is a list of expressions which are likely to come up in weather forecasts.

| | | | |
|---|---|---|---|
| yìhmyiht | hot | gōnchou | dry |
| hòhnláahng | cold | tīnchìhng | fine |
| wānnyúhn | warm | tīnyām | overcast |
| chīnglèuhng | cool | mahtwàhn | cloudy |
| chiuhsāp | humid | fūngsai kèuhnggihng | windy |

When rain, fog, snow, or thunderstorms are predicted, the "existential" **yáuh** is used. For example:

| | | | |
|---|---|---|---|
| yáuh yúh | (there will be) rain | yáuh lèuihbouh | thunderstorms |
| yáuh mèihyúh | light rain | yáuh mouh | fog |
| yáuh jaauhyúh | showers | yáuh syut | snow |

For forecasting rain or snow, we use verb-object constructions with the verb **lohk**, which means "to come down" or to "fall" but, unlike the English, takes an object:

| | |
|---|---|
| lohk-yúh | to rain |
| lohk-syut | to snow |

When *change* in weather is predicted, the verb **jyún**, which means "to change," is used:

| | | | |
|---|---|---|---|
| jyún yiht | to turn hot | jyún láahng | to turn cold |
| jyún lèuhng | to turn cool | jyún chìhng | to turn fine |

# Unit 12: *The weather*

Weather forecasts often predict wind directions. In Cantonese, the verb **chēui** is used before the word for the direction and the word for "wind," **fūng**. For example, **chēui dūng fūng** predicts "easterly winds."

| | |
|---|---|
| **chēui dūng fūng** | easterly winds |
| **chēui nàahm fūng** | southerly winds |
| **chēui sāi fūng** | westerly winds |
| **chēui bāk fūng** | northerly winds |

Weather forecasts also predict highest temperatures, lowest temperatures, and relative humidities. Below are the related vocabulary items:

| | |
|---|---|
| **heiwān** | air temperature |
| **jeui gōu heiwān** | highest temperature |
| **jeui dāi heiwān** | lowest temperature |
| **sēungdeui sāpdouh** | relative humidity |

> ### Temperature and humidity
>
> Normally, the Celsius scale (centigrade) is used, and since this is taken for granted, only the word for "degree," namely **douh**, is used when referring to temperatures. Hence, 10°C is **sahp douh**, while 20°C is **yih-sahp douh**. Relative humidities, on the other hand, are expressed in percentages. Note the Cantonese structure. For example, 50% is **baak fahn jī** *ńgh-sahp*. Here, the figure 50 (**ńgh-sahp**) comes *after* the expression for %: **baak fahn jī**; **baak** means "one hundred" and **fahn** means "parts," and the whole expression **baak fahn jī ńgh-sahp** translates literally into "one hundred parts fifty." Hence, 60% is **baak fahn jī luhk-sahp** and 65% is **baak fahn jī luhk-sahp ńgh**, etc.

## Idioms and structures (CD2; 39)

The items in the list below appear in the same order as they do in the dialogues above. The *italicized* items are *new* items. In the notes, numbers in brackets refer to the expressions listed below.

| | |
|---|---|
| 1 Náusāilàahn yìhgā dī tīnhei dímyéung a? | How is the weather in New Zealand right now? |
| 2 mhaih géi *syūfuhk* | it doesn't feel very *comfortable* |
| 3 *Yuhchāak* tīngyaht *wúih* chēui bāk fūng. | *It is predicted* that winds will be northerly tomorrow. |

## The possessive dī (1)

The **dī** in this context is used to indicate possession, specifying that the weather being discussed is that of the present moment in New Zealand. Notice that the "possessor" of the weather is **yìhgā** rather than **Náusāilàahn**; thus the expression is very similar in structure to "the present moment's weather in New Zealand" in English. A similar expression is **Hèunggóng gāmyaht *dī* tīnhei**, which means "today's weather in Hong Kong."

## Asking about the weather (2)

To ask a general question about the weather, you can use the question word **dímyéung**:

| | |
|---|---|
| Tīngyaht dī tīnhei *dímyéung* a? | What will the weather be like tomorrow? |

or you can ask a choice-type question:

| | |
|---|---|
| Tīngyaht dī tīnhei *hóu-mh-hóu* a? | Will the weather be good tomorrow? |

You can also ask about certain characteristics of the weather with a choice-type question:

| | |
|---|---|
| Tīngyaht *yiht-mh-yiht* a? | Will it be cold tomorrow? |
| Tīngyaht *hóu-mh-hóutīn* a? | Will it be fine tomorrow? |
| Tīngyaht *yáuh móuh yúh lohk* a? | Will there be rain tomorrow? |

## Predicting the future (3)

When predicting things that are likely to happen in the future, we use the modal **wúih**. **Wúih** can be used before an adjective, as in:

Unit 12: *The weather*

**Tīngyaht *wúih* hóutīn.**   It will be fine tomorrow.

It can be used before the "existential" verb **yáuh**, as in:

**Tīngyaht *wúih* yáuh mouh.**   It will be foggy tomorrow.

It can also be used before other verbs, as in:

**Hauhyaht *wúih* lohk-yúh.**   It will rain the day after tomorrow.
**Jāumuht *wúih* jyún lèuhng.**   It will turn cool during the weekend.

## Exercise 1 Weather forecast

Here is a forecast of tomorrow's weather in Guangzhou. Read the forecast or listen to the audio recording. Then complete the table.

Tīngyaht tīnhei yìhmyiht tùhng chìuhsāp. Jeui gōu heiwān daaih-yeuk sāam-sahp yih douh. Jeui dāi heiwān yih-sahp-baat douh. Sēungdeui sāpdouh baak fahn jī chāt-sahp baat ji baak fahn jī baat-sahp gáu.

General description:
Highest temperature:
Lowest temperature:
Relative humidity:   %–   %

## Vocabulary

### Wishing others well (CD2; 35)

Below are a number of idiomatic expressions used in wishing others well during festive seasons or on special occasions:

| | |
|---|---|
| **Singdaan faailohk!** | Merry Christmas! |
| **Sānnìhn faailohk!** | Happy New Year! |
| **Sāangyaht faailohk!** | Happy birthday! |
| **Yātlouh seuhnfūng!** | Have a good flight! |
| **Gūnghéi faatchòih!** | greeting said at Chinese New Year |

## The months of the year (CD2; 36)

In Cantonese, the months do not have special names, but are simply called "the first month" (**yāt-yuht**), "the second month" (**yih-yuht**) and so on. Here is a list of the twelve months in Cantonese:

| | | | |
|---|---|---|---|
| yāt-yuht | January | chāt-yuht | July |
| yih-yuht | February | baat-yuht | August |
| sāam-yuht | March | gáu-yuht | September |
| sei-yuht | April | sahp-yuht | October |
| ńgh-yuht | May | sahp-yāt-yuht | November |
| luhk-yuht | June | sahp-yih-yuht | December |

## Days of the month

To refer to a particular day of the month, the word **houh** (lit. "number") is used. The "first" is **yāt-houh**, the "second" is **yih-houh**, the "third" is **sāam-houh**, etc. If the month is also given in a date, then the month comes *before* the day. Below are a few examples:

| | |
|---|---|
| yāt-yuht yāt-houh | first of January |
| chāt-yuht gáu-houh | ninth of July |
| sahp-yih-yuht yih-sahp-ńgh-houh | twenty-fifth of December |

## Dialogue 3

**(CD2; 37)**

It is Christmas Day and Jimmy is flying out to New York to visit his brother Oscar this evening. He is telephoning Oscar from Hong Kong, asking him about the weather in New York.

(a) What is the weather in New York like now?
(b) What is the average temperature?
(c) What is the outlook for next week?
(d) What advice does Oscar give to Jimmy about the clothes to bring to New York?

| | |
|---|---|
| JIMMY: | Singdaan faailohk! |
| OSCAR: | Singdaan faailohk! |
| JIMMY: | Oscar, Náuyeuk yìhgā dī tīnhei dímyéung a? |

Unit 12: *The weather*

OSCAR: Náuyeuk yìhgā hóu dūng a, lohk-gán syut a, heiwān daaih-yeuk lìhng hah yih-sahp douh.
JIMMY: Gám, sái-mh-sái daaih dō-dī sāam lèih Náuyeuk a?
OSCAR: Jeui hóu daaih dō-dī sāam lèih lā.
JIMMY: Hóu lā.
OSCAR: Bātgwo mhóu daaih taai dō sāam wo, yānwaih hah go láih baai tīnhei wúih nyúhn fāan dī.
JIMMY: Hóu lā. Gám, tīngyaht gin lā.
OSCAR: Hóu lā. Yātlouh seuhnfūng.

## Dialogue 4

**(CD2; 38)**
It's a December day in Hong Kong. On the radio the weather forecaster is giving some weather information as well as advice for rivers.

(a) What will the weather be like today?
(b) What advice is given to people who are leaving home?
(c) What advice is given to drivers?

WEATHER FORECASTER: Yuhchāak gāmyaht tīnhei wúih hòhnláahng tùhng yáuh yúh. Daaihgā chēut-gāai geidāk jeuk dō gihn sāam, tùhngmàaih daai fāan bá jē la. Juhng yáuh, yìhgā lohk-gán yúh. Daaihgā yiu síusām jā-chē a.

## Idioms and structures (CD2; 39)

The items in the list below appear in the same order as they do in the dialogues above. The *italicized* items are *new* items. In the notes, numbers in brackets refer to the expressions listed below.

1 *lìhng hah* yih-sahp douh
2 *Jeui hóu* daaih dō-dī sāam lèih lā.
3 Bātgwo *mhóu* daaih taai dō sāam wo

20° *below zero*
*It might be best* to bring more clothes.
But *don't* bring too many clothes

4 **nyúhn fāan dī**  it will become warm again
5 **tīngyaht gin là**  see you tomorrow
6 **Daaihgā** chēut gāai *geidāk* jeuk dō gihn sāam  Everyone must *remember* to put on more clothes when going out
7 **Daaihgā yiu *síusām* jā-chē a.**  Everyone has to drive *carefully*.

## Sub-zero temperatures (1)

**Lìhng** means "zero" and **hah** means "below" or "under"; thus **lìhng hah yih-sahp douh** is "twenty degrees below zero." Similarly, **lìhng hah sahp douh** is "minus ten degrees."

## Giving advice (2, 3)

When giving advice in Cantonese, the two modals **jeui hóu** (similar in meaning to "had better") and **yiu** (similar in meaning to "should") can be used before the verb. To advise somebody *not* to do something, **mhóu** "don't" is used before the verb. To say that it is not necessary to do something, **msái** is used. Below are some examples:

**Gāmyaht wúih yáuh jaauyúh. Néih chēut gāai *jeui hóu* daai bá jē.**
There will be showers today. You'd better take your umbrella when you go out.

**Gāmmáahn wúih hóu dung. Néih *yiu* jeuk dō gihn sāam a.**
It will be cold tonight. You have to put on more clothes.

**Gāmyaht tīnhei hóu dūng. *Mhóu* heui yàuhséui la.**
It's very cold today. Don't go swimming.

**Tīnhei wúih jyún yiht. *Msái* jeuk taai dō sāam la.**
The weather is getting hotter. There's no need to wear too many clothes.

## Fāan to indicate change back to normal (4)

The word **fāan** here has the meaning of "back to normal." Thus the expression **nyúhn fāan dī** has the connotation of "going back to the warm weather which we had before."

Unit 12: *The weather*

## "See you" (5)

The verb **gin** means "to see." **Tīngyaht gin lā** is equivalent to "See you tomorrow" in English and is often used to close a conversation.

## Everyone (6)

**Daaihgā** is a pronoun which means "everyone," and is very often used in broadcast messages to appeal to the general public. For example, **Daaihgā yiu síusām jā-chē a** is an appeal to the listeners to drive carefully.

## Adverbs of manner (7)

Adverbs of manner, like most other adverbs, are put *before* the verbs they modify. For example:

**Daaihgā yiu *síusām* jā-chē a.**   We must drive *carefully*.
**Daaihgā *maahn-máan* hàahng a.**   Please walk slowly.

### Exercise 2 The weather in China

The two newspaper cuttings below provide information about two major cities in China, namely Shanghai (Seuhnghói) and Guangzhou (Gwóngjāu). You have friends who plan to go to these cities at different times of the year, and they have come to consult you for the appropriate weather information. Complete the conversation which follows by using the information provided.

| Shanghai temperature range and average rainfall | | | |
|---|---|---|---|
| | Temperature high (°C) | Temperature low (°C) | Number of days with rainfall | Monthly rainfall (in cm) |
| January | 8 | 0 | 10 | 4.8 |
| April | 19 | 9 | 13 | 9.1 |
| July | 33 | 24 | 11 | 14.7 |
| October | 24 | 13 | 9 | 7.4 |

**WHEN TO GO** Although Shanghai's climate is subtropical, it does have a distinct change of seasons. Spring weather is usually warm but unsettled. Summer is hot and humid, with the highest incidence of rainy days of all the seasons. Autumn is the best season for visiting: warm and relatively dry. Winter, the longest season, is cold, but although the temperatures often go below freezing, snow is unusual.

### Guangzhou temperature range and average rainfall

|         | Temperature high (°C) | Temperature low (°C) | Number of days with rainfall | Monthly rainfall (in cm) |
|---------|-----------------------|----------------------|------------------------------|--------------------------|
| January | 18                    | 9                    | 7                            | 2.2                      |
| April   | 25                    | 18                   | 15                           | 17.3                     |
| July    | 33                    | 25                   | 16                           | 20.5                     |
| October | 29                    | 19                   | 6                            | 8.6                      |

**WHEN TO GO** Guangzhou is in a subtropical weather belt. In summer it is hot and humid, the rainfall heavy, with numerous thunderstorms. No pronounced winter season exists; although occasional days can be very cold, generally winter is mild and pleasant. In spring the weather starts to get warmer and the humidity higher; the rainy season begins in April and continues through September, about 80 per cent of the yearly average of 162 cm falling in these six months. Autumn is a delightful season with warm days, low humidity, and infrequent rainfall.

The province is frequently affected by typhoons in August and September. Northerly breezes prevail in October through February; southerly winds are more evident in the other months.

The most pleasant time to visit Guangzhou is October through March.

*Conversation 1:*

JOHN: Ngóh yāt-yuht yiu heui Seuhnghói. Seuhnghói yāt-yuht dung-mh-dung a?

YOU: (a) Seuhnghói yāt-yuht dōu géi dung a. Heiwān ...

JOHN: Gám, sái-mh-sái daaih hóu dō sāam a?

Unit 12: *The weather*

YOU: (b)
JOHN: Seuhnghói yāt-yuht yáuh móuh yúh lohk a? Sái-mh-sái daai bá jē a?
YOU: (c)

*Conversation 2:*
CARMEN: Ngóh sei-yuht wúih heui Gwóngjāu. Gwóngjāu ei-yuht dī tīnhei dím a?
YOU: (d) Gwóngjāu sei-yuht ...
CARMEN: Gám, heiwān daaihyeuk géidō douh a?
YOU: (e)
CARMEN: Gám, chìuh-mh-chìuhsāp a?
YOU: (f)

*Conversation 3:*
RICHARD: Ngóh sahp-yuht heui Gwóngjāu. Néih jī-mh-jī Gwóngjāu sahp-yuht dī tīnhei wúih dím ga?
YOU: (g)
RICHARD: Wúih-mh-wúih lohk-yúh a?
YOU: (h)
RICHARD: Gám, sái-mh-sái daai bá jē heui a?
YOU: (i)

## Exercise 3 Predicting the future

Translate the following sentences into Cantonese, using **wúih** for predictions. The first one has been done for you as an example.

(a) It will rain tomorrow.
   **Tīngyaht wúih lohk-yúh.**
(b) The weather will become cooler the day after tomorrow.
(c) The weather will become hot next week.
(d) It will be very windy on Saturday.
(e) There will be thunderstorms on Sunday.
(f) It will be humid tomorrow.

## Exercise 4 When will they come home?

Mr. and Mrs. Chan's children all live abroad, but they are all coming home this year to celebrate their parents' fortieth wedding anniversary. Mr. and Mrs. Chan are looking at their calendar to remind themselves when each of their children will come home to Hong Kong. Using the information provided below, complete the conversation between Mr. Chan and Mrs. Chan.

| MR. CHAN: | Simon géisìh fāan Hēunggóng a? |
| MRS. CHAN: | Simon baat-houh sīngkèih-yih jauh fāan Hēunggóng la. |
| MR. CHAN: | Gám, Samuel nē? |
| MRS. CHAN: | Samuel àh? (a) Samuel ... |
| MR. CHAN: | Gám, Keith nē? |
| MRS. CHAN: | (b) |
| MR. CHAN: | Teresa yauh géisìh fāan lèih a? |
| MRS. CHAN: | (c) |

**March**

| M | T | W | T | F | S | S |
|---|---|---|---|---|---|---|
| Simon back in HK | 1 | 2 | 3 Samuel | 4 back from UK | 5 | 6 |
| 7 | ⑧ | 9 | ⑩ | 11 | 12 | 13 |
| ⑭ | 15 | 16 | 17 | ⑱ | 19 | 20 |
| Teresa back 21 | 22 | 23 | 24 | 25 Keith back from Australia | 26 | 27 |
| 28 | 29 | 30 | 31 | | | |

## Recognizing Chinese characters

| 炎熱 | hot | 晴朗 | fine |
| 寒冷 | cold | 陰暗 | overcast |
| 溫暖 | warm | 密雲 | cloudy |
| 清涼 | cool | 有雨 | rainy |

Unit 12: *The weather*

## Communicative activities

1 Talk about the weather in your hometown. What is it like during the winter? What is it like during the summer?
2 Pair up with a Cantonese-speaking classmate or colleague. Try to find out about where the person grew up and what the climate is like there.

## Cultural point

Hong Kong is in a tropical storm belt where tropical cyclones (or typhoons) are common. Tropical cyclones typically occur between the months of May and November, and are particularly common in September. Advisory warnings are issued by the Hong Kong observatory whenever a tropical cyclone centered within 800 km of Hong Kong poses a threat to the territory. Advisory bulletins include the tropical cyclone warning signal issued and its significance, the latest position and expected movement of the center of the tropical cyclone, information on the wind strength, rainfall, and sea level in the territory and advice on precautionary measures. The signals are not on an even scale, but are according to the following sequence 1, 3, 8, 9, 10. Below are the official signal levels for Hong Kong:

**T 1**

This is a standby signal, indicating that a tropical cyclone is centered within about 800 km of Hong Kong and may affect the territory.

Strong wind is expected or blowing generally in Hong Kong near sea level, with a sustained speed of 41–62 km/h and gusts which may exceed 110 km/h, and the wind condition is expected to persist. Winds are normally expected to become generally stronger in Hong Kong within 12 hours after the issue of this signal. Winds over offshore waters and on high ground may reach gale force.

**NW** 西北　**SW** 西南　**NE** 東北　**SE** 東南

Gale or storm force wind is expected or blowing generally in Hong Kong near sea level, with a sustained wind speed of 63–117 km/h from the quarter indicated and gusts which may exceed 180 km/h.

Gale or storm force wind is increasing or expected to increase significantly in strength.

Hurricane force wind is expected or blowing with sustained wind speed reaching upwards from 118 km/h and gusts that may exceed 220 km/h.

# Unit Thirteen
# Yīfuhk

The clothes we wear

In Unit 13 you will learn about:

- describing what people are wearing
- colors

## Dialogue 1

**(CD2; 40)**
CHAN Syut Wai and Emily have been shopping together. They have met John in a café, and they are showing him what they bought.

(a) What did Emily buy?
(b) What did CHAN Syut Wai buy?
(c) What did CHAN Syut Wai buy for John?

| | |
|---|---|
| JOHN: | Wā! Néihdeih máaih-jó gam dō yéh àh? |
| CHAN SYUT WAI: | Haih a. Dī yéh hóu pèhng a. |
| EMILY: | Haih a. Néih tái. Ngóh máaih-jó léuhng gihn sēutsāam, léuhng tìuh bunjihtkwàhn, tùhng yāt deui hàaih a. |
| JOHN: | Gám néih nē, CHAN Syut Wai? Néih máaih-jó dī mātyéh a? |
| CHAN SYUT WAI: | Ngóh máaih jó yāt tou toujōng, yāt gihn ngoihtou, tùhng léuhng gihn sēutsāam. Néih tái leng-mh-leng? |
| JOHN: | Haih géi leng wo. |
| CHAN SYUT WAI: | Juhng yáuh. Ngóh máaih-jó yāt yeuhng yéh béi néih. |
| JOHN: | Mātyéh lèih ga? |
| CHAN SYUT WAI: | Ngóh máaih-jó nī tìuh tāai béi néih. Néih jūng-mh-jūngyi a? |
| JOHN: | Jūngyi. Dōjeh. |

## Dialogue 2

**(CD2; 41)**
John and Carmen are looking at a photograph of John's colleagues, which was taken on a trip to Beijing. John is telling Carmen who's who in his office.

(a) Who is the man wearing a coat and a hat?
(b) Who is the man wearing a scarf?
(c) Who is the woman wearing a skirt and high-heeled shoes?

| | |
|---|---|
| CARMEN: | Yí, nī go jeuk daaihlāu, daai móu ge haih bīngo a? |
| JOHN: | Nī go daai-jó móu ge haih Ben, ngóhdeih go lóuhbáan. |

Unit 13: *The clothes we wear*

| CARMEN: | Kéuih jauh haih Ben àh? Gám, nī go laahm-jó géng gān ge, fèih-féi-déi ge yauh haih bīngo a? |
|---|---|
| JOHN: | Laahm-jó génggān nī go haih Teddy. Teddy gaaklèih, jeuk kwàhn tùhng gōujāanghàaih gó go haih kéuih taai-táai. |
| CARMEN: | Nī go jauh haih Teddy go taai-táai àh? |
| JOHN: | Haih a, jeuk kwàhn tùhng gōujāanghàaih, chèuhng tàuhfaat nī go jauh haih Teddy go taai-táai laak. |

## Vocabulary

### Clothing

Below is a list of clothing. Notice the different classifiers that are used. Try reading each item aloud. If you have the audio for this book, model your pronunciation on the recording.

Men's wear **(CD2; 42)**

| yāt gihn sēutsāam | a shirt |
|---|---|
| yāt tou sāijōng | a suit |
| yāt tìuh (sāijōng) fu | a pair of trousers/slacks |
| yāt tìuh tāai | a tie |
| yāt gihn ngoihtou | a jacket |
| yāt deui (pèih)hàaih | a pair of (leather) shoes |
| yāt deui maht | a pair of socks |
| yāt déng móu | a hat/a cap |

Ladies' wear **(CD2; 43)**

| yāt gihn sēutsāam | a blouse |
|---|---|
| yāt tìuh kwàhn | a dress, a skirt |
| yāt tìuh bunjihtkwàhn | a skirt |
| yāt tìuh (sāijōng) fu | a pair of slacks |
| yāt tou toujōng | a suit |
| yāt gihn ngoihtou | a jacket |
| yāt deui sīmaht | a pair of pantyhose |
| yāt deui (pèih)hàaih | a pair of (leather) shoes |
| yāt deui gōujāanghàaih | a pair of high-heeled shoes |

## Casual wear (CD2; 44)

| | |
|---|---|
| yāt gihn tīsēut | a T-shirt |
| yāt tìuh ngàuhjáifu | a pair of jeans |
| yāt tìuh dyúnfu | a pair of shorts |
| yāt deui bōhàaih | a pair of sports shoes |
| yāt deui lèuhnghàaih | a pair of sandals |

## Warm clothes (CD2; 45)

| | |
|---|---|
| yāt gihn lāangsāam | a woollen sweater/jumper |
| yāt gihn (daaih)lāu | a(n) (over)coat |
| yāt tìuh génggān | a scarf |
| yāt deui sáumaht | a pair of gloves |

---

**Classifiers for items of clothing**

**Gihn** is the classifier used for tops such as **sēutsāam** "shirt" and **ngoihtou** "jacket," **tìuh** is the classifier used for **fu** "slacks" and **kwàhn** "dress and skirt," while **deui** is the classifier for all things that come in pairs, such as kinds of **hàaih**, **maht**, and **sáumaht** "shoes, socks, and gloves."

---

## Exercise 1 The spending spree

The Chans are going to Canada. Mrs. Chan has just gone shopping for warm clothes, and Mr. Chan is finding out what she has bought for the family. Read the conversation between Mr. and Mrs. Chan. Then note down what Mrs. Chan has bought.

MRS. CHAN: Néih tái. Ngóh máaih-jó géi dō sāam.
MR. CHAN: Haih wo. Néih máaih-jó dī mātyéh a?
MRS. CHAN: Néih tái. Ngóh máaih-jó sāam gihn daaihlāu, sei gihn lāangsāam. Juhng yáuh sāam tìuh génggān.
MR. CHAN: Haih wo. Dī génggān hóu leng wo.
MRS. CHAN: Haih a. Dī génggān hóu leng ga. Bātgwo dōu msyun hóu gwai.
MR. CHAN: Gám, nī bāau haih mātyéh lèih ga?
MRS. CHAN: Nī bāau haih sáumaht. Ngóh júngguhng máaih-jó ńgh deui sáumaht.
MR. CHAN: Wā! Gam dō àh?

Unit 13: *The clothes we wear*

# Idioms and structures (CD2; 48)

The items in the list below appear in the same order as they do in the dialogues above. The *italicized* items are *new* items. In the notes, numbers in brackets refer to the expressions listed below.

1 *Wā* — an exclamation showing surprise
2 **Néihdeih máaih-jó gam dō yéh àh?** — You bought so many things?
3 **Néih tái.** — Look.
4 **Néih tái leng-mh-leng?** — Do you think they are pretty?
5 *Haih* géi leng *wo.* — They *are* quite pretty.
6 **Ngóh máaih-jó yāt yeuhng yéh *béi néih*.** — I bought something *for you*.
7 **Mātyéh lèih ga?** — What is it? (showing curiosity)
8 **Nī go *jeuk daaihláu, daai móu* ge haih bīngo a?** — Who is this one *wearing a coat and a hat*?
9 *lóuhbáan* — boss

## Question to indicate recognition and slight surprise (2)

Here **Néihdeih máaih-jó gam dō yéh àh?** is another question which shows recognition and slight surprise. The word **gam** helps indicate the recognition. A genuine question (for instance, if John is asking Carmen on the phone) would be **Néihdeih máaih-jó hóu dō yéh àh?** To both questions a positive response is **Haih a** while a negative one would be **Mhaih aak** "No, not really."

## Haih ... wo (5)

To comment on something being quite pretty, you can say **Géi leng wo.** However, when you are *asked* to judge whether something is pretty and a positive answer is expected, you can make the emphatic statement *Haih* **géi leng *wo*.** The **haih** used before the adjective **leng** coupled with the particle **wo** (see Unit 5) help convey the message "They *are* quite pretty."

## The verbs for "putting on" (8)

**Jeuk** is the Cantonese verb which means "to wear" or "to put on." However, there are a few other verbs which are used specifically for certain kinds of clothes. For example, for **tāai** "tie," the verb **dá** is used, while **daai** is used for **móu** "hat/cap." For **génggān** "scarf," the verb **laahm**, which literally means "to wrap around the body," is used.

To say what clothes somebody has put on, the aspect marker **-jó** is often used, as follows:

**Mary *jeuk-jó* tou toujōng tùhng gōujāanghàaih.**
Mary is wearing a suit and high-heeled shoes.

**Tīnhei hóu dung. Jimmy *laahm-jó* tìuh génggān.**
The weather is cold. Jimmy has put on a scarf.

When information about clothes is used to describe people for identification purposes, the aspect marker **-jó** is not used, and the classifiers are omitted. For example:

***Jeuk sāijōng** gó go haih ngóh bàh-bā.*
The one wearing a suit is my father.

***Daai móu** gó go haih Peter.*
The one wearing a cap is Peter.

***Jeuk tīsēut, ngàuhjáifu** gó go néuihjái hóu leng.*
The girl wearing a T-shirt and jeans is very pretty.

## Vocabulary

### Colors (CD2; 46)

| | | | | |
|---|---|---|---|---|
| hùhngsīk | red | | hàaksīk | black |
| wòhngsīk | yellow | | jísīk | violet, purple |
| làahmsīk | blue | | fēsīk | brown |
| luhksīk | green | | cháangsīk | orange |
| baahksīk | white | | fūisīk | gray |

**Sīk** by itself means "color." Thus **hùhngsīk**, for example, literally means "red color."

# Unit 13: *The clothes we wear*

## Dialogue 3

**(CD2; 47)**

Sam and Elza are discussing the clothes they wear to work. Sam teaches at a university while Elza works in a bank.

(a) What does Sam wear to work?
(b) Does he usually wear a tie?
(c) What does Elza wear to work?
(d) What does Elza wear when she does not have to go to work?

ELZA: Sam, néih pìhngsìh jeuk mātyéh sāam fāan-gūng ga?
SAM: Ngóh hái daaihhohk gaau-syū, sóyíh msái jeuk dāk taai sīmàhn. Ngóh dōsou dōu haih jeuk sēutsāam tùhng sāi fu.
ELZA: Sái-mh-sái dá tāai a?
SAM: Msái yātdihng dá tāai. Bātgwo ngóh dūngtīn tīnhei dung jauh dōsou dá tāai, hahtīn tīnhei yiht jauh hóu síu dá laak. Néih nē, Elza? Néih fāan-gūng sái-mh-sái jeuk dāk hóu sīmàhn a?
ELZA: Yiu a. Ngóh fāan ngàhnhòhng, yātdihng yiu jeuk kwàhn tùhng jeuk gōujāanghàaih. Dūngtīn jauh dōsou jeuk tou-jōng. Bātgwo ngóh fongga msái fāan-gūng jauh jeuk fāan tīsēut, ngàuhjáifu tùhng bōhàaih, gámyéung syūfuhk dī.

## Idioms and structures (CD2; 48)

The items in the list below appear in the same order as they do in the dialogue above. The *italicized* items are *new* items. In the notes, numbers in brackets refer to the expressions listed below.

| | | |
|---|---|---|
| 1 | **Ngóh hái *daaihhohk gaau-syū*** | I *teach* at a *university* |
| 2 | **msái jeuk dāk taai *sīmàhn*** | (I) do not have to be very *smartly dressed* |
| 3 | ***Msái yātdihng* dá tāai** | I *don't necessarily* have to wear a tie. |
| 4 | **ngóh *dūngtīn* tīnhei dung jauh dōsou dá tāai** | *In winter* when the weather is cold I usually wear a tie. |
| 5 | ***hahtīn*** | (in) summer |

| | |
|---|---|
| 6 Ngóh fāan *ngàhnhòhng* | I work in a *bank* |
| 7 ngóh ... jauh jeuk *fāan* tīsēut ... | (lit.) I will go *back to* wearing T-shirts |

## "University" (1)

**Daaihhohk** is "university," and it literally means "big school." **Síuhohk** (lit. "little school"), on the other hand, is "primary school," and **jūnghohk** (lit. "middle school") is "secondary school."

## Gaau-syū (1)

The verb-object construction **gaau-syū** means "teach," literally "teach books" (**syū** = book).

## Dress code (2)

To comment on *how* somebody is dressed, the resultative particle **dāk** is used after the verb **jeuk**, which is then followed by an adjective. Resultative structure is used to indicate the result or extent of the action of the verb. Below are some examples:

| | |
|---|---|
| **Kéuih *jeuk dāk* hóu sīmàhn.** | He is very smartly dressed. |
| **Kéuih *jeuk dāk* hóu chèuihbín.** | She is very casually dressed. |
| **Dī hohksāang *jeuk dāk* hóu jíngchàih.** | The students are very neatly dressed. |

To say whether one needs to dress up for an occasion, the modals **yiu** "have to," **msái** "don't have to," and **hóyíh** "can" are used. For example:

**Chàhn sīnsāang fāan-gūng *yiu* jeuk dāk hóu sīmàhn.**
Mr. Chan has to dress up smartly when he goes to work.

**Richard fāan-gūng *msái* jeuk dāk taai sīmàhn.**
Richard does not have to dress up too smartly when he goes to work.

**Ngóh sīngkèih-luhk fāan-gūng *hóyíh* jeuk ngàuhjáifu tùhng bōhàaih.**
On Saturdays I can go to work in jeans and sports shoes.

## The idiomatic use of the verb fāan to mean "to work in" (6)

The expression **Ngóh fāan ngàhnhòhng** is another way of saying **Ngóh hái ngàhnhòhng fāan-gūng** "I work in a bank"; **fāan** is the verb taken from **fāan-gūng**.

## The particle fāan to mean "back to" (7)

**Fāan** in the expression **ngóh jauh jeuk *fāan* tīsēut ...** has the meaning of "going back to," and conveys the idea that Elza usually wears T-shirts and other casual clothes.

## Exercise 2 Grace's friends

Grace is showing a photograph of her friends in Japan to John and Carmen. Read the conversation, then label the picture with the correct names.

GRACE: Nī géi go dōu haih ngóh hái Yahtbún dī hóu pàhng-yáuh.
JOHN: Nī go jeuk dāk hóu sīmàhn ge haih bīngo a?
GRACE: Kéuih haih Saito. Kéuih haih ngóh tùhnghohk.

CARMEN: Nī go nē? Nī go jeuk hùhngsīk kwàhn ge néuihjái nē?
GRACE: Nī go néuihjái haih Saito go mùih-múi. Kéuih giujouh Mariko.
JOHN: Gám, nī léuhng go nē? Nī léuhng go jeuk dāk hóu chèuih-bín ge nàahmjái nē?
GRACE: Kéuihdeih haih Hama tùhng Hideki. Nī go jeuk hāaksīk tīsēut tùhng ngàuhjáifu ge haih Hama. Kéuih haih Hideki go gòh-gō. Jeuk hāaksīk tīsēut tùhng dyúnfu ge haih Hideki. Kéuih haih dàih-dái.

## Exercise 3 Old friends

Your friends have come to your home for dinner. After dinner you show them your photos. You are looking at a photo of your college friends taken ten years ago on the snowy mountains. You are telling your dinner guests the names of each of them by describing their appearance and the clothes they were wearing. Complete the monologue by referring to the picture.

YOU: Jóbīn nī go jeuk fu, laahm-jó génggān, daai-jó sáumaht ge néuihjái ...

# Unit 13: The clothes we wear

## Exercise 4 What you wear to work

You are talking with a friend about the clothes that you have to wear to work and the clothes that you like wearing when going out in the evening and on the weekends. Complete the conversation below with true information about yourself.

YOUR FRIEND: Ngóh múih yaht fāan-gūng yiu jeuk sāijōng dá tāai. Néih nē? Néih sái-mh-sái a?
YOU: Ngóh ...
YOUR FRIEND: Bātgwo ngóh yehmáahn tùhng sīngkèih-luhk sīngkèih yaht heui gāai jauh mjūngyi jeuk sāijōng dá tāai laak. Ngóh jūngyi jeuk dāk chèuihbín dī. Ngóh jūngyi jeuk ngàuhjáifu tùhng tīsēut dō-dī. Gám, néih nē?
YOU: Ngóh ...

## Recognizing Chinese characters

| | |
|---|---|
| 紅色 | red |
| 黃色 | yellow |
| 藍色 | blue |
| 綠色 | green |
| 白色 | white |
| 黑色 | black |

## Communicative activities

1 Describe what your partner is wearing. Make sure you include the colors of their clothing and whether they are casually or smartly dressed.
2 Have a Cantonese-speaking friend describe over the phone what he or she is wearing that day. If you are artistically inclined, do a sketch of what you hear and check later for accuracy.

## Cultural point

### Clothing in Hong Kong

With its small size (1,054 km²/407 sq. miles) and relative lack of natural resources, Hong Kong's economy has always relied on exports. A big part of that export market is textiles. One can find the entire spectrum of clothing for sale in Hong Kong from chic brands to HK$10 shirts hawked by street vendors. Moreover, tailors stand ready to make any kind of custom clothing you desire. Many of the tailors (as in many places in southeast Asia) are from the local Indian community.

# Unit Fourteen
# Léuihhàhng gīngyihm
Traveling experiences

### In Unit 14 you will learn about:

- discussing past experiences
- asking "how often," "how long," and "when"
- describing countries and cities

## Dialogue 1

**(CD2; 49)**
Richard and John are discussing their traveling experiences.
(a) How many times has John been to China?
(b) When did he go to China?
(c) Has Richard been to China?
(d) When did Richard go to Taiwan?

| | |
|---|---|
| RICHARD: | John, néih yáuh móuh heui-gwo Jūnggwok a? |
| JOHN: | Yáuh a, ngóh heui-gwo Jūnggwok la. |
| RICHARD: | Gám, néih heui-gwo géidō chi Jūnggwok a? |
| JOHN: | Ngóh heui-gwo léuhng chi. |
| RICHARD: | Néih géisìh heui ga? |
| JOHN: | Ngóh chìhnnín heui-gwo yāt chi, gauhnín heui-gwo yāt chi. Néih nē? Néih heui-gwo Jūnggwok meih a? |
| RICHARD: | Ngóh meih heui-gwo Jūnggwok, bātgwo ngóh heui-gwo Tòihwāan. |
| JOHN: | Néih géisìh heui Tòihwāan ga? |
| RICHARD: | Ngóh seuhng go yuht heui Tòihwāan ge. |

## Dialogue 2

**(CD2; 50)**
HO Syut Hwa and CHAN Syut Wai are talking about the sports they have played lately.
(a) Has CHAN Syut Wai played any tennis this year?
(b) Why hasn't CHAN Syut Wai done any swimming this year?
(c) Why hasn't HO Syut Hwa played any sports this year?

| | |
|---|---|
| HO SYUT HWA: | CHAN Syut Wai, néih gāmnín yáuh móuh yàuh-gwo séui a? |
| CHAN SYUT WAI: | Móuh a, ngóh gāmnín móuh yàuh-gwo séui a. Gāmnín tīnhei taai dung la. Bātgwo ngóh dá-gwo géi chi móhngkàuh. Néih nē, HO Syut Hwa? Néih gāmnín yáuh móuh jouh-gwo wahnduhng a? |
| HO SYUT HWA: | Móuh a. Ngóh gāmnín hóu mòhng, móuh sìhgaan jouh wahnduhng, sóyíh móuh yàuh-gwo séui, yauh móuh dá-gwo móhngkàuh. |

## Vocabulary

**(CD2; 51)**
Below are some commonly used expressions about past time. Try reading each item aloud. If you have the audio material for this book, you can model your pronunciation on the recording.

| | |
|---|---|
| gāmnín | this year |
| gauhnín | last year |
| chìhnnín | the year before last |
| nī go yuht | this month |
| seuhng go yuht | last month |
| chìhn go yuht | the month before last |
| nī go láihbaai | this week |
| seuhng go láihbaai | last week |
| chìhn go láihbaai | the week before last |
| sāam nìhn chìhn | three years ago |
| sāam go yuht chìhn | three months ago |
| sāam go láihbaai chìhn | three weeks ago |

Note that in the last three expressions, **chìhn** means "ago." However, both **yuht** and **láihbaai** take the classifier **go**, while **nìhn** does not. **Nìhn** is the same word as **nín** in **gāmnín**, **gauhnín**, and **chìhnnín**, but the pronunciation has undergone a tone change.

## Idioms and structures

The items in the list below appear in the same order as they do in the dialogues above. The *italicized* items are *new* items. In the notes, numbers in brackets refer to the expressions listed below.

1 ***néih yáuh móuh heui-gwo Jūnggwok a?*** — Have you ever been to China?

2 ***néih heui-gwo géidō chi Jūnggwok a?*** — How many times have you been to China?

3 ***Néih géisìh heui ga?*** — When did you go?

4 ***Néih gāmnín yáuh móuh jouh-gwo wahnduhng a?*** — Have you *done any sports* this year?

5 **Ngóh gāmnín** *hóu mòhng*    I have been *very busy* this year.
6 **móuh** *sìhgaan* **jouh-wahnduhng**    (I haven't had) *time* to do sports

## Asking about and describing experiences (1)

To ask whether somebody has had the experience of doing something, you can form a choice-type question with the two existential verbs **yáuh** and **móuh**, and use the aspect marker **-gwo** after the main verb:

**Néih** *yáuh móuh* **heui-*gwo* Oujāu a?**    Have you been to Australia?

**Néih** *yáuh móuh* **gin-*gwo* doihsyú a?**    Have you seen kangaroos before?

A positive answer to the first question would then be:

*Yáuh* **a, ngóh heui-*gwo* Oujāu.**    Yes, I have been to Australia.

And a negative answer would be:

*Móuh* **a, ngóh** *móuh* **heui-*gwo* Oujāu.**    No, I have not been to Australia.

A second way to ask the same first question is to offer the two choices of **heui-gwo** and **meih heui-gwo**, **meih** being the adverb for incomplete action. However, in such an interrogative pattern the verb **heui** and the aspect marker **-gwo** are not repeated in the negative option, resulting in the following question:

**Néih heui-gwo Oujāu** *meih* **a?**    Have you been to Australia?

And to ask the second question in the same way, you say:

**Néih gin-gwo doihsyú** *meih* **a?**    Have you seen kangaroos before?

Positive answers to the questions above can be either long or short, as follows:

**Ngóh heui-gwo Oujāu. / Heui-gwo.**
**Ngóh gin-gwo doihsyú. / Gin-gwo.**

Negative answers can also be long or short:

**Ngóh meih heui-gwo Oujāu. / Meih heui-gwo.**
**Ngóh meih gin-gwo doihsyú. / Meih gin-gwo.**

## Asking about frequency (2)

A possible follow-up question to whether somebody has experienced something is to ask how many times. The Cantonese expression for asking this is **géidō chi**. Read the following exchange:

A: **Néih yáuh móuh heui-gwo Oujāu a?**
   Have you been to Australia?
B: **Yáuh a, ngóh heui-gwo Oujāu.**
   Yes, I have been to Australia.
A: **Néih heui-gwo *géidō chi* Oujāu a?**
   How many times have you been to Australia?
B: **Ngóh heui-gwo *léuhng chi* Oujāu.**
   I've been to Australia twice.

The point to bear in mind about the pattern is the word order. The expression of frequency comes between the verb-and-aspect marker **heui-gwo** and its object **Oujāu**, so that the literal translation of the Cantonese **Ngóh heui-gwo léuhng chi Oujāu** is "I have been two times (to) Australia." Here is a further exchange to illustrate the structure:

A: **Néih gāmnín yàuh-gwo séui meih a?**
   Have you done any swimming this year?
B: **Yàuh-gwo.**
   Yes, I have.
A: **Néih gāmnín yàuh-gwo *géidō chi* séui a?**
   How many times have you been swimming this year?
B: **Ngóh gāmnín yàuh-gwo *sāam chi* séui.**
   I've been swimming three times this year.

## Asking when (3)

When discussing experiences, another possible follow-up question is "When ...?" The Cantonese word for "when" is **géisìh**. Read the following exchanges:

A: **Néih yáuh móuh heui-gwo Oujāu a?**
Have you been to Australia?
B: **Yáuh a, ngóh heui-gwo Oujāu.**
Yes, I have been to Australia.
A: **Néih *géisìh* heui ga?**
So, when did you go?
B: **Ngóh *gauhnín* heui ge.**
I went last year.
C: **Néih yáuh móuh gin-gwo sāyùh a?**
Have you ever seen sharks before?
D: **Yáuh a, ngóh gin-gwo sāyùh la.**
Yes, I have seen sharks before.
C: **Néih *géisìh* gin ga?**
When did you see them?
D: **Ngóh *sāam nìhn chìhn* hái Oujāu gin ge.**
I saw them in Australia three years ago.

Notice that in the follow-up question to "When ...?" the destination or the object can be omitted, and so can the aspect marker **-gwo**. **Ga** is often used instead of **a** as the interrogative (question) particle in such a follow-up question. In answer to a follow-up question, **ge** is often used as a sentence-final particle. In Cantonese, time expressions always come *before* the verb, hence **Ngóh *gauhnín* heui ge**.

## Vocabulary

### Major cities of the world (CD2; 52)

Here is a list of some of the world's major cities. Read each item aloud, or if you have the audio material for this book, you can model your pronunciation on the recording.

| | | | |
|---|---|---|---|
| **Lèuhndēun** | London | **Sāamfàahnsíh** | San Francisco |
| **Lohkchaamgēi** | Los Angeles | **Dūnggīng** | Tokyo |
| **Máhnèihlāai** | Manila | **Dōlèuhndō** | Toronto |
| **Náuyeuk** | New York | **Wāngōwàh** | Vancouver |
| **Bālàih** | Paris | | |

## Describing countries (CD2; 53)

You may want to say what you like about a particular country. Below are some of the probable reasons for liking a country.

| | |
|---|---|
| Fūngging hóu leng. | The scenery is good. |
| Wàahngíng hóu gōnjehng. | The environment is clean. |
| Gāautūng hóu fōngbihn. | The transportation is convenient. |
| Dī yàhn hóu hóu. | The people are nice. |
| Máaih-yéh hóu pèhng. | Things are very cheap. |
| Dī yéh hóu hóusihk. | The food is delicious. |

### Dialogue 3

**(CD2; 54)**

Peter is asking John about his recent trip to the United States.

(a) When did John go to the United States?
(b) Which cities did he visit?
(c) How long did he stay in each?

PETER: John, néih seuhng go yuht haih-mh-haih heui-gwo Méihgwok a?
JOHN: Haih a. Ngóh ngāam-ngāam hái Méihgwok fāan lèih.
PETER: Néih heui-jó Méihgwok bīndouh a?
JOHN: Ngóh heui-jó Sāamfàahnsíh tùhng Lohkchaamgēi. Ngóh heui taam-pàhngyáuh.
PETER: Néih heui-jó Sāamfàhnsíh géinoih a?
JOHN: Ngóh heui-jó Sāamfàahnsíh ńgh yaht.
PETER: Gám, Lohkchaamgēi nē? Néih hái Lohkchaamgēi làuh-jó géidō yaht a?
JOHN: Ngóh hái Lohkchaamgēi jauh làuh-jó luhk yaht.

### Dialogue 4

**(CD2; 55)**

Jimmy is asking William about his impressions of Japan, which he visited once.

(a) How does William find Japan?
(b) What are the things he likes about Japan?
(c) What are the things he doesn't like about Japan?

JIMMY: William, néih gak, heui-gwo Yahtbún haih-mh-haih a?
WILLIAM: Haih a.
JIMMY: Néih géisìh heui ga?
WILLIAM: Ngóh chìhnnín heui ge.
JIMMY: Gám, néih jūng-mh-jūngyi Yahtbún a?
WILLIAM: Ngóh hóu jūngyi Yahtbún a. Yahtbún dī fūngging hóu leng, jāuwàih dōu hóu gōnjehng, dī yàhn hóu hóu, hóu yáuh láihmaauh, bātgwo máaih-yéh hóu gwai.
JIMMY: Dī yéh hóu-mh-hóusihk ga?
WILLIAM: Màh-má-déi lā, tùhngmàaih sihk-yéh dōu hóu gwai.

## Exercise 1 Your favorite place

Of all the places you have visited, which is your favorite country or city? Using Dialogue 4 as a model, explain why you like this place best.

YOU: Ngóh jeui jūngyi ... yānwaih ...

## Idioms and structures

The items in the list below appear in the same order as they do in the dialogues above. The *italicized* items are *new* items. In the notes, numbers in brackets refer to the expressions listed below.

| 1 | **néih seuhng go yuht haih-mh-haih heui-gwo Méihgwok a?** | You went to the United States last month, didn't you? |
|---|---|---|
| 2 | **Ngóh *ngāam-ngāam* hái Méihgwok fāan lèih.** | I have *just* come back from the United States. |
| 3 | **Ngóh heui *taam-pàhngyáuh*.** | I went to *visit friends*. |
| 4 | ***Néih heui-jó Sāamfàhnsíh géinoih a?*** | *How long did you stay in San Francisco?* |
| 5 | **Néih hái Lohkchaamgēi làuh-jó géidō yaht a?** | How many days did you *stay* in Los Angeles? |

Unit 14: Traveling experiences

6 **jāuwàih dōu hóu gōnjehng**   It's very clean *everywhere*.
7 **hóu yáuh láihmaauh**   very *polite*

## Asking for confirmation (1)

The question asks for confirmation of some information, hence **haih-mh-haih heui-gwo Méihgwok a?** rather than **yáuh móuh heui-gwo Méihgwok a?** or **heui-gwo Méihgwok meih a?** The most appropriate translation into English is the tag question: "You went to the United States last month, didn't you?"

## Taam (3)

The verb **taam** can only take human objects and means "to pay somebody a visit." Thus, **heui Méihgwok *taam*-pàhngyáuh** is correct but *****taam* Méihgwok** is wrong.

## Asking about the length of an activity (4, 5)

Apart from asking when somebody has visited a country, one might also enquire how long he or she stayed there. For this the question word **géinoih** "how long" is used. Read the exchange below:

A: **Néih yáuh móuh heui-gwo Yahtbún a?**
   Have you ever been to Japan?
B: **Yáuh a. Heui-gwo yāt chi. Gauhnín heui ge.**
   Yes, I have, once. I went last year.
A: **Gám, néih heui-jó *géinoih* a?**
   How long did you stay there?
B: **Ngóh heui-jó sahp yaht.**
   I was there for ten days.

Notice that two different aspect markers, namely **-gwo** and **-jó**, are used with the verb **heui** in this dialogue. **-gwo** is used to refer to an experience, as evident in the question **Néih yáuh móuh *heui-gwo* Yahtbún a?** "*Have* you *ever been* to Japan?" and the statement **Heui-gwo yāt chi** "I *have been* once." **-jó**, on the other hand, focuses on new information about a completed action which is already known about. In the dialogue above, after A has heard that B has been to Japan once, A then asks **néih *heui-jó* géinoih a?** "How long *did* you *stay there?*," and B answers **Ngóh heui-jó sahp yaht** "*I was there for ten days,*" both of which show recognition of the fact, now known, that B has been to Japan.

Another point worth noting is the word order. Whereas time expressions in Cantonese usually precede the verb, phrases of duration usually *follow* the verb, hence **Ngóh heui-jó sahp yaht**.

## Exercise 2 Where have they been?

Translate the following sentences into Cantonese, using **-gwo** to refer to experiences. The first one has been done for you as an example.

(a) I went to England last year.
 **Ngóh gauhnín heui-gwo Yīnggwok.**
(b) I went to Japan the month before last.
(c) He went to France last week.
(d) She went to China two months ago.
(e) We went to Taiwan five years ago.
(f) They went to Canada four weeks ago.

## Jāuwàih (6)

The Cantonese word **jāuwàih** is a noun which means "the surroundings," and so the sentence **jāuwàih dōu hóu gōnjehng** is literally "The surroundings are all very clean."

## Yáuh láihmaauh (7)

In the expression **yáuh láihmaauh**, **yáuh** is a verb which means "to have" while **láihmaauh** is a noun which means "good manners," hence "polite." The expression for "impolite" is **móuh láihmaauh**.

Unit 14: *Traveling experiences*

## Exercise 3 Globe-trotters

Winnie, Kitty, and Sally are bragging about their wide traveling experiences. Read the conversation. Then make a record of the girls' traveling experiences and decide which of the three has traveled the most.

WINNIE: Ngóh jeui jūngyi heui-léuihhàhng ga laak. Ngóh heui-gwo sāam chi āujāu, léuhng chi Méihgwok, yāt chi Yahtbún, tùhng yāt chi Oujāu.

KITTY: Gám, néih yáuh móuh heui-gwo Jūnggwok tùhng Tòihwāan a?

WINNIE: Móuh wo.

KITTY: Ngóh heui-gwo ńgh chi Jūnggwok, sei chi Tòihwāan, léuhng chi Yahtbún. Ngóh dōu yáuh heui-gwo āujāu, Méihgwok, tùhng Oujāu, múih douh heui-gwo léuhng chi.

SALLY: Gám ngóh heui dāk jeui dō léuihhàhng la. Ngóh heui-gwo yāt chi Yandouh, sāam chi Fēileuhtbān, léuhng chi Yahtbún, sei chi Jūnggwok, tùhng ńgh chi Tòihwāan. Āujāu ngóh heui-gwo yāt chi, Méihgwok sei chi, Gānàhdaaih sāam chi. Juhng yáuh, ngóh heui-gwo sāam chi Oujāu, tùhng léuhng chi Náusāilàahn.

## Exercise 4 Expressing frequency

To familiarize yourself with the structures for expressing frequency of past experiences, answer the following questions with the number given. The first one has been done for you as an example.

(a) **Néih heui-gwo géidō chi Yahtbún a?** (3)
 **Ngóh heui-gwo sāam chi Yahtbún.**

(b) Néih heui-gwo géidō chi Dākgwok a? (5)

(c) Néih nī go yuht tái-gwo géidō chi hei a? (2)

(d) Néih nī go láihbaai dá-gwo géidō chi móhngkàuh a? (2)

(e) Néih gāmnín heui-gwo géidō chi léuihhàhng a? (4)

## Exercise 5 Where have the Chans been?

Mr. and Mrs. Chan love traveling. They have done quite a bit this year, and their neighbors Mr. and Mrs. Wong are asking them about their travels. Complete the conversation with the information given on the calendar.

| April | | | | | | |
|---|---|---|---|---|---|---|
| M | T | W | T | F | S | S |
|  |  | Philippines |  |  | 1 | 2 | 3 |
| 4 | 5 | 6 | 7 | 8 | 9 | 10 |
| 11 | 12 | 13 | 14 | 15 India | 16 | 17 |
| 18 | 19 | 20 | 21 | 22 | 23 | 24 |
| 25 | 26 | 27 | 28 | 29 | 30 |  |
| India | | | | | | |

| May | | | | | | |
|---|---|---|---|---|---|---|
| M | T | W | T | F | S | S |
|  |  |  |  |  |  | 1 |
| 2 | 3 | 4 | 5 | 6 | 7 | 8 |
| 9 | 10 | 11 Taiwan | 12 | 13 | 14 | 15 |
| 16 | 17 | 18 | 19 | 20 | 21 | 22 |
| 23 | 24 | 25 | 26 | 27 | 28 | 29 |
| 30 | 31 |  |  |  |  |  |

MR. WONG: Chàhn sīnsāang, Chàhn táai, néihdeih gāmnín yáuh móuh heui-gwo léuihhàhng a?
MR. CHAN: Yáuh a. Ngóhdeih gāmnín heui-gwo sāam go gwokgā la.
MR. WONG: Bīn sāam go gwokgā a?
MRS. CHAN: (a) Ngóhdeih heui-jó ...
MRS. WONG: Néihdeih géisìh heui ... ga?
MR. CHAN: (b) Ngóhdeih ...
MR. WONG: Néihdeih heui-jó géinoih a?
MRS. CHAN: (c)
MRS. WONG: Gám, juhng yáuh nē?
MRS. CHAN: (d)
MRS. WONG: Gám, juhng yáuh yāt go gwokgā nē?
MRS. CHAN: (e)

## Exercise 6 Where have you been?

Using Exercise 1 above as a model, write out your traveling experiences in Cantonese below.

YOU: **Ngóh heui-gwo ...**

## Recognizing Chinese characters

| 倫敦 | London |
| 馬尼拉 | Manila |
| 紐約 | New York |
| 巴黎 | Paris |

Unit 14: *Traveling experiences*

| 三藩市 | San Francisco |
| 東京 | Tokyo |
| 多倫多 | Toronto |
| 溫哥華 | Vancouver |

## Communicative activities

1 With a Cantonese-speaking partner, talk about a favorite vacation that you have experienced. Where did you go? What kind of places did you visit while there? What was your favorite thing to do? Engage your partner with the same questions.
2 Play the role of a traveler planning a round-the-world trip. Have a partner play the role of travel agent. Switch roles and repeat.

## Cultural point

### Tourism in Hong Kong

According to the Hong Kong tourism commission, Hong Kong received nearly 30 million visitors in 2008. Tourism-related expenditures of the same year were estimated at HK$159.0 billion. People come to Hong Kong for many reasons, but shopping and eating are among the most popular pastimes. In fact, many tourists do nothing else *but* shop and eat. Because of its history as a British colony, Hong Kong has a unique blend of East and West. Hong Kong has an amazing array of shopping opportunities ranging from second-hand goods street markets to glitzy malls to boutiques with world-class fashion. It is also a place to buy Chinese traditional goods and cutting-edge electronics.

Besides shopping and dining, visitors come to enjoy some of the most spectacular views found anywhere in the world, including the harbor, the Giant Buddha of Lantau Island, and scenic beaches.

# Unit Fifteen
# Dá-dihnwá
On the telephone

In Unit 15 you will learn about:

- telephone conversations
- how to invite somebody out
- how to arrange to meet somebody

Unit 15: *On the telephone*

## Dialogue 1

**(CD2; 57)**

CHAN Wing Sang is out of the office for a while and his colleague Jimmy is answering the phone for him.

(a) Who is calling?
(b) What message does he leave?
(c) What is his phone number?

| | |
|---|---|
| MR. WONG: | Wái, mgōi néih giu CHAN Wing Sang tēng-dihnwá. |
| JIMMY: | Deui mjyuh, CHAN Wing Sang hàahnghōi-jó. Chíng mahn bīnwái wán kéuih a? |
| MR. WONG: | Ngóh haih Wòhng sīnsāang a. Néih haih bīnwái a? |
| JIMMY: | Ngóh haih CHAN Wing Sang go tùhngsih Jimmy. Wòhng sīnsāang, sái-mh-sái làuh go háuseun a? |
| MR. WONG: | Hóu ā. Mgōi néih giu kéuih dá fāan dihnwá béi ngóh ā. Ngóh go dihnwá haih sāam-luhk-lìhng-sāam-luhk-chāt-baat. |
| JIMMY: | Sāam-luhk-lìhng-sāam-luhk-chāt-baat. Hóu, ngóh giu CHAN Wing Sang dá fāan dihnwá béi néih lā. |
| MR. WONG: | Hóu. Mgōi saai, Jimmy. |
| JIMMY: | Bāai-baai. |
| MR. WONG: | Bāai-baai. |

## Dialogue 2

**(CD2; 58)**

John is alone at home. The telephone rings and John picks it up.

(a) Where is Carmen?
(b) What message does Susan leave?
(c) Does she want Carmen to call her back?

| | |
|---|---|
| JOHN: | Wái. |
| SUSAN: | Wái, chíng mahn Carmen hái-mh-hái douh a? |
| JOHN: | Deui mjyuh, Carmen chēut-jó gāai wo. Néih bīnwái wán kéuih a? |
| SUSAN: | Ngóh haih Susan a. Néih haih-mh-haih John a? |
| JOHN: | Haih a. |
| SUSAN: | John, néih hó-mh-hóyíh tùhng ngóh làuh go háu-seun béi Carmen a? |

JOHN: Hóyíh. Néih góng lā.
SUSAN: Mgòi néih wah béi Carmen tēng, tīngyaht lohk-yúh jauh mheui dá móhngkàuh laak.
JOHN: Hóu lā. Ngóh wah béi kéuih tēng lā. Gám, sái-mh-sái giu Carmen dá-fāan béi néih a?
SUSAN: Msái la.
JOHN: Hóu lā. Bāai-baai.
SUSAN: Bāai-baai.

 Vocabulary

**(CD2; 59)**
Cantonese speakers have certain conventions when talking on the telephone. Below is a list of the common expressions used. Try reading each item aloud. If you have the audio for this book, you can model your pronunciation on the recording.

| | |
|---|---|
| dá-dihnwá | to make a phone call |
| tēng-dihnwá | to answer the phone |
| dáng (yāt) dáng/dáng (yāt) jahn | to wait a minute |
| mhái douh | not here |
| hàahnghōi-jó | has/have gone out |
| làuh (yāt go) háuseun | leave a message |
| dá gwo (dihnwá) lèih | to call again |
| dá fāan (dihnwá) béi néih | to call you back |
| daap cho sin | wrong number |
| góng-gán | line engaged |
| noihsin | extension |

 Idioms and structures

The items in the list below appear in the same order as they do in the dialogues above. The *italicized* items are *new* items. In the notes, numbers in brackets refer to the expressions listed below.

1 ***Wái, mgōi néih giu CHAN Wing Sang tēng-dihnwá.***  Hello, can I speak to CHAN Wing Sang, please?

2 ***Deui mjyuh, CHAN Wing Sang hàahnghōi-jó.***  Sorry, CHAN Wing Sang is not in at the moment.

3 **Ngóh haih CHAN Wing Sang go tùhngsih.**  I am CHAN Wing Sang's colleague.
4 **Mgōi néih giu kéuih dá fāan dihnwá béi ngóh ā.**  Please ask him to return my call.
5 **Bāai-baai.**  Bye-bye.

## Greeting on the phone (1)

To open a telephone conversation, Cantonese speakers say **wái**, whether calling or answering.

## Asking for somebody on the phone (1)

To ask for somebody on the phone, you can go straight into it by saying:

**Wái, mgōi néih giu ... tēng-dihnwá.**  Hello, can I speak to ... please?

Or you can first ask whether somebody is there:

**Wái, chíng mahn ... hái-mh-hái douh a?**  Hello, is ... there, please?

## Answering the phone (2)

When a caller asks to speak to somebody else, you might answer:

**Hóu, mgōi dáng yāt jahn.**  Please wait a minute.

When a caller asks whether somebody else is in, you might say:

**Hái douh. Mgōi dáng yāt jahn.**  Yes, he's here. Just a minute.

If someone asks to speak to you, you say:

**Ngóh haih.**  Speaking.

If somebody asked for is not in, you might say:

**Deui mjyuh, kéuih mhái douh wo.**  I'm sorry, he's not in.

or

**Deui mjyuh, kéuih hàahnghōi-jó wo.**  I'm sorry, he's gone out.

You may wish to ask who is calling, by saying:

> **Chíng mahn bīnwái wán kéuih a?**   May I ask who's calling, please?

You may also want to ask whether the caller needs to leave a message:

> **Néih sái-mh-sái làuh go háuseun a?**   Would you like to leave a message?

## Colleagues and classmates (3)

The noun **tùhngsih** "colleague" is made up of **tùhng**, which means "together with," and **sih**, which means "to work." Thus **tùhngsih** is "someone you work with," while **tùhnghohk** "classmate" is "someone you learn with," **hohk** meaning "to learn."

## Leaving a message (4)

To ask to leave a message, you can say:

> **Mgōi néih tùhng ngóh làuh go háuseun ā.**
> Could you leave a message for me, please?

In leaving a message, you can say who you are, and then say you'll call back another time:

> **Mgōi néih wah béi kéuih tēng Chàhn sīnsāang wán-gwo kéuih. Ngóh wúih sei dím jūng dá gwo làih.**
> Please tell him/her that Mr. Chan called, and I'll call again at 4 o'clock.

You can also ask to have the person return your call:

> **Ngóh haih Chàhn sīnsāang. Mgōi néih giu kéuih dá fāan dihn-wá béi ngóh ā.**
> This is Mr. Chan. Please tell him/her to call me back.

You may also leave your own telephone number for someone to call back. "Telephone number" is **dihnwá houhmáh** in Cantonese (though many people just say **dihnwá** in colloquial speech), and the actual number is cited digit by digit:

Ngóh go dihnwá (houhmáh) haih ńgh-chāt-lìhng-gáu-baat-lìhng-sei.
My phone number is 5709804.

## Saying goodbye (5)

The conventional way of saying goodbye at a meeting or on the telephone is **joi gin**, which literally means "see you again." However, in Hong Kong, because of the Western influence, people tend to say **bāai-baai** instead. **Bāai-baai** is borrowed from the colloquial English "bye-bye," but when we say it in Cantonese we have to abide by the rules of Cantonese, and get the tones right!

## Exercise 1 Taking messages

Your colleague, Pam, has gone out for a while and says she's coming back at about four o'clock. You have promised to take messages for her. Complete the following conversation between you and a caller.

CALLER:  Wái, mgōi néih giu Pam tēng-dihnwá.
YOU:     (a) Deui mjyuh, Pam ...
CALLER:  Chíng mahn kéuih géi dím jūng fāan lèih a?
YOU:     (b) Pam wah kéuih ...
CALLER:  Mgōi hó-mh-hóyíh tùhng ngóh làuh go háuseun a?
YOU:     (c)
CALLER:  Mgōi néih giu kéuih hái ńgh dím jūng chìhn dá fāan dihnwá béi ngóh ā.
YOU:     (d) Hóu, ngóh giu kéuih ...
CALLER:  Hóu laak. Mgōi saai. Bāai-baai.
YOU:     (e) Msái mgōi ...

## Vocabulary

### Leisure activities (CD2; 60)

Below is a list of popular activities that you might invite somebody out for. Try reading each item aloud. If you have the audio for this book, you can model your pronunciation on the recording.

| | |
|---|---|
| heui tái-hei | to go to the cinema |
| sihk máahnfaahn | to have dinner |
| heui yám-yéh | to have a drink |
| heui yám-jáu | to go for a drink |
| heui yám-gafē | to go for a coffee |
| heui tiu-móuh | to go to a dance |
| heui yàuh-séui | to go swimming |
| heui dá-bō | to play a ballgame |
| heui tēng-yāmngohk | to go to a concert |

## Specifying the day

When arranging to meet somebody, we need to make it clear which day we are talking about. Read the examples below:

| | |
|---|---|
| (nī go) sīngkèih-yaht | this (coming) Sunday |
| (nī go) sīngkèih-yāt | this (coming) Monday |
| (nī go) sīngkèih-yih | this (coming) Tuesday |
| hah (go) sīngkèih-yaht | Sunday |
| hah (go) sīngkèih-yāt | Monday |
| hah (go) sīngkèih-yih | Tuesday |

Note that the other term for week, **láihbaai**, can be substituted for **sīngkèih** in the above expressions.

## Dialogue 3

**(CD2; 61)**

John is at home and calls Richard to extend an invitation.

(a) What activity is John suggesting?
(b) Who's going?
(c) How will they meet up?

| | |
|---|---|
| JOHN: | Wái. |
| RICHARD: | Wái, neih haih John a? |
| JOHN: | Haih, ngóh haih John. |
| RICHARD: | Ngóh haih Richard. John, tīngmáahn dāk-mh-dākhàahn a? Yáuh móuh hīngcheui heui tái-héi a? |
| JOHN: | Dākhàahn a. Tái géi dímjūng a? |
| RICHARD: | Mjī. Dáng ngóh séuhng-mohng tái háh sìhgāan sīn. |

(Richard comes back on the phone after finding the show times online.)

RICHARD: Wái. John, Tīngmáahn chāat dím tùhng sahp dím jūng dōu yáuh héi tái. Néih séung tái géi dím jūng a?
JOHN: Tái chāat dím jūng lā, hóu mā?
RICHARD: Hóu. Ngóh dou heiyún houh, faat go dyún sheuhn béi néih.
JOHN: Hóu lā. Tīngmáahn gin.
RICHARD: Tīngmáahn gin.

## Dialogue 4

**(CD2; 62)**
William wants to buy a new cell phone plan but he is not sure which one is best for his needs. He calls his friend Linda for her opinion.

(a) What plan does Linda have?
(b) What plan does her brother have?
(c) What plan does William choose?

LINDA: Wái.
WILLIAM: Wái. Linda, ngóh haih William.
LINDA: William, dím a?
WILLIAM: Géi hóu. Ngóh séung chēut bou saugēi, Néih wah bīngo toih tùhng maaih gaaiwahk hou a? Néih tùhng néih gōgo yuhng gán mātyéh gaaiwahk a?
LINDA: Ngóh yuhng gán Hēung Góng Dihnsheun ge yuhtfai gaaiwahk, ngóh gōgo jauh yuhng gán chúhjik kāak.
WILLIAM: Yātgo yuht, yau géi dō fānjūng a? Dihnwah yáuhmóuh dāk seuhng mòhng ga?
LINDA: Ngóh ge gaaiwahk múih go yuht yáuh yāt chīn yi baak fānjūng, bāau móuhhaang dyúnseuhn, dihnwah yí gīng yáuh WiFi.
WILLIAM: Néih gōgo nē?
LINDA: Kéiuh ge chúhjikkāak haih múih faanjung luhk sīn, múih chi jeui síu yiu jāan jik ńgh sahp mān. Daahnhaaih Keiuh dihn waah mouh WiFi. Kéiuh gaaiwahk pèhng hóudō.
WILLIAM: Gam, ngóhnám ngoh yīnggōi wuih máaih chúhjik kāak lak. Mgōi néih bōngmòhng!
LINDA: Msai mgōi.

 Idioms and structures

The items in the list below appear in the same order as they do in the dialogues above. The *italicized* items are *new* items. In the notes, numbers in brackets refer to the expressions listed below.

1 **Tīngmáahn dāk-mh-dākhàahn a?** — Are you free tomorrow night?
2 **Yáuh móuh hīngcheui heui tái-héi a?** — Are you interested in seeing a movie?
3 **Dākhàahn a.** — (I am) free.
4 **Dáng ngóh séuhng-mohng tái *háh* sìhgāan sīn.** — Let me go online and check the times.
5 **Ngóh dou heiyún houh, faat go dyún seuhn béi néih.** — I'll text you when I get to the movie theater.
6 **Néih tùhng néih gōgo yuhng gán mātyéh gaaiwahk a?** — Which plan do you and your (older) brother have?
7 **yuhtfai gaaiwahk, chúhjik kāat** — monthly plan, prepaid card

8 **Dihnwah yáuhmóuh dāk**     Can you go on the Internet?
   **seuhng mòhng ga?**
9 **bāau móuhhaang dyúnseuhn**     including unlimited texting

## Inviting someone out (1, 2)

To invite someone out, it is common to begin by asking if he or she is free on a certain day:

> **Néih sīngkèih yaht yehmáahn *dāk-mh-dākhàahn* a?**
> *Are you free* on Sunday evening?

**Dākhàahn** is the adjective for "free," and in the example above it is used to form a choice-type question. If the answer is positive, another question can be asked, this time to find out if the person is interested in a certain type of activity:

> **Néih *yáuh móuh hingcheui* tùhng ngóh heui tái-héi a?**
> *Are you interested in* going to a movie with me?

The choice-type question above is formed with the existential verbs **yáuh** and **móuh**, followed by the noun for "interest," **hingcheui**. In Dialogue 4, **yáuhmóuh** is also used, in **Dihnwah yáuhmóuh dāk séung mòhng ga?** "Can you go on the Internet?"

Another way of suggesting an activity is to use the expression **bātyùh** with the sentence-final particle **ā**:

> **Tīnhei gam yiht, *bātyùh* heui yàuh-séui *ā*.**
> The weather is so hot. *Why don't we* go swimming?

> **Daaihgā dōu dākhàahn. *Bātyùh* heui tái-hei *ā*.**
> We're all free. *Why don't we* go to see a movie?

Or you can come straight to the point in inviting somebody out:

> **Ngóh séung chéng néih heui yāmngohkwúi. Mjī néih dāk-mh-dākhàahn nē?**
> I'd like to invite you to a concert. I was wondering whether you were free?

The pattern **Mjī ... nē** is a way of asking a question, and functions exactly like the English pattern "I was wondering whether ...."

## The aspect marker -háh (4)

**-háh** is an aspect marker used after a verb to indicate that an action is to be taken for a short while. For example, when John says he'll look up the times online, that should take just a moment, as is indicated in **Dáng ngóh séuhng-mohng tái háh sìhgāan sīn** "Let me go online and check the times."

## Exercise 2 Housewarming

Amy has moved into a new flat and wants to invite Kitty to her new home for dinner. She phones Kitty to discuss a date. Read the conversation, then answer the following questions:

(a) Why can't Kitty make it on Tuesday evening?
(b) Why can't she make it on Wednesday evening?
(c) What day do Amy and Kitty eventually agree on?
(d) What time does Amy expect Kitty?

AMY: Wái, haih-mh-haih Kitty a?
KITTY: Haih a. Néih haih Amy àh?
AMY: Kitty, ngóh séung chéng néih làih ngóh ngūkkéi sihk máahn-faahn a. Néih hah sīngkèih-yih dāk-mh-dākhàahn a?
KITTY: Hah sīngkèih-yih mdāk a. Ngóh yiu tùhng Peter heui tēng-yāmngohk a.
AMY: Gám, láihbaai-sāam máahn nē?
KITTY: Láihbaai-sāam máahn dōu mdāk a. Ngóh yiu fāan-hohk a. Bātyùh láihbaai-ńgh máahn ā, hóu-mh-hóu? Láihbaai-ńgh máahn ngóh béigaau dākhàahn.
AMY: Hóu lā. Gám jauh láihbaai-ńgh máahn lā. Néih yehmáahn chāt dím bun lèih douh ngóh ngūkkéi, dāk-mh-dāk?
KITTY: Dāk, móuh mahntàih.

## Exercise 3 When are you free?

Your friend Stephen is leaving Hong Kong at the end of the week, and has phoned to suggest having a drink together after work some time this week. You have a very busy week, and you are trying desperately to fit in a time for Stephen. Complete the conversation with reference to the diary:

# Unit 15: On the telephone

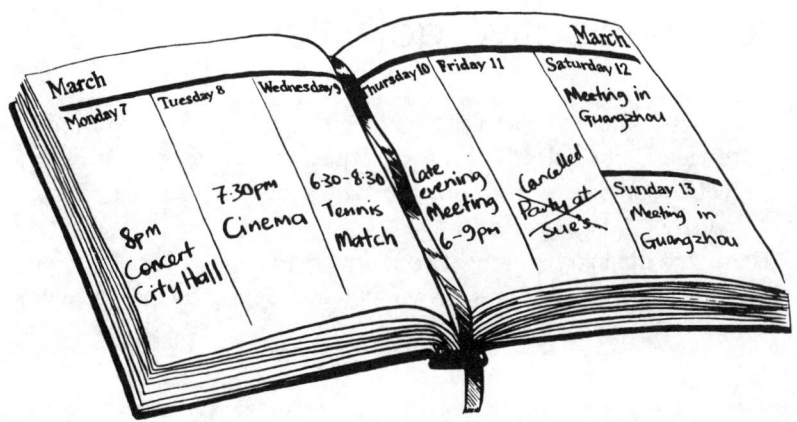

STEPHEN: Wái, ngóh haih Stephen a. Ngóh sīngkèih-luhk jauh fāan Méihgwok la. Néih nī go láihbaai géisìh dākhàahn tùhng ngóh yám-yéh a?
YOU: Ngóh nī go láihbaai hóu mòhng a.
STEPHEN: Sīngkèih-sāam máahn dāk-mh-dāk?
YOU: (a) Mdāk a. Ngóh yiu ...
STEPHEN: Gám sīngkèih-sei nē?
YOU: (b) Sīngkèih-sei ...
STEPHEN: Sīngkèih-yih nē?
YOU: (c) ... Bātyùh ...
STEPHEN: Hóu lā. Dou sìh gin lā.

## Recognizing Chinese characters

| | |
|---|---|
| 大會堂 | City Hall |
| 文化中心 | Cultural Center |
| 藝術中心 | Arts Center |
| 演藝學院 | Academy for Performing Arts |

## Communicative activities

1 With a Cantonese-speaking partner, role-play several telephone conversations based on the dialogues in this lesson. Call and invite your partner to a concert or a movie or see if a certain manager is in the office.
2 You are planning a party at your house. Play the role of the host while your partner plays the various friends as you call to invite them. Switch roles and try again.

## Cultural points

### Cell phones and numbers

Hong Kong and China generally are passionate about mobile (cell) phones. You will find more models of phones in Hong Kong than in almost any other place in the world. The choice of phone number is quite important, particularly in business. For example, the number eight (八 **baat**) is considered lucky and therefore highly desirable in a phone number, because it sounds a little like the word for prosper (發 **faat**). In contrast, the number four (四 **sei**) is undesirable, because it sounds a little like the word for death (死 **séi**). This practice of number selection extends to all sorts of domains in Chinese culture. A license plate with eights can command huge sums in government auctions, flight numbers to and from China often contain 8, and the opening ceremony of the 2008 Summer Olympics in Beijing began at 8 seconds and 8 minutes past 8 p.m. (local time) on August 8, 2008.

### Visiting a Chinese home

Visiting a Chinese home for dinner or for other formal activities invokes certain customs. It is considered polite to bring a gift or certain foods. Traditionally, it has been common to bring nicely packaged seasonal fruit (but for reasons mentioned above, never *four* of anything!). It is also common to bring a gift box of imported chocolates or similar items. Many supermarkets often have sections just for gifts of this sort, including special gift bags. During holiday seasons, such as the mid-autumn festival, you might bring a special item like moon cake.

# Translations of dialogues

## Unit 6

**1**

CARMEN: Mrs. Lam, your furniture is really beautiful.
MRS. LAM: Thank you. I like my furniture very much too.
CARMEN: How much did this sofa cost?
MRS. LAM: I bought this sofa for $12,500.
CARMEN: So, how about the dining table?
MRS. LAM: The dining table cost $7,000. The dining chairs were $800 each.
JOHN: I especially like this coffee table. How much was it?
MRS. LAM: The coffee table cost $4,600.

**2**

JOHN: Jack, I would like to buy a decent tennis racket. About how much would one cost?
JACK: A decent tennis racket would cost about $1,000.
JOHN: So how about a nice pair of running shoes? How much would they cost?
JACK: A pair of running shoes would cost about $500.
CARMEN: I would like to buy a bicycle. How much would that cost?
JACK: A good bicycle would cost about $8,000.

**3**

KATHY: BAAK Yu Ping, is sending a letter in Hong Kong expensive?
BAAK YU PING: Sending a letter in Hong Kong is quite cheap.
KATHY: So how much is it to send a letter?
BAAK YU PING: Sending a local letter costs only $1.40.

KATHY: That is really cheap! So how much would it cost to send a postcard to the U.S.?
BAAK YU PING: Sending a postcard to the U.S. would cost $2.40. To send a letter to the U.S. would cost $3.00 each.
KATHY: So how about a surface letter? How much would that cost?
BAAK YU PING: Sending a surface letter would be cheaper—$2.00 each.

## Unit 7

1

EMILY: Carmen, how do you get to work in the morning?
CARMEN: I usually take the subway to work.
EMILY: So how long does it take to go by subway?
CARMEN: It takes about 45 minutes.
EMILY: Does it really take as long as 45 minutes?
CARMEN: It does.
EMILY: So how about you, John? What means of transportation do you take to go to work?
JOHN: I drive to work.
EMILY: So how long does it take by car?
JOHN: It takes about 25 minutes by car. What about you Emily? How do you get to work?
EMILY: I don't need to take any means of transportation. I walk to work. I walk for half an hour and that's all it takes.
CARMEN: That is pretty quick!

2

HO SYUT HWA: Jack, where do you live?
JACK: I live on an outlying island.
HO SYUT HWA: So do you need to take a ferry to work?
JACK: Yes.
HO SYUT HWA: So how long does the ferry take?
JACK: The ferry takes an hour and ten minutes. So how about you, HO Syut Hwa? How do you get to work?
HO SYUT HWA: I usually take a taxi to work. It takes about ten minutes and I am there.

## 3

JOHN: Richard, do you need to commute to work?
RICHARD: Yes, I do. I have to take the subway and a bus to work.
JOHN: So how long does it take?
RICHARD: I leave home at 8 a.m., and then walk 10 minutes to the subway station. Then I take a half-hour subway ride and afterwards a 20-minute bus ride. I arrive at work about 9 a.m.
JOHN: So how long does it take altogether?
RICHARD: From home to the office it takes about an hour.

## 4

MRS. WONG: Mrs. Lam, how do you get to school in the morning?
MRS. LAM: I live far away. It takes an hour for me to get to the school. I have to walk for 10 minutes first to get to the train station, then I take a 25-minute train ride and transfer to the subway for 20 minutes. Finally, I have to walk another 10 minutes and only then do I arrive at the school.
MRS. WONG: So it really does take a whole hour (to get to work)!

# Unit 8

## 1

JOHN: Mrs. Lam, your house is quite large.
MRS. LAM: Yes, I suppose it is quite large.
JOHN: So how many rooms does it have in all?
MRS. LAM: In all it has two large rooms and four smaller rooms: a sitting room, a dining room, three bedrooms, and a study. It also has a kitchen, two bathrooms, and a domestic worker's room.
CARMEN: So how many people are in your family in all?
MRS. LAM: There are six people altogether. My husband and I, my mother and father, as well as my son Kenny and daughter Angel.
CARMEN: How old are Kenny and Angel?
MRS. LAM: Kenny is eight years old and Angel is seven.

## 2

| | |
|---|---|
| JOHN: | Mrs. Lam, where is your husband? |
| MRS. LAM: | My husband is still at his office. He is having a meeting. I'm sure he will be back at 7. |
| JOHN: | And what about your father and mother? |
| MRS. LAM: | My mother is in the kitchen cooking and my father is in his room watching television. |
| CARMEN: | And what about Kenny and Angel? |
| MRS. LAM: | Kenny went swimming and Angel is at school. |
| CARMEN: | Where did Kenny go swimming? |
| MRS. LAM: | He went swimming at the pool. |
| JOHN: | So what is Angel doing at the school? |
| MRS. LAM: | Angel went to the school to sing. They will return home around 6:30. |

# Unit 9

## 1

| | |
|---|---|
| MRS. LAM: | Angel, your clothes aren't washed yet. Can you wash them for me? |
| ANGEL: | No mom! I have to go swimming. |
| MRS. LAM: | So how about you, Kenny? Will you help me wash the clothes, OK? |
| KENNY: | OK. No problem. |

## 2

| | |
|---|---|
| MRS. LAM: | Kenny, can you help to clear the table? |
| KENNY: | OK. |
| MRS. LAM: | And Angel, can you please wash the dishes? |
| ANGEL: | OK, I'll wash (the dishes). |
| MRS. LAM: | So George, can you empty the trash bin? |
| MR. LAM: | I can. |

## 3

| | |
|---|---|
| MR. LAM: | I am looking for someone to type several letters for me. Who is free? |
| VICKY: | I have time. I can do it for you, Mr. Lam. |

## Translations of dialogues

MR. LAM: Thanks, Vicky. Is there anyone who can help me do some photocopying?
WONG PUI WAN: I'll help you make copies, Mr. Lam.
MR. LAM: Thank you so much, WONG Pui Wan.
WONG PUI WAN: You are welcome.

### 4

MRS. LAM: There is a lot of ironing to be done. Who can help get the clothes ironed? Kenny, how about you?
KENNY: No, I am watching soccer. How about Angel?
ANGEL: OK. I will help you iron.
MRS. LAM: Thanks, Angel. Another thing, the floor is dirty, who can help sweep?
MR. LAM: I can help sweep.
MRS. LAM: Thanks, George. So Kenny, when will you finish watching soccer?
KENNY: There are still fifteen more minutes to go and then I'll finish watching it.
MRS. LAM: So when you have finished watching soccer, help me clean the windows, all right?
KENNY: All right, no problem.

## Unit 10

### 1

SALLY: Mom, my handbag is missing. Do you know where my handbag is?
MRS. CHAN: Look! Your handbag is on the sofa.
SALLY: Oh, right. So how about my gloves? I can't find them.
MRS. CHAN: Your gloves are on the easy chair. Do you see them?
SALLY: I can see them now. Thanks, mom.

### 2

MR. CHAN: I can't find my eyeglasses!
MRS. CHAN: Look! Aren't those your glasses on the coffee table? Do you see them?
MR. CHAN: Where? ... Oh, I see them. On the coffee table, as you said.

| | |
|---|---|
| SYLVAN: | Mom, have you seen my comb? I've lost it. |
| MRS. CHAN: | Did you say your comb? Look! Isn't that your comb on top of the television? |
| SYLVAN: | Oh, right. What about my socks? Have you seen them? |
| MRS. CHAN: | Your socks are on the floor. Look, under the dining table. |
| SYLVAN: | I see them now. Thanks, mom. |

### 3

| | |
|---|---|
| AUNTIE KATE: | Sally, I want to buy a pair of shoes. Do you know where I can find a shoe store is? |
| SALLY: | I know there is a shoe store opposite the subway station. The shoes are really nice there. |
| AUNTIE KATE: | So is the shoe store close to here? |
| SALLY: | Very close. It is just a walk of about ten minutes. |
| AUNTIE KATE: | So is there a dress shop nearby? I also want to buy some clothes. |
| SALLY: | There is one, it's diagonally across from the shoe store. |
| AUNTIE KATE: | That's great! |

### 4

| | |
|---|---|
| AUNTIE KATE: | Sylvan, I want to go see a movie. Where is the nearest theater to your house? |
| SYLVAN: | The nearest movie theater to here is the Capitol Cinema. Even so it's quite far away. It takes about 25 minutes to walk there. |
| AUNTIE KATE: | So how long would it take by taxi? |
| SYLVAN: | It is fast by taxi, ten minutes and you are there. |

## Unit 11

### 1

| | |
|---|---|
| WAITER: | Sir, what would you like to eat? |
| JOHN: | A bowl of won-ton noodles please and a bowl of congee with mixed meat. |
| WAITER: | Good. One bowl of won-ton noodles and one bowl of congee with mixed meat. Would you like a plate of |

| | |
|---|---|
| | **yauchoi** (vegetables with oyster sauce) as well? The choisum is excellent today. |
| JOHN: | Excellent. I would like a plate of **yauchoi** too then. |

(*Some time later.*)

| | |
|---|---|
| JOHN: | Waiter, the bill please. |
| WAITER: | That will be a total of $28. Please pay at the front. |

## 2

| | |
|---|---|
| WAITER: | Sir, how many are there (in your party)? |
| MR. LAM: | Four, please. |
| WAITER: | Four? This way. |
| MR. LAM: | OK, thank you. |
| WAITER: | What tea would you like to drink? |
| MRS. LAM: | A pot of jasmine tea please and a pot of Pu-erh tea. |

(*After a few minutes the waiter comes back with the teas.*)

| | |
|---|---|
| WAITER: | A pot of jasmine and a pot of Pu-erh. What kind of **dímsām** would you like? |
| MRS. LAM: | Two baskets of Hagaau, one basket of Siumaai, and two baskets of Chasiubaau. |
| KENNY: | I would also like a plate of custard tarts. |
| ANGEL: | And a basket of Fangwo. |
| WAITER: | Very good. Two baskets of Hagaau, one basket of Siumaai, one basket of Fangwo, two baskets of Chasiubaau, and one plate of custard tarts. |

(*Some time later the Lams are ready to go.*)

| | |
|---|---|
| MR. LAM: | Waiter, the bill please. |
| WAITER: | Very good. |

(*The waiter returns.*)

| | |
|---|---|
| WAITER: | $192 please. |
| MR. LAM: | Here is $200. Keep the change. |
| WAITER: | Thank you. |

## 3

| | |
|---|---|
| SALESPERSON: | Welcome. |
| CARMEN: | One cheeseburger, one large French fries, and one small cola please. |
| SALESPERSON: | To eat here or take away? |

| | |
|---|---|
| CARMEN: | To take away. |
| SALESPERSON: | $17.50 please. |
| CARMEN: | Here is $20. |
| SALESPERSON: | Thank you. Your change is $2.50. |
| CARMEN: | Thank you. |

### 4

| | |
|---|---|
| LEIH MAN CHUNG: | Carmen, do you like Japanese food? |
| CARMEN: | I do. I like eating Japanese food. |
| LEIH MAN CHUNG: | So is Japanese food your favorite? |
| CARMEN: | No, it isn't. I really like Chinese food. |
| LEIH MAN CHUNG: | So which do you like more? |
| CARMEN: | Between Japanese and Chinese food, I like Chinese food better. How about you, LEIH Man Chung? |
| LEIH MAN CHUNG: | I don't like Japanese food. I like French and Chinese food, but I like French food better than Chinese food. |
| CARMEN: | So you are just like John. John likes French the best too. |

## Unit 12

### 1

| | |
|---|---|
| PAUL: | Peter, how is the weather in New Zealand right now? |
| PETER: | New Zealand is quite cold right now—it's about 10°C, but nice and sunny. So how about Hong Kong? |
| PAUL: | Hong Kong is really hot right now—about 30°C. It is really humid and not very comfortable. |

### 2

| | |
|---|---|
| FORECASTER: | It is predicted that winds will be northerly tomorrow. The weather will be cold with light rain. The high will be around 15°C and the low around 11°C. |

### 3

| | |
|---|---|
| JIMMY: | Merry Christmas! |
| OSCAR: | Merry Christmas! |

# Translations of dialogues

| | |
|---|---|
| JIMMY: | Oscar, how is the weather in New York right now? |
| OSCAR: | New York is really cold right now. It is snowing and about −20°C. |
| JIMMY: | So do I need to bring more clothes? |
| OSCAR: | It might be best to bring more (clothes). |
| JIMMY: | OK. |
| OSCAR: | But don't bring too many clothes because it will get warm again next week. |
| JIMMY: | OK. See you tomorrow, then. |
| OSCAR: | OK. Have a good flight. |

## 4

| | |
|---|---|
| WEATHER FORECASTER: | It is predicted that today's weather will be cold and rainy. Everyone must remember to put on more clothes when going out and to bring their umbrellas. Also, it is currently raining so everyone has to drive carefully. |

# Unit 13

## 1

| | |
|---|---|
| JOHN: | Wow! You bought so many things? |
| CHAN SYUT WAI: | I have. Things are so cheap. |
| EMILY: | Yes. Look. I bought two blouses, two skirts, and a pair of shoes. |
| JOHN: | And what about you, CHAN Syut Wai? What did you buy? |
| CHAN SYUT WAI: | I bought a (women's) suit, a jacket, and two blouses. Do you think they are pretty? |
| JOHN: | They are quite pretty! |
| CHAN SYUT WAI: | Also, I bought something for you. |
| JOHN: | What is it? |
| CHAN SYUT WAI: | I bought a tie for you. Do you like it? |
| JOHN: | I do. Thanks. |

## 2

| | |
|---|---|
| CARMEN: | Hey, who is the one wearing the overcoat and a hat? |
| JOHN: | The one wearing a hat is Ben, our boss. |
| CARMEN: | So that is Ben? Who is the heavier one wearing a scarf? |

JOHN: The one wearing a scarf is Teddy. The one next to Teddy wearing a skirt and high heels is his wife.
CARMEN: Oh, so that is Teddy's wife?
JOHN: Right. The one wearing high heels and with long hair is Teddy's wife.

### 3

ELZA: Sam, what do you usually wear to work?
SAM: I teach at a university so I don't need to dress up too much. I usually wear a shirt and slacks.
ELZA: Do you need to wear a tie?
SAM: I don't necessarily have to wear a tie. But when it gets colder in the winter I usually wear a tie, and when it is hot in the summer I rarely wear one. And how about you, Elza? Do you have to dress up for work?
ELZA: I do. I work in a bank and so I have to wear a skirt and high heels. During the winter I usually wear a suit. But when I am on vacation and don't need to go to work, I wear a T-shirt, jeans, and casual shoes—it is more comfortable that way.

## Unit 14

### 1

RICHARD: John, have you ever been to China?
JOHN: I have been to China.
RICHARD: So how many times have you been to China?
JOHN: I have been twice.
RICHARD: When did you go?
JOHN: I went once the year before last, and once last year. How about you? Have you been to China?
RICHARD: I have never been to China, but I have been to Taiwan twice.
JOHN: When did you go to Taiwan?
RICHARD: I went to Taiwan last month.

### 2

HO SYUT HWA: CHAN Syut Wai, have you been swimming this year?

# Translations of dialogues

CHAN SYUT WAI: No, I have not been swimming this year. The weather this year has been too cold, but I have played tennis a few times. How about you, HO Syut Hwa? Have you done any sports this year?

HO SYUT HWA: No. I have been very busy this year. I haven't had time to do sports, so I haven't been swimming or played tennis.

### 3

PETER: John, you went to the United States last month, didn't you?
JOHN: I did. I have just come back from the United States.
PETER: Where did you go in the U.S.?
JOHN: I went to San Francisco and Los Angeles. I went to visit friends.
PETER: How long did you stay in San Francisco?
JOHN: I was in San Francisco for five days.
PETER: So how about Los Angeles? How many days did you stay in Los Angeles?
JOHN: I stayed in Los Angeles for six days.

### 4

JIMMY: William, you've been to Japan, haven't you?
WILLIAM: I have.
JIMMY: When did you go?
WILLIAM: I went the year before last.
JIMMY: So did you like Japan?
WILLIAM: I really liked Japan. The scenery in Japan is really beautiful. It is very clean everywhere, the people are nice and very polite. However, shopping is really expensive.
JIMMY: Is the food tasty?
WILLIAM: It is just OK and it is really expensive.

# Unit 15

### 1

MR. WONG: Hello, can I speak to CHAN Wing Sang, please.
JIMMY: Sorry, CHAN Wing Sang is not in at the moment. May I ask who is calling?

MR. WONG: I am Mr. Wong. Who is this?
JIMMY: I am CHAN Wing Sang's colleague Jimmy. Would you like to leave a message, Mr. Wong?
MR. WONG: OK. Please ask him to return my call. My phone number is 3603678.
JIMMY: 3603678. OK, I will have CHAN Wing Sang return your call then.
MR. WONG: OK, thank you so much, Jimmy.
JIMMY: Bye-bye.
MR. WONG: Bye-bye.

## 2

JOHN: Hello.
SUSAN: Hello, is Carmen in, please?
JOHN: Sorry, Carmen has gone out. May I ask who is calling?
SUSAN: This is Susan. Is that John?
JOHN: Yes.
SUSAN: John, may I leave a message for Carmen?
JOHN: Yes, you may. What is it?
SUSAN: Please tell Carmen that if it rains tomorrow, we won't be playing tennis.
JOHN: OK. I will tell her then. Does Carmen need to return your call?
SUSAN: No, that is not necessary.
JOHN: OK. Goodbye.
SUSAN: Goodbye.

## 3

JOHN: Hello.
RICHARD: Hello, is that John?
JOHN: Yes, this is John.
RICHARD: This is Richard. John, are you free tomorrow night? Are you interested in seeing a movie?
JOHN: I am free. What time is the movie?
RICHARD: I don't know. Let me go online and check the times.

*(Richard comes back on the phone after finding the show times online.)*

RICHARD: Hello. John, there is both a 7 p.m. and a 10 p.m. showing tomorrow night. Which do you want to see?

## Translations of dialogues

JOHN: How about the 7 p.m. showing?
RICHARD: OK. I'll text you when I get to the theater.
JOHN: Great. I'll see you tomorrow.
RICHARD: See you tomorrow.

## 4

LINDA: Hello.
WILLIAM: Hello. Linda, this is William.
LINDA: William, how are you doing?
WILLIAM: Pretty well. I want to get a cell phone, and I want to ask you which phone company and cell phone plan you think is the best. Which plan do you and your (older) brother have?
LINDA: I am using a monthly plan from Hong Kong Telecom and my brother has a prepaid card.
WILLIAM: How many minutes do you have each month? Can you go on the Internet?
LINDA: My plan has 1,200 minutes a month, including unlimited texting and the cell phone already has WiFi.
WILLIAM: How about your brother's?
LINDA: His prepaid card is $0.06 per minute, he needs to add a value of at least $50 each time, but his phone doesn't have WiFi. His plan is much cheaper.
WILLIAM: I think that I will buy the prepaid plan then. Thanks for your help.
LINDA: No problem.

# Key to the exercises

## Unit 1

Dialogues

**1** (a) New Zealand. (b) The U.S. **2** (a) Australia. (b) English and German. (c) Canada. (d) English and French. **3** (a) Japan. (b) Japanese, English, and Putonghua (Mandarin).

Exercise 1

(a) (i). (b) (i). (c) (ii). (d) (ii).

Exercise 3

(b) Kéuih giujouh Pierre Gagnon. Kéuih haih Faatgwok yàhn. Kéuih sīk góng Faatmán tùhng Sāibāanngàhmán. (c) Kéuih giujouh Paola Giannini. Kéuih haih Yidaaihleih yàhn. Kéuih sīk góng Yidaaihleihmán, Faatmán tùhng Yīngmán. (d) Kéuih giujouh Kim Yoo Sung. Kéuih haih Hòhngwok yàhn. Kéuih sīk góng Hòhnmán, Yahtmán tùhng Yīngmán.

Exercise 4

**Raul**: Filipino; speaks English, Spanish, and Tagalog. **Jane**: Australian; speaks English, French, and Italian. **Bruce**: American; speaks English, German, French, and Spanish. **Antonia**: Canadian; speaks English, French, and Italian. (a) 4. (b) 6. (c) Bruce. (d) English. (e) Spanish and Italian. (f) Tagalog and German.

## Unit 2

Dialogues

**1** (a) Mangoes. (b) 4. (c) $20. **2** (a) Oranges. (b) 6. (c) $15. **3** (a) Grapes. (b) One pound. (c) $20.

# Key to the exercises

## Exercise 1
(a) (i). (b) (iii). (c) (i). (d) (ii).

## Exercise 2
(a) Dī léi ... yāt go. (b) Dī sāigwā ... yāt bohng. (c) Dī muhkgwā ... yāt bohng. (d) Dī bōlòh ... yāt go. (e) Dī laihjī ... yāt bohng.

## Exercise 3
(a) Sei mān yāt bohng. (b) Nǵh mān yāt go. (c) Sahp mān sāam go. (d) Sahp mān sei go. (e) Gáu mān yāt go.

## Exercise 4
(a) (i) Sahp mān sāam go. (ii) Hóu, yāt dā pìhnggwó. (iii) Dōjeh sei-sahp mān lā. (iv) Dōjeh. (b) (i) Sahp yih mān yāt bohng. (ii) Hóu, sāam bohng laihjī. (iii) Dōjeh yih-sahp luhk mān lā. (iv) Jáau fāan sei mān. (v) Dōjeh.

## Exercise 5
(a) Hawker A. (b) $86.

## Exercise 6
Grapes—$15 a pound; kiwifruit—$3 each; apples—$3 each; papayas—$8 a pound; water-melons—$2 a pound; oranges—$10 for 4; pears—$10 for 4.

## Exercise 7
(b) Ngóh yiu yih-sahp go Méihgwok cháang. (c) Ngóh yiu léuhng bohng Méihgwok tàihjí. (d) Ngóh yiu sāam go Fēileuhtbān bōlòh. (e) Ngóh yiu baat go Fēileuhtbān mōnggwó. (f) Ngóh yiu yāt dā (*or* sahp-yih go) Oujāu léi.

# Unit 3

## Dialogues

**1** (a) Swimming, playing tennis, and listening to music. (b) Listening to music, reading, and watching television. **2** (a) Window-shopping and watching movies. (b) He likes watching movies, traveling, and taking pictures, but he doesn't like window-shopping. **3** (a) Once a week. (b) Saturday. **4** (a) About twice a week. (b) About twice a year.

Exercise 1

(b) Kéuih mjūngyi yàuh-séui. (c) Kéuih géi jūngyi tái-syū. (d) Ngóhdeih mhaih géi jūngyi tái-dihnsih. (e) Kéuihdeih mjūngyi cheung-gō.

Exercise 2

Kéuih yauh jūngyi tek-jūkkàuh. Kéuih fùhng sīngkèih-yaht tek-jūkkàuh. Kéuih yauh jūngyi páau-bouh. Kéuih fùhng sīngkèih-sāam tùhng sīngkèih-nǵh páau-bouh. Kéuih yauh jūngyi dá-làahmkàuh. Kéuih fùhng sīngkèih-yih tùhng sīngkèih-sei dá-làahmkàuh. Kéuih yauh jūngyi cháai-dāanchē. Kéuih fùhng sīngkèih-luhk cháai-dāanchē.

Exercise 3

(a) (iii). (b) (iii). (c) (ii).

Exercise 4

(b) Ngóh yāt go láihbaai hàahng léuhng chi gāai. (c) Ngóh yāt go yuht tái léuhng chi hei. (d) Ngóh yāt go láihbaai yàuh sāam chi séui. (e) Ngóh yāt nìhn heui sei chi léuihhàhng.

Exercise 6

Example answer: Emily tùhng WONG Git dōu jūngyi tái-hei.

## Unit 4

### Dialogues

**1** (a) 4:30. (b) 5:30. **2** (a) 7 p.m. (b) 4:30 p.m. (c) 9:30 a.m. **3** (a) 7:15 a.m. (b) 11:30 p.m. (c) John gets up at 8:30 a.m. and goes to bed at about 12 midnight. **4** (a) 9:30 p.m. (b) 6:30 p.m. and 11 p.m. (c) 7:30 p.m. **5** (a) At 6 this evening. (b) At 8:30 this evening. (c) Horse-racing is shown at 9:35 tomorrow evening.

### Quick practice 1

(a) seuhngjau gáu dīm sahp. (b) seuhngjau sahp-yāt dím chāt. (c) seuhngjau sahp dím sei. (d) hahjau nǵh dím sahp-yāt. (e) hahjau luhk dím nǵh. (f) hahjau sāam dím baat. (g) seuhngjau chāt dím bun.

### Quick practice 2

(b) sei dím yāt go jih. (c) sahp dím léuhng go jih. (d) gáu dím sahp go jih. (e) sāam dím gáu go jih.

# Key to the exercises

## Exercise 1

(b) Yìhgā (haih) sāam dím chāt. / Yìhgā (haih) sāam dím sāam-sahp ńgh fān. (c) Yìhgā (haih) gáu dím sahp-baat fān. (d) Yìhgā (haih) sahp-yāt dím ńgh-sahp yih fān. (e) Yìhgā (haih) ńgh dím sāam. / Yìhgā (haih) ńgh dím sahp-ńgh fān. / Yìhgā (haih) ńgh dím yāt go gwāt.

## Exercise 2

(a) (i). (b) (ii). (c) (iv). (d) (ii).

## Exercise 3

(a) ... Kéuih yehmáahn baat dímjūng sihk-máahnfaahn, yìhnhauh sahp-yih dím fan-gaau. (b) Carmen seungjau chāt dím bun héi-sān, gáu dímjūng fāan-gūng. Kéuih hahjau sahp-yih dím bun sihk-ngaan, yìhnhauh ńgh dím sāam fong-gūng. Kéuih yehmáahn baat dímjūng sihk-máahnfaahn, yìhnhauh yāt dímjūng fan-gaau. (c) Richard seungjau chāt dím sāam héi-sān, gáu dímjūng fāan-gūng. Kéuih hahjau yāt dímjūng sihk-ngaan, yìhnhauh ńgh dím bun fong-gūng. Kéuih yehmáahn chāt dímjūng sihk-máahnfaahn, yìhnhauh sahp-yāt dím bun fan-gaau.

## Exercise 4

(a) Gāmmáahn chāt dím yāt tùhng sahp-yāt dím gáu yáuh sānmán tái. (b) Gāmmáahn chāt dím ńgh tùhng sahp-yih dím yih yáuh tīnhéi tái. (c) Yáuh. Gāmmáahn baat dím bun yáuh géiluhkpín tái. (d) Gāmmáahn gáu dím bun yáuh héi tái. (e) Gāmmáahn móuh móhngkàuh tái.

# Unit 5

## Dialogues

**1** (a) John is tall, not too fat and not too thin, and wears glasses. (b) CHAN Syut Wai is fairly thin, not too tall, has short hair, and does not wear glasses. **2** (a) He is tall, thin, wears glasses, has short hair, and is good-looking. (b) She is rather short, has long hair, does not wear glasses, is quite pretty, and looks quite young. **3** (a) Both are 49. (b) 12. (c) 11.

## Exercise 2

(b) 52. (c) 38. (d) 71. (e) 96. (f) 49.

## Exercise 3

From left to right: Li Ming (Chinese), Michael (American), Christine (French), and Judy (English).

## Exercise 4

(b) Martin gāmnín ńgh-sahp yih seui. Kéuih fèih-féi-déi, mhaih géi gōu, daai ngáahngéng, dyún tàuhfaat. (c) Pam gāmnín sei-sahp gáu seui. Kéuih mhaih géi fèih, mhaih géi sau, daai ngáahngéng. (d) Clara gāmnín sahp-chāt seui. Kéuih géi gōu, géi sau, chèuhng tàuhfaat, móuh daai ngáahngéng. Kéuih géi leng ga. (e) Jimmy gāmnín sahp-sāam seui. Kéuih géi ngái, géi sau, daai ngáahngéng, dyún tàuhfaat.

# Unit 6

## Dialogues

**1** (a) $12,500. (b) $7,000; $800 each. (c) $4,600. **2** (a) About $1,000. (b) About $500. (c) About $8,000. **3** (a) $0.80. (b) $2.30. (c) $1.80.

## Quick practice 1

(b) yih-baak ńgh-sahp luhk mān. (c) yāt-chīn chāt-baak baat-sahp gáu mān. (d) ńgh-chīn luhk-baak yih-sahp mān. (e) yāt-maahn ńgh-chīn mān. (f) sāam-maahn chāt-chīn ńgh-baak mān. (g) gáu-sahp sāam maahn chāt-chīn mān. (h) ńgh-sahp-luhk maahn yih-chīn yāt-baak mān. (i) yāt-baak ńgh-sahp yih maahn mān. (j) sei-baak luhk-sahp baat maahn gáu-chīn mān.

## Quick practice 2

(b) yāt-chīn lìhng sāam-sahp mān. (c) yih-maahn chāt-chīn lìhng ńgh mān. (d) ńgh-sahp maahn lìhng sei-baak mān. (e) yāt-baak gáu-sahp maahn lìhng baat-baak mān.

## Quick practice 3

(b) ńgh-baak géi mān. (c) sei-chīn yih-baak géi mān. (d) sāam-maahn luhk-chīn géi mān. (e) sahp-géi maahn mān. (f) gáu-sahp yih maahn géi mān. (g) yāt-baak yih-sahp-géi maahn mān. (h) sei-baak-géi maahn mān.

Key to the exercises 259

## Quick Practice 4

(b) gáu go yāt. (c) nǵh go bun. (d) baat go yih. (e) go sei. (f) luhk hòuhjí.

## Exercise 1

Japan—$12,000; Hawaii—$12,000; Korea—$8,500; the Philippines—$4,000.

## Exercise 2

5 oranges—$12.50; 4 apples—$6.80; 1 water-melon—$14; total—$33.30.

## Exercise 3

(b) Nī jēung chāantói maaih baat-chīn yih-baak nǵh-sahp mān. (c) Dī chāanyih gáu-baak yāt-sahp mān yāt jēung. (d) Jēung sōfá chāt-chīn baat-baak mān. (e) Nī jēung ōnlohkyí yāt-chīn lìhng nǵh-sahp mān.

## Exercise 4

(b) Chris jeui ngái. (c) Diana jeui sau. (d) Chris jeui fèih. (e) Sally fèih-dī. (f) Raul sau-dī. (g) Elsie yáuh daai ngáahngéng. (h) Terry yáuh wùsōu.

## Exercise 5

(b) Méihgwok pìhnggwó sāam mān yāt go. (c) Jūnggwok pìhnggwó léuhng mān yāt go. (d) Yahtbún pìhnggwó y'ah-nǵh mān yāt go. (e) Jūnggwok pìhnggwó jeui pèhng. (f) Yahtbún pìhnggwó jeui gwai. (g) Méihgwok pìhnggwó pèhng-dī.

## Exercise 6

(b) Carmen sau-gwo Emily. (c) Nī jēung chàhgēi dái-gwo go jēung. (d) Go jēung chāanyí leng-dī. (e) Ngóh go móhngkàuhpáak gwai-dī. (f) Nī jēung sōfá jeui pèhng. (g) Carmen ga dāanchē jeui dái.

# Unit 7

## Dialogues

**1** (a) The subway; 45 minutes. (b) He drives; 25 minutes. (c) On foot; 30 minutes. **2** (a) By ferry; 1 hour 10 minutes. (b) By taxi; 10 minutes.

**3** (a) 2. (b) 10 minutes. (c) 30 minutes. (d) 20 minutes. (e) 1 hour.
**4** (a) over 1 hour. (b) 10 minutes. (c) 25 minutes. (d) 20 minutes. (e) 10 minutes.

### Exercise 1

(b) sāam-sahp luhk fānjūng. (c) sei-sahp ńgh fānjūng *or* gáu go jih. (d) ńgh-sahp ńgh fānjūng *or* sahp-yāt go jih. (e) yāt go jūngtàuh ńgh-sahp fānjūng *or* yāt go jūngtàuh sahp go jih. (f) léuhng go jūngtàuh chāt fānjūng.

### Exercise 2

**Jim**: Home → walk (15 minutes) → ferry (50 minutes) → walk (10 minutes) → office.
**Bill**: Home → walk (5 minutes) → bus (15 minutes) → MTR (30 minutes) → office.

### Exercise 3

(b) ńgh go jūngtàuh ńgh-sahp ńgh fānjūng. (c) luhk yaht. (d) yāt go sīngkèih/láihbaai lìhng sei yaht. (e) sāam go yuht. (f) léuhng nìhn lìhng sahp-yāt go yuht.

### Exercise 4

(b) léuhng go bun jūngtàuh. (c) sei go bun jūngtàuh. (d) ńgh yaht bun. (e) gáu go bun sīngkèih/láihbaai. (f) chāt go bun yuht. (g) ńgh nìhn lìhng luhk go yuht.

### Exercise 6

(c) Ngóh hàahng sei go jih jauh fāan dou gūngsī *laak*. (d) Ngóh yiu hàahng sei go jih *sīnji* fāan dou gūngsī *a*. (e) Ngóh daap ńgh sahp fānjūng fóchē, joi hàahng sāam go jih, jauh fāan dou gūngsī *laak*. (f) Ngóh yiu daap ńgh sahp fānjūng fóchē, joi hàahng sāam go jih, sīnji fāan dou gūngsī *a*.

### Exercise 7

**1** (i) Daap-féigéi yiu yēt chìhn yih-baak yāt sahp mān. (ii) Yiu daap sāam-sahp fānjūng. (iii) Daap-syùhn yiu yāt-baak sei-sahp chāt mān. (iv) Daap-syùhn yiu yāt go jūngtàuh sei-sahp ńgh fānjūng. **2** (i) Daap-bāsí pèhng-dī. Daap-fóchē yiu yāt-baak gáu-sahp mān, daap-bāsí yiu baat sahp mān jēk. (ii) Daap-fóchē yiu léuhng go jūngtàuh gáu go jih,

*Key to the exercises* 261

daap-bāsí jauh yiu sāam go jūngtàuh laak. (iii) Daap-syùhn yiu yāt-baak sei-sahp chāt mān, yiu daap yāt go jūngtàuh sei go jih. **3** Daap-féigéi jeui dái.

# Unit 8

## Dialogues

**1** (a) 6: 1 sitting room, 1 dining room, 3 bedrooms and 1 study. (b) 6: Mrs. Lam and her husband, her parents, her son Kenny and her daughter Angel. (c) Kenny is eight and Angel is seven. **2** (a) Mr. Lam is still at the office. (b) He is in his room. (c) She is in the kitchen. (d) Kenny has gone to the swimming pool. (e) Angel has gone to her school.

## Exercise 1

(b) HO Syut Hwa jyú-gán faahn. (c) Kéuih cheung-gán gō. (d) Kéuih dá-gán làahmkàuh. (e) Kéuih tái-gán dihnsih.

## Exercise 2

(a) He is having a meeting. (b) He is watching television. (c) She is cooking. (d) He is swimming. (e) She is singing.

## Exercise 3

(b) Ngóh daap deihtit fāan-gūng. (c) Kéuih jūngyi tái-héi. (d) Ngóh múihfùhng láihbaai-yih dá-móhngkàuh. (e) Ngóh màh-mā fan-gán gaau. (f) Ngóh bàh-bā jūngyi tēng-yāmngohk. (g) Ngóh taai-táai jūngyi jyúh-yéhsihk. (h) Ngóh jèh-jē wáan-gán yàuhheigēi.

## Exercise 4

(a) Ngóhdeih gāan ngūk yáuh yāt go haaktēng, yāt go faahntēng, léuhng gāan seuihfóng, yāt go chyùhfóng tùhng yūt go chisó. (b) Ngóhdeih gāan ngūk yáuh yāt go haaktēng, yāt go faahntēng, sāam gāan seuihfóng, sāam gāan chūnglèuhngfóng, yāt go chyùhfóng tùhng yāt gāan gūngyàhnfóng.

## Exercise 5

(a) Chàhn sīnsāang hái faahntēng yám-gán bējáu. (b) Kéuih hái haaktēng tái-gán dihnsih. (c) Kéuih hái haaktēng tái-gán syū.

## Exercise 6

(a) Kéuih heui-jó hàahng-gāai. (b) Kéuih heui-jó tái-jūkkàuh. (c) Kenny heui-jó dá-móhngkàuh. (d) Angel heui-jó tēng-yāmngohk.

# Unit 9

## Dialogues

**1** (a) Washing clothes. (b) Kenny. **2** (a) Kenny. (b) Angel. (c) Mr. Lam. **3** (a) Vicky. (b) WONG Pui Wan. **4** (a) Angel. (b) Mr. Lam. (c) Kenny.

## Exercise 1

| | |
|---|---|
| making the beds | ✓ |
| washing the dishes | ✓ |
| buying food for dinner | ✗ |
| washing the clothes | ✗ |
| hanging the clothes out | ✓ |
| vacuum-cleaning | ✓ |
| cleaning the windows | ✓ |

## Exercise 2

(a) Néih hó-mh-hóyíh bōng ngóh dá léuhng fūng seun a? (b) Gám, hó-mh-hóyíh bōng ngóh je sāam bún syū a? (c) Dāk, móuh mahntàih. (d) Gám, tùhng ngóh máaih jēung fóchēfēi, dāk-mh-dāk? (e) Hóu aak. (f) Msái mgōi.

## Exercise 3

(a) Ngóh dōu mdākhàahn a. Ngóh wáan-gán yàuhheigēi a. (b) Deui mjyuh. Ngóh dōu mdāk a. Ngóh tái-gán boují a.

# Unit 10

## Dialogues

**1** (a) On the sofa. (b) On the easy chair. **2** (a) On the coffee table. (b) On the television set. (c) On the floor under the dining table. **3** (a) Opposite the subway station. (b) About 10 minutes' walk away. (c) Diagonally across from the shoe store. **4** (a) Capitol Cinema. (b) About 25 minutes. (c) 10 minutes.

# Key to the exercises

## Exercise 1

(b) Bá jē hái sōfá gaaklèih. (c) Go ngáahngéng hái deihhá seuhngmihn. (d) Go chàhbūi hái syūgá seuhngmihn. (e) Deui tōháai hái chàhgēi hahmihn. (f) Go séuibūi hái dihnsih gei seuhngmihn. (g) Jī bāt hái séuibūi tùhng chàhbūi jūnggāan.

## Exercise 2

(a) bookstore—next to supermarket, opposite flower shop; drugstore—diagonally across from bookstore, next to flower shop; electrical appliance store—diagonally across from movie theater, next to shoe shop; bakery—opposite movie theater, next to supermarket; sweet shop—between movie theater and dress shop.

## Exercise 3

Hái sōfá seuhngmihn yáuh yāt go sáudói, yāt jek maht, yāt jek sáumaht, tùhng yāt bá jē. Hái sōfá gaaklèih ge deihhá yáuh yāt go ngàhnbāau, yāt bá sō, yāt jek tōháai. Hái dihnsihgēi seuhngmihn yáuh yāt go séuibūi. Hái dihnsihgēi gaaklèih ge deihhá yáuh yāt jek chàhbūi, léuhng jī bāt, tùhng sāam béng luhkyíngdáai. Dihnsihgēi hahmihn go luhkyínggēi mgin-jó.

## Exercise 4

(a) Tim Tim jeui káhn. (b) Mhaih. (c) Wing Sing jeui daaih. (d) Dōu msyun hóu yúhn, daaihyeuk yiu hàahng sāam go jih. (e) Yáuh léuhng gāan, Quicken tùhng Good Foot. (f) Quicken káhn-dī. (g) Hàahng léuhng go jih jauh dou laak.

# Unit 11

## Dialogues

**1** (a) A bowl of won-ton noodles and a bowl of congee with mixed meat. (b) A plate of vegetables with oyster sauce (Yauchoi). (c) $28. **2** (a) A pot of jasmine tea and a pot of Pu-erh tea. (b) 2 baskets of shrimp dumplings (Hagaau), 1 basket of pork dumplings (Siumaai), 2 baskets of barbecued-pork buns (Chasiubaau), 1 basket of shrimp and bamboo-shoot dumplings (Fangwo), and a plate of custard tarts (Daahntaat). (c) $192. (d) $200. **3** (a) 1 cheeseburger, 1 large French fries, and 1 small cola. (b) Taking away. (c) $17.50. **4** (a) Chinese food. (b) French food. (c) French food.

## Exercise 1

**Food**: 2 hamburgers, 3 hot-dogs, 2 large French fries. **Drinks**: 2 cups of tea, 2 cups of coffee, and 1 orange juice.

## Exercise 2

Richard's favorite place: India. Carmen's: China. John's: Japan.

## Exercise 3

(a) Sāam wún yùhdáanmihn y'ah sei mān, léuhng dihp yàuhchoi sahp-yih mān, yāt wún gahpdáijūk jauh sahp-yāt mān. Júngguhng sei'ah chāt mān lā. (b) Jáau fāan ngh'ah sāam mān. (c) Dōjeh. (d) Sei wún wàhntānmihn, sā'ah luhk mān, léuhng wún yùhdáanmihn, sahp-luhk mān, sāam wún ngàuhyuhkjūk, sā'ah mān, léuhng dihp yàuhchoi, sahp-yih mān. Júngguhng gáu'ah sei mān lā. (e) Jáau fāan sei-baak lìhng luhk mān. (f) Dōjeh.

## Exercise 5

(b) Ngóh bàh-bā jūngyi heui yám-chàh dō-gwo heui tái-hei. *or* Heui yám-chàh tùhng heui tái-hei, ngóh bàh-bā jūngyi heui yám-chàh dō-dī. *or* Heui yám-chàh tùhng heui tái-hei, ngóh bàh-bā béigaau jūngyi heui yám-chàh. (c) Ngóh gòh-gō jūngyi dá-làahmkàuh dō-gwo dá-móhng-kàuh. *or* Dá-làahmkàuh tùhng dá-móhngkàuh, ngóh gòh-gō jūngyi dá-làahmkàuh dō-dī. *or* Dá-làahmkàuh tùhng dá-móhngkàuh, ngóh gòh-go béigaau jūngyi dá-làahmkàuh. (d) Kéuih màhmā jūngyi tēng-sāuyāmgēi dō-gwo tái-dihnsih. *or* Tēng-sāuyāmgēi tùhng tái-dihnsih, kéuih màh-mā jūngyi tēng-sāuyāmgēi dō-dī. *or* Tēng-sāuyāmgēi tùhng tái-dihnsih, kéuih màh-mā béigaau jūngyi tēng-sāuyāmgēi. (e) Ngóh mùih-múi jūngyi hohk-Faatmán dō-gwo hohk-Dākmán. *or* Hohk Faatmán tùhng hohk-Dākmán, ngóh mùih-múi jūngyi hohk-Faatmán dō-dī. *or* Hohk-Faatmán tùhng hohk-Dākmán, ngóh mùih-múi béigaau jūngyi hohk-Faatmán.

# Unit 12

## Dialogues

**1** (a) Quite cold, with temperatures around 10°C, but fine. (b) Very hot, around 30°C, very humid. **2** (a) Cold, with northerly winds and light rain. (b) Yes. (c) 15°C; 11°C. **3** (a) Very cold, with snow. (b) Around

−20°C. (c) Warmer. (d) To bring more clothes but not too many.
**4** (a) Cold and rainy. (b) To wear more clothes. (c) To drive carefully.

### Exercise 1

Hot and humid; 32°C; 28°C; 78%–89%.

### Exercise 2

(a) Seuhnghói yāt-yuht dōu géi dung a. Heiwān lìhng douh ji baat dou. (b) Yiu a. (c) Seuhnghói yāt-yuht mhaih géi dō yúh lohk, hóyíh mdaai jē. (d) Gwóngjāu sei-yuht béigaau nyúhn, tùhngmàaih wúih lohk-yúh. (e) Heiwān daaihyeuk sahp-baat douh ji yih-sahp ńgh douh. (f) Hóu chìusāp. (g) Gwóngjāu sahp-yuht wānnyúhn tùhng gōnchou, béigaau syūfuhk. (h) Mhaih géi dō yúh lohk. (i) Msái la.

### Exercise 3

(b) Hauhyaht wúih jyún lèuhng. (c) Hah go láihbaai tīnhei wúih jyún yiht. (d) Sīngkèih-luhk wúih hóu daaihfūng. (e) Sīngkèih-yaht wúih yáuh lèuihbouh. (f) Tīngyaht wúih chìuhsāp.

### Exercise 4

(a) Samuel sahp-houh sīngkèih-sei hái Yīnggwok fāan lèih. (b) Keith jauh sahp-baat-houh sīngkèih-ńgh hái Oujāu fāan lèih. (c) Teresa jauh sahp-sei-houh sīngkèih-yāt fāan Hēunggóng.

## Unit 13

### Dialogues

**1** (a) 2 blouses, 2 skirts, and 1 pair of shoes. (b) 1 suit, 1 jacket, and 2 blouses. (c) A tie. **2** (a) Ben. (b) Teddy. (c) Teddy's wife. **3** (a) A shirt and slacks. (b) Not always. He usually wears one in winter, but not in summer. (c) A skirt and high-heeled shoes, and usually a suit in winter. (d) A T-shirt, jeans, and sports shoes.

### Exercise 1

3 coats, 4 woollen jumpers, 3 scarves, and 5 pairs of gloves.

### Exercise 2

From left to right: Hideki, Hama, Mariko, and Saito.

Exercise 3

Jóbín nī go jeuk fu, laahm-jó génggān, daai-jó sáumaht ge néuihjái haih Sandy. Gaaklèih nī go daai-jó móu, jeuk daaihlāu, daai ngáahngéng ge nàahmjái haih Andy. Nī go dá tāai, laahm-jó génggān ge haih Timmy. Kéuih gaaklèih nī go daai-jó móu tùhng sáumaht ge néuihjái haih Beverly.

## Unit 14

Dialogues

**1** (a) Twice. (b) Last year and the year before last. (c) No. (d) Last month. **2** (a) Yes. (b) It was too cold. (c) Too busy. **3** (a) Last month. (b) San Francisco and Los Angeles. (c) 5 days in San Francisco and 6 in Los Angeles. **4** (a) He likes it very much. (b) The beautiful scenery, the clean surroundings, and the nice, polite people. (c) Shopping and food are very expensive.

Exercise 2

(b) Ngóh chìhn go yuht heui-gwo Yahtbún. (c) Kéuih seuhng go yuht heui-gwo Faatgwok. (d) Kéuih léuhng go yuht chìhn heui-gwo Jūnggwok. (e) Ngóhdeih ńgh nìhn chìhn heui-gwo Tòiwāan. (f) Kéuihdeih sei go láihbaai chìhn heui-gwo Gānàhdaai.

Exercise 3

**Winnie**: 3 times to Europe, twice to the U.S., once to Japan, and once to Australia. **Kitty**: 5 times to China, 4 times to Taiwan, twice to Japan, twice to Europe, the U.S., and Australia. **Sally**: once to India, 3 times to the Philippines, twice to Japan, 4 times to China, 5 times to Taiwan, once to Europe, 4 times to the U.S., 3 times to Canada, 3 times to Australia, and twice to New Zealand. Sally is the most widely traveled girl.

Exercise 4

(b) Ngóh heui-gwo ńgh chi Dākgwok. (c) Ngóh nī go yuht tái-gwo léuhng chi hei. (d) Ngóh nī go láihbaai dá-gwo léuhng chi móhngkàuh. (e) Ngóh gāmnín heui-gwo sei chi léuihhàhng.

# Key to the exercises

## Exercise 5

(a) Ngóhdeih heui-jó Fēileuhtbān, Yandouh, tùhng Tòihwāan ... (b) Ngóhdeih sei-yuht heui Fēileuhtbān ge ... (c) Ngóhdeih heui-jó luhk yaht ... (d) Ngóhdeih juhng yáuh heui Yandouh. Dōu haih sei-yuht heui. Heui-jó baat yaht ... (e) Juhng yáuh, ngóhdeih ńgh-yuht heui-jó luhk yaht Tòihwāan.

## Unit 15

### Dialogues

**1** (a) Mr. Wong. (b) He wants CHAN Wing Sang to ring him back. (c) 3603678. **2** (a) She has gone out. (b) That they will not be playing tennis if it rains tomorrow. (c) No. **3** (a) Going to a movie. (b) John and Richard. (c) John will text Richard when he arrives at the theater. **4** (a) Monthly plan from Hong Kong Telecom. (b) Prepaid card. (c) Prepaid card.

### Exercise 1

(a) Deui mijyuh, Pam mhái douh wo, *or* Deui mijyuh, Pam hàahnghō-jó wo. (b) Pam wah kéuih daaihyeuk sei dím jūng fāan lèih. (c) Dāk, móuh mahntaih. (d) Hóu, ngóh giu kéuih hái ńgh dím jūng chìhn dá fāan dihnwá béi néih. (e) Msái mgōi. Bāai-baai.

### Exercise 2

(a) She has to go to a concert with Peter. (b) She has a class on Wednesday evening. (c) Friday. (d) 7:30 p.m.

### Exercise 3

(a) Mdāk a. Ngóh yiu dá-móhngkàuh a. (b) Sīngkèih-sei máahn ngóh yiu hōi-wúi a. (c) Sīngkèih-yih máahn dōu mdāk wo. Ngóh yiu heui tái-hei. Bātyùh sīngkèih-ńgh ā.

# Cantonese–English glossary

## Abbreviations for grammatical terms

| | |
|---|---|
| adv | adverb |
| adj | adjective |
| asp | aspect marker |
| conj | conjunction |
| cl | classifier |
| dem | demonstrative |
| i | interjection |
| ie | idiomatic expression |
| m | measure |
| mv | modal verb |
| n | noun |
| num | numeral |
| prep | preposition |
| prt | particle |
| prn | pronoun |
| pw | place word |
| qw | question-word |
| tw | time word |
| v | verb |
| v-o | verb-object construction |
| v-prt | verbal particle |

## A

**ā** (*prt*)
**a** (*prt*)
**àh** (*prt*)
**ak** (*prt*)
**ā ma** (*prt*)
**Aujāu** (*pw*) Europe
**A-yī** aunt

## B

**bá** (*cl*) classifier for long slender objects such as combs and umbrellas
**baahksīk** (*adj*) white
**bāai-baai** (*ie*) bye-bye!
**baak** (*num*) hundred
**baakmaahn** (*num*) million
**baat** (*num*) eight
**baat'ah** (*num*) eighty (elided form)
**baat-yuht** (*tw*) August
**bāau** (*n/m*) packet
**bāau** (*v*) to include
**Bāgēisītáan** (*pw*) Pakistan
**Bāgēisītáanwá** (*n*) any of the languages of Pakistan
**bàh-bā** (*n*) father
**bāk** (*adj*) north
**Bākgīng** (*pw*) Beijing/Peking
**Bālàih** (*pw*) Paris
**bāsí** (*n*) bus
**bāsíjaahm** (*n*) bus stop
**bāt** (*n*) pen
**bātgwo** (*conj*) but
**bātyùh** (*ie*) why don't ...?
**béi** (*v*) to give
**béi-chín** (*v-o*) to pay
**béigaau** (*adv*) comparatively
**bējáu** (*n*) beer
**béng** (*cl*) classifier for audio- and video-tapes

# Cantonese–English glossary

| | | |
|---|---|---|
| bīn (+ cl/dem) (qw) | which? | |
| bīndouh (qw) | where? | |
| bīngo (qw) | who? | |
| bīnwái (qw) | who? | |
| bōhàaih (n) | sports shoe | |
| bohng (m) | pound (in weight) | |
| bōlòh (n) | pineapple | |
| bōng(sáu) (v) | to help | |
| bougou (n) | report | |
| boulām (n) | plum | |
| bóuléi (n) | Pu-erh (dark) tea | |
| būi (n/m) | cup | |
| bún (cl) | classifier for books | |
| bun (n) | half | |
| búngóng (adj) | local (in Hong Kong) | |
| bunjihtkwàhn (n) | skirt | |
| bunyeh (tw) | after midnight | |

## C

| | |
|---|---|
| cháai-dāanchē (v-o) | to ride a bicycle |
| chāandang (n) | dining chair |
| cháang (n) | orange |
| cháangjāp (n) | orange juice |
| cháangsīk (adj) | orange (color) |
| chāantói (n) | dining table |
| chāanyí (n) | dining chair |
| chàh (n) | tea |
| chàhbūi (n) | cup |
| chàhgēi (n) | coffee table |
| chàhmmáahn (tw) | yesterday evening, last night |
| chàhmyaht (tw) | yesterday |
| chāsīubāau (n) | steamed barbecued-pork bun |
| chāt (num) | seven |
| chāt'ah (num) | seventy (elided form) |
| chāt-yuht (tw) | July |
| chē (n) | car |
| chēfòhng (n) | garage |
| chèhdeuimihn (adv) | diagonally across the road |
| chéng (v) | to invite |
| chèuhng (adj) | long |
| chēui (v) | to blow |
| chèuihbín (adj) | casual (in dress) |
| chēung (n) | window |
| cheung-gō (v-o) | to sing |
| chēungyún (n) | spring roll |
| chēut (cl) | classifier for movies and documentaries |
| chēut-gāai (v-o) | to go out |
| chēutmihn (adv) | outside |
| chēut-mùhnháu (v-o) | to leave home |
| chi (n) | a time |
| chìhn (adv) | ago, the one (week, month, year, etc.) before last |
| chìhng (adj) | fine (weather) |
| chìhnmihn (adv) | in front (of) |
| chìhnnín (tw) | the year before last |
| chín (n) | money |
| chīn (num) | thousand |
| chīnglèuhng (adj) | cool |
| chíng mahn (ie) | may I ask |
| chisó (n) | toilet |
| Chìuhjāuwá (n) | Chiu Chow dialect |
| chìuhsāp (adj) | humid |
| chīukāp-síhchèuhng (n) | supermarket |
| chòhng (n) | bed |
| choi (n) | food, cuisine |
| choimáh (n) | horse-racing |
| choisām (n) | a Chinese green vegetable, choisum |
| chúhjik kāat (n) | prepaid (phone) card |
| chūng-lèuhng (v-o) | to take a bath/shower |
| chyùhfóng (n) | kitchen |

## D

| | |
|---|---|
| dá (v) | to hit, to type |
| dā (num) | a dozen |
| daahntāat (n) | custard tart |
| daai (v) | to put on (eyeglasses, a cap, a hat, etc.); to take, to bring |
| daaih (adj) | large |
| daaihfūng (adj) | windy |
| daaihgā (prn) | everyone |
| daaihhohk (n) | university |

# Cantonese-English glossary

| | | | |
|---|---|---|---|
| daaihlāu (n) | overcoat | deui (m) | pair |
| daaihlóu (n) | elder brother | deuimihn (adv) | opposite, across the road |
| Daaihwuih-tòhng-Yāmngohk-tēng (pw) | City Hall Concert Hall | deui mjyuh (ie) | Sorry! |
| | | dī (prn) | some |
| | | -dī (prt) | |
| daaihyeuk (adv) | roughly, approximately | dihnchē (n) | streetcar, tram |
| | | dihnchējaahm (n) | streetcar, tram stop |
| dāan (n) | bill | dihng (conj) | or (in questions with two alternatives) |
| dāanchē (n) | bicycle | | |
| daap (v) | to take (a means of transport) | | |
| | | dihnheipóu (n) | electrical appliance store |
| daap cho sin (ie) | wrong number (on the phone) | | |
| | | dihnseun (n) | telecom |
| dá-bō (v-o) | to play a ballgame | dihnsih (n) | television |
| dá-dihnwá (v-o) | to make a phone call | dihnsihgēi (n) | television set |
| dái (adj) | good value | dihnsihkehk (n) | television drama |
| dāi (adj) | low | dihnwá (n) | telephone |
| dàih-dái (n) | younger brother | dihnyíng (n) | movie |
| dá-jih (v-o) | to type | dihp (m) | plate |
| dāk (v-prt) | | dīksí (n) | taxi |
| dāk (adj) | OK, all right | dīksíjaahm (n) | taxi rank |
| Dākgwok (pw) | Germany | dím (qw) | how? |
| dākhàahn (adj) | free, not busy | dim (n) | shop, store |
| Dākmán (n) | German (language) | dím(jūng) (tw) | o'clock |
| dāk-mh-dāk (ie) | is it all right? | dím maaih a? (ie) | what is the price? |
| dá-làahmkàuh (v-o) | to play basketball | dímsām (n) | snacks, generally steamed, served in a tea-house |
| dá-móhngkàuh (v-o) | to play tennis | | |
| | | dímyéung (qw) | what does he/she look like?; how?, what? |
| dáng (v) | to wait | | |
| dang (n) | chair | | |
| dáng ngóh lèih gaaisiuh ... (ie) | let me introduce ... | díp (n) | plate |
| | | dō (adj) | many, much |
| dáng yāt jahn/ dáng (ie) | wait a minute | doihsyú (n) | kangaroo |
| | | dōjeh (ie) | thank you (for a gift) |
| dá-tāai (v-o) | to put on a tie | dōjeh saai (ie) | thank you very much |
| deihhá (n) | floor | | |
| deihtit (n) | subway, underground railway (in Hong Kong, MTR or Mass Transit Railway) | Dōlèuhndō (pw) | Toronto |
| | | dōsou (adv) | mostly |
| | | dóu (v-prt) | |
| | | dōu (adv) | also, still |
| | | dou (prt) | |
| deihtitjaahm (n) | subway (MTR), underground station | douh (adv) | there |
| | | dóu-laahpsaap (v-o) | to empty the trash bin |
| déng (cl) | classifier for headgear | | |

|  |  |
|---|---|
| duhk-syū (v-o) | to study |
| dūng (adj) | east |
| dung (adj) | cold |
| Dūnggīng (pw) | Tokyo |
| dūngtīn (tw) | winter |
| dyún (adj) | short |
| dyúnfu (n) | shorts |
| dyún seuhn (n) | text message |

## F

| | |
|---|---|
| faahntēng (n) | dining room |
| faai (adj) | quick; in a short time |
| fāan (v-prt) | |
| fāan (v) | to return |
| fāan ... (ie) | to work at/in ... |
| fāan-gūng (v-o) | to go to work |
| fāan-hohk (v-o) | to go to school |
| Faatgwok (pw) | France |
| Faatmán (n) | French (language) |
| fādim (n) | flower shop |
| fan-gaau (v-o) | to sleep |
| fān(jūng) (n) | minute |
| fángwó (n) | steamed shrimp and bamboo-shoot dumpling |
| fāyún (n) | garden |
| fēi (n) | ticket |
| fēifaatpóu (n) | barber's shop |
| fēigēi (n) | airplane |
| fēigēichèuhng (n) | airport |
| fèih (adj) | fat |
| Fēileuhtbān (pw) | the Philippines |
| Fēileuhtbānwá (n) | any of the languages of the Philippines |
| fēsīk (adj) | brown |
| fóchē (n) | train |
| fóchējaahm (n) | rail station |
| fógei (n) | waiter |
| fóng (n) | room |
| fōngbihn (adj) | convenient |
| fong-gūng (v-o) | to leave work |
| fu (cl) | classifier for eyeglasses |
| fu (n) | trousers, slacks |
| fuhgahn (adv) | nearby |
| fuhkjōngdim (n) | dress shop |
| fùhng (adv) | whenever |
| fūisīk (adj) | gray |
| fūng (cl) | classifier for a letter |
| fūng (n) | wind |
| fūnggíng (n) | scenery |
| fūngsai kèuhnggihng (adj) | windy |
| fūnyìhng gwōnglàhm (ie) | Welcome! |

## G

| | |
|---|---|
| ga (cl) | classifier for vehicles |
| ga (prt) | |
| gāai (n) | street, road |
| gāaisíh (n) | market |
| gāaiwahk (n) | (call) plan |
| gaaklèih (adv) | beside |
| gāan (cl) | classifier for houses, rooms and shops |
| gaau-syū (v-o) | to teach (in school or university) |
| gāautūng (n) | transportation |
| gafē (n) | coffee |
| gahpdáijūk (n) | congee with mixed meat |
| gājē (n) | elder sister |
| gakèih (n) | holiday |
| ga la (prt) | |
| ga laak (prt) | |
| gám ... (ie) | so ..., then ... |
| gam (adv) | so, such |
| gāmmáahn (tw) | this evening, tonight |
| gāmnín (tw) | this year |
| gam noih (ie) | such a long time |
| gāmyaht (tw) | today |
| gámyéung (adv) | in this way, like this |
| -gán (asp) | progressive aspect marker |
| Gānàhdaaih (pw) | Canada |
| gānjyuh (adv) | and then |
| gāsī (n) | furniture |
| gáu (num) | nine |
| gáu'ah (num) | ninety (elided form) |
| gauhnín (tw) | last year |
| gáu-yuht (tw) | September |

| | | | |
|---|---|---|---|
| ge (prt) | | gōu-gōu-sau-sau (ie) | tall and thin |
| géi (adv) | quite | gōujāanghàaih (n) | high-heeled shoe |
| géi (num) | several | Gūnghéi faat- | greeting at |
| gei (v) | to send something by post | chòih (ie) | Chinese New Year |
| gēichèuhng (n) | airport | gūngsī (n) | office |
| geidāk (v) | to remember | gūngyàhnfóng (n) | servant's room |
| géidímjūng (qw) | what time? | gwai (adj) | expensive |
| géidō (qw) | how much, how many? | gwai (adv) | honorably |
| | | gwāt (n) | a fifteen-minute unit of time |
| géidō seui (ie) | how old? | | |
| géiluhkpín (n) | documentary | -gwo (prt) | |
| géinoih (qw) | how long (a period of time)? | -gwo (asp) | experiential aspect marker |
| gei-seun (v-o) | to send something by post | gwokgā (n) | country |
| | | Gwóngjāu (pw) | Guangzhou/Canton |
| géisìh (qw) | when? | Gwóngjāuwá/ | Cantonese |
| génggān (n) | scarf | Gwóngdūngwá (n) | (language) |
| gihn (cl) | classifier for items of clothing | **H** | |
| gin (v) | to see | hàahng (v) | to walk |
| giujouh (v) | to be called, named | hàahng-gāai (v-o) | to go window-shopping |
| gó (dem) | that | | |
| go (cl) | classifier for people, roundish objects such as apples and custard tarts, containers such as bowls and cups, physical spaces such as rooms and airports, and many abstract concepts such as measures of time | hàahnghōi-jó (ie) | not in, gone out |
| | | hàahng-louh (v-o) | to walk |
| | | hàaih (n) | shoe |
| | | hàaihpóu (n) | shoe store |
| | | haakfóng (n) | guest room |
| | | hāaksīk (adj) | black |
| | | haaktēng (n) | sitting room |
| | | hāgáau (n) | steamed shrimp dumpling |
| | | háh (asp) | delimitative aspect marker |
| go (num) | unit | hah (adj) | next (week, month or year) |
| góbīn (adv) | over there | | |
| gòh-gō (n) | elder brother | hah (prep) | below, under |
| gokdāk (v) | to feel | hahjau (tw) | afternoon |
| gōn(chou) (adj) | dry | hahmihn (adv) | under, beneath |
| góng (v) | to speak | hahtīn (tw) | summer |
| góng-gán (ie) | line busy (on the phone) | Hahwāiyìh (pw) | Hawaii |
| | | hái (v) | to be in/at |
| | | hái (prep) | in/at a place, at a time |
| gōnjehng (adj) | clean | hái douh sihk (ie) | eat-in |
| gōu (adj) | tall, high | haih (v) | to be |
| gōudaaih (adj) | big (in body build) | haih nē (ie) | by the way |

|  |  |  |  |
|---|---|---|---|
| hauhmihn (adv) | behind | jaauhyúh (n) | shower (of rain) |
| hauhsāang (adj) | young | jā-chē (v-o) | to drive a car |
| háuseun (n) | message | jái (n) | son |
| hei (n) | movie, film | jān haih (ie) | really |
| héifūn (v) | to like | jāp (v) | to tidy up |
| héi-sān (v-o) | to get up | jāp-chòhng (v-o) | to make the bed |
| heiwān (n) | temperature | jāp-tói (v-o) | to clear the table |
| heiyún (n) | movies, cinema | jáu (v) | to leave |
| heui (v) | to go | jāu (n) | continent |
| heui-gāai (v-o) | to go out | jauh (conj) | (if ...) then |
| heui-léuihhàhng (v-o) | to go traveling | jāuwàih (n) | surroundings |
| | | jē (n) | umbrella |
| Hēunggóng (pw) | Hong Kong | je (v) | to borrow |
| hēungjīu (n) | banana | jèih-jē (n) | elder sister |
| hēungpín (n) | jasmine tea | jēk (prt) | |
| hingcheui (n) | interest | jek (cl) | classifier for single pieces of footwear, gloves, windows, animals, boats, dumplings, bananas and hot-dogs |
| hohkhaauh (n) | school | | |
| hohksāang (n) | student | | |
| Hòhngwok (pw) | Korea | | |
| hòhnláahng (adj) | cold | | |
| Hòhnmán (n) | Korean (language) | | |
| hóitāan (n) | beach | jeui (adv) | most |
| hōi-wúi (v-o) | to be at/have a meeting | jeui hauh (adv) | finally |
| | | jeui hóu ... (ie) | it might be better to ... |
| hólohk (n) | cola | | |
| honbóubāau (n) | hamburger | jeuk (v) | to wear |
| hóu (adj) | good, decent | jēung (cl) | classifier for pieces of furniture with flat surfaces and for other flat objects |
| hóu (adv) | very, quite | | |
| hòuhjí (n) | a ten-cent unit of money | | |
| | | jī (cl) | classifier for long, slender objects such as pens |
| houh(máh) (n) | number | | |
| hóusihk (adj) | delicious | | |
| hóutái (adj) | good to see (of a movie or television program) | | |
| | | jī(dou) (v) | to know |
| | | jih (n) | a five-minute unit of time |
| hóutīn (adj) | fine, sunny (weather) | | |
| hóuwáan (adj) | fun to do, fun to visit, etc. | jihgéi (prn) | self |
| | | jik (n) | value |
| hóyíh (mv) | can, could | jīngchàih (adj) | neat (in dress) |
| hùhngsīk (adj) | red | jīsí honbóubāau (n) | cheeseburger |
| hūngyàuh (n) | air-mail | | |
| | | jísīk (adj) | purple, violet |
| **J** | | jīujóu (tw) | early morning |
| ja (prt) | | -jó (asp) | perfective aspect marker |
| jāan (v) | to add | | |
| jáau (v) | to give as change | jóbīn (adv) | on the left |

| | | | |
|---|---|---|---|
| joi (adv) | and, again | laak (prt) | |
| jóuchāan (n) | breakfast | lāangsāam (n) | woollen sweater, jumper |
| jouh (v) | to do; is shown (of a movie or television program) | làh (prt) | |
| | | láihbaai (n) | week |
| jouh-wahnduhng (v-o) | to play sports | láihbaai-luhk (tw) | Saturday |
| | | láihbaai-ngh (tw) | Friday |
| juhng (adv) | still; in addition | láihbaai-sāam (tw) | Wednesday |
| jūnggāan (adv) | in the middle, between | láihbaai-sei (tw) | Thursday |
| | | láihbaai-yaht (tw) | Sunday |
| júngguhng (adv) | in total, altogether | láihbaai-yāt (tw) | Monday |
| Jūnggwok (pw) | China | láihbaai-yih (tw) | Tuesday |
| jūnghohk (n) | secondary school | laihjī (n) | lychee |
| júngjaahm (n) | terminal, terminus | láihmaauh (n) | good manners |
| Jūngmán (n) | Chinese (language) | lāu (n) | coat |
| jūngtàuh (n) | hour | làuh (v) | to stay, to leave something behind (e.g. a message) |
| jūngyi (v) | to like | | |
| jyú (v) | to cook | | |
| jyú-faahn (v-o) | to cook a meal | léi (n) | pear |
| jyuh (v) | to live | lèih (prep) | from |
| jyún (v) | to become, to turn; to change | lèihdóu (n) | outlying island |
| | | leng (adj) | pretty; fresh (of fruit) |
| jyun (v) | to change (transportation) | lengjái (adj) | handsome |
| | | Lèuhndēun (pw) | London |
| jyú-yéhsihk (v-o) | to cook (food) | léuhng (num) | two |
| | | lèuhng (adj) | cool |
| **K** | | lèuhnghàaih (n) | sandals |
| kàhmmáahn (tw) | yesterday evening, last night | leuhtsī (n) | lawyer |
| | | lèuihbouh (n) | thunderstorm |
| kàhmyaht (tw) | yesterday | léuihmihn (adv) | inside |
| káhn (adj) | near | lìhng (num) | zero |
| kāp-chàhn (v-o) | to vacuum-clean | lìhng hah (ie) | below zero (of temperatures) |
| kèihsaht (adv) | actually | | |
| kèihyihgwó (n) | kiwifruit | lihngngoih (adv) | besides |
| kèuhnggihng (adj) | strong | līk jáu (ie) | take-away |
| kéuih (prn) | he, him, she, her, it | lō (prt) | |
| kéuihdeih (prn) | they, them | lohk (v) | to fall (rain, snow) |
| kwàhn (n) | dress, skirt | Lohkchaamgēi (pw) | Los Angeles |
| **L** | | lohk-syut (v-o) | to snow |
| lā (prt) | | lohk-yúh (v-o) | to rain |
| la (prt) | | lohng-sāam (v-o) | to hang clothes out to dry |
| laahm (v) | to put on (a scarf) | | |
| làahmsīk (adj) | blue | lóuh (adj) | old |
| láahng (adj) | cold | lóuhbáan (n) | boss |
| laahpsaap (n) | trash, rubbish | lóuhsī (n) | teacher |

# Cantonese-English glossary

| | | | | |
|---|---|---|---|---|
| luhk (*num*) | six | | mgōi màaih-dāan (*ie*) | The bill, please! |
| luhk'ah (*num*) | sixty (elided form) | | mgōi saai (*ie*) | Thanks a lot! |
| luhksīk (*adj*) | green | | mgōi tái-sou (*ie*) | The bill, please! |
| luhkyíngdáai (*n*) | video-tape | | mhái douh (*ie*) | not here |
| luhkyínggēi (*n*) | video-recorder | | mhaih géi (*adv*) | not that much |
| luhk-yuht (*tw*) | June | | mihnbāaupóu (*n*) | bakery |
| lùhng (*n/m*) | bamboo basket for steaming dimsum | | mìhngseunpín (*n*) | postcard |
| lùhngjéng (*n*) | Lung-ching (light) tea | | mjī (*v*) | to wonder |
| | | | mòhng (*adj*) | busy |
| | | | móhngkàuh-páak (*n*) | tennis racket |

## M

| | | | | |
|---|---|---|---|---|
| | | | mōnggwó (*n*) | mango |
| m- (*adv*) | negative marker | | móu (*n*) | hat, cap |
| máahn (*tw*) | evening | | móuh (*v*) | negative of **yáuh** |
| maahn (*num*) | ten thousand | | mouh (*n*) | fog |
| máahnfaahn (*n*) | dinner | | móuhhaang (*adj*) | unlimited |
| maahn-máan (*adv*) | slowly | | móuh mahntàih (*ie*) | No problem! |
| máaih (*v*) | to buy | | | |
| maaih (*v*) | to sell | | msái (*mv*) | need not |
| máaih-fēi (*v-o*) | to buy tickets | | msái jáau laak (*ie*) | Keep the change! |
| máaih-sung (*v-o*) | to buy food (for meals) | | msái mgōi (*ie*) | Not at all! (polite response to **mgōi**) |
| máaih-yéh (*v-o*) | to go shopping | | muhkgwā (*n*) | papaya |
| maat-chēung (*v-o*) | to clean the windows | | mùhnháu (*n*) | entrance |
| màhfàahn (*adj*) | problematic, troublesome | | (mùih-)múi (*n*) | younger sister |
| màh-mā (*n*) | mother | | | |
| màh-má-déi (*ie*) | not that much | | **N** | |
| Máhnèihlāai (*pw*) | Manila | | nàahm (*adj*) | south |
| Màhnfa-Jūngsām (*pw*) | Cultural Center | | nàahmjái (*n*) | boy, young man |
| | | | nàahmyán (*n*) | man |
| màhngeuihdim (*n*) | stationery shop | | Náusāilàahn (*pw*) | New Zealand |
| maht (*n*) | sock | | Náuyeuk (*pw*) | New York |
| máhtàuh (*n*) | ferry pier | | nē (*prt*) | |
| mahtwàhn (*adj*) | cloudy | | nē (*i*) | |
| māmìh (*n*) | mom, mum | | néih (*prn*) | you (singular) |
| mān (*m*) | dollar | | néihdeih (*prn*) | you (plural) |
| mātyéh (*qw*) | what? | | néih hóu (*ie*) | How are you? |
| mdāk a (*ie*) | not OK | | néui (*n*) | daughter |
| meih (*adv*) | not yet | | néuihjái (*n*) | girl, young woman |
| Méihgwok (*pw*) | the U.S. | | néuihyán (*n*) | woman |
| mèihyúh (*n*) | light rain, drizzle | | ngáahngéng (*n*) | eyeglasses |
| méng (*n*) | name | | ngāam-ngāam | just, a short while ago |
| mgin-jó (*ie*) | (gone) missing | | | |
| mgōi (*ie*) | thank you (for a favor); please | | ngāam saai laak (*ie*) | That's great! |

| | | | | |
|---|---|---|---|---|
| ngàhnbāau (n) | purse | | Sāamfàahnsíh (pw) | San Francisco |
| ngàhnhòhng (n) | bank | | sāam-yuht (tw) | March |
| ngái(sai) (adj) | short (in body build) | | sāanggwó (n) | fruit |
| ngàuhjáifu (n) | jeans | | sāanggwódong (n) | fruit-stall |
| ngàuhyuhkjūk (n) | congee with beef | | sāangyaht faailohk (ie) | Happy birthday! |
| ńgh (num) | five | | sahp (num) | ten |
| ńgh'ah (num) | fifty (elided form) | | sahp-maahn (num) | hundred thousand |
| ńgh-yuht (tw) | May | | sahp-yāt-yuht (tw) | November |
| ngóh (prn) | I, me | | sahp-yih-yuht (tw) | December |
| ngóhdeih (prn) | we, us | | sahp-yuht (tw) | October |
| ngoihtou (n) | jacket | | sái (v) | to wash |
| ngūk (n) | house, flat | | sāi (adj) | west |
| ngūkkéi (n) | home | | sai (adj) | small |
| ngūkkéiyàhn (n) | family member | | Sāibāanngàh (pw) | Spain |
| nī (dem) | this | | Sāibāanngàh-mán (n) | Spanish (language) |
| nībīn (adv) | over here | | sái-díp (v-o) | to wash the dishes |
| nīdouh (adv) | here | | sāigwā (n) | water-melon |
| nìhn (n/m) | year | | sāijōng (n) | men's suit |
| noih (adj) | long (time) | | sāijōngfu (n) | trousers, slacks |
| noihsin (n) | telephone extension | | sailóu (n) | younger brother |
| nyúhn (adj) | warm | | sái-sāam (v-o) | to wash clothes |
| | | | sái-wún (v-o) | to wash the dishes, to wash up |
| **O** | | | | |
| ōnlohkyí (n) | easy chair | | sānmán (n) | news |
| Oujāu (pw) | Australia | | sānnìhn faailohk (ie) | Happy New Year! |
| | | | sāp (adj) | humid |
| **P** | | | sau (adj) | thin |
| páau-bouh (v-o) | to run (for exercise) | | sáudói (n) | handbag |
| páaubouhhàaih (n) | running shoe | | saugēi (n) | cell (mobile) phone |
| pàhngyáuh (n) | friend | | sáumaht (n) | glove |
| pèhng (adj) | cheap | | sáusīn (adv) | first of all |
| pèihhàaih (n) | leather shoe | | sāyùh (n) | shark |
| pìhnggwó (n) | apple | | sèhng (adj/adv) | whole; fully, completely |
| pìhngsìh (adv) | usually, generally | | sei (num) | four |
| pìhngyàuh (n) | surface mail | | sei'ah (num) | forty (elided form) |
| -póu (n) | shop, store | | sei-yuht (tw) | April |
| Póutūngwá (n) | Putonghua/ Mandarin (language) | | seuhng (adj) | previous (week, month or year) |
| | | | seuhng (adv) | on, above, over |
| **S** | | | | |
| sā'ah (num) | thirty (elided form) | | | |
| saai (v-prt) | | | | |
| sāam (n) | clothes | | | |
| sāam (num) | three | | | |

# Cantonese–English glossary

| | | | |
|---|---|---|---|
| Seuhnghói (pw) | Shanghai | síubā (n) | minibus |
| Seuhnghóiwá (n) | Shanghainese (language) | síuhohk (n) | primary school |
| | | síujé (n) | Miss, young lady |
| seuhngjau (tw) | in the morning | sīumáai (n) | steamed pork dumpling |
| seuhngmihn (adv) | on, above | | |
| seuhng mohng (v-o) | to go online | síusām (adj/adv) | careful(ly) |
| | | síusíu (adj/adv) | a little, some |
| séui (n) | water | sō (n) | comb |
| seui (n) | years of age | sōfá (n) | sofa |
| séuibūi (n) | (drinking) glass | sou-deih (v-o) | to sweep the floor |
| seuihfóng (n) | bedroom | | |
| seun (n) | letter | sóyíh (conj) | so, as |
| séung (mv) | to want to, to wish to | sūksuk | uncle |
| sēungdeui-sāpdouh (n) | relative humidity | sung (n) | food for cooking a meal |
| sēutsāam (n) | shirt, blouse | syū (n) | book |
| sìhgaan (n) | time | syūdim (n) | bookstore |
| sihk (v) | to eat | syūfóng (n) | study |
| sihk-jóuchāan (v-o) | to have breakfast | syūfuhk (adj) | comfortable |
| | | syūgá (n) | bookcase, bookshelves |
| sihk-máahn-faahn (v-o) | to have dinner | | |
| | | syūgúk (n) | bookstore |
| sihk-ngaan (v-o) | to have lunch | syùhn (n) | boat, ferry |
| sihk-yéh (v-o) | to eat | syùhtíu (n) | chips, French fries |
| sihou (n) | hobby | syun (v) | can be regarded as ... |
| sīk (mv) | can, to know how to | | |
| sīk (n) | color | syut (n) | snow |
| Sīknèih (pw) | Sydney | | |
| sīmàhn (adj) | smart (in dress) | **T** | |
| sīmaht (n) | pantyhose | -táai (n) | Mrs. |
| sīn (adv) | first, firstly | tāai (n) | (neck-)tie |
| sing (v) | to be surnamed | taai-táai (n) | Mrs., wife |
| singdaan faailohk (ie) | Merry Christmas! | taam-pàhngyáuh (v-o) | to visit friends |
| sīngkèih (n) | week | tái (v) | to see, to watch, to look at, to read |
| sīngkèih-luhk (tw) | Saturday | | |
| sīngkèih-ńgh (tw) | Friday | tái-boují (v-o) | to read the newspaper |
| sīngkèih-sāam (tw) | Wednesday | | |
| sīngkèih-sei (tw) | Thursday | tái-dihnsih (v-o) | to watch television |
| sīngkèih-yaht (tw) | Sunday | tái-dihnyíng (v-o) | to watch a movie |
| sīngkèih-yāt (tw) | Monday | tái-hei (v-o) | to watch a movie |
| sīngkèih-yih (tw) | Tuesday | tàihjí (n) | grape |
| sīnji (adv) | only then | tái-jūkkàuh (v-o) | to watch soccer, football |
| sīnsāang (n) | Mr., teacher, husband | tái-syū (v-o) | to read (books) |
| | | táiyuhk (n) | sports |

| | | | |
|---|---|---|---|
| tàuhfaat (n) | hair | wá | language |
| tek-jūkkàuh (v-o) | to play soccer, football | wàahngíng (n) | the environment |
| tēng (v) | to listen (to) | wáan-yàuhheigēi (v-o) | to play electronic games |
| tēng (n) | sitting room, dining room | wah ... tēng (v) | to tell |
| | | wahnduhng (n) | sports |
| tēng-dihnwá (v-o) | to answer the phone | wàhntānmihn (n) | won-ton noodles |
| tēng-sāuyāmgēi (v-o) | to listen to the radio | wái (cl) | classifier for people |
| | | wái (ie) | Hello! (greeting on the phone) |
| tēng-yāmngohk (v-o) | to listen to music | wán (v) | to look for |
| tīm (adv) | in addition | Wāngōwàh (pw) | Vancouver |
| tīnchìhng (adj) | fine (weather) | wānnyúhn (adj) | warm |
| tīngmáahn (tw) | tomorrow evening/night | wihngchìh (n) | swimming pool |
| | | wo (prt) | |
| tīngyaht (tw) | tomorrow | wòhngsīk (adj) | yellow |
| tīngyaht gin lā (ie) | See you tomorrow! | wùh (m) | pot |
| tīnhei (n) | weather | wùhsōu (n) | moustache, beard |
| tīnyām (adj) | overcast | wúih (mv) | shall, will |
| tīsēut (n) | T-shirt | wūjōu (adj) | dirty |
| tìuh (cl) | classifier for long slender objects such as trousers, streets, and sharks | wún (n/m) | bowl |
| | | **Y** | |
| tiu-móuh (v-o) | to dance | y'ah (num) | twenty (elided form) |
| tōháai (n) | slipper | yàhn (n) | person, people |
| tòhnggwó (n) | sweets | yaht (n) | day |
| tòhnggwódim (n) | sweet shop | Yahtbún (pw) | Japan |
| tòihfūng (n) | typhoon | Yahtmán (n) | Japanese (language) |
| Tòihwāan (pw) | Taiwan | yám (v) | to drink |
| tong-sāam (v-o) | to iron clothes | yám-bējáu (v-o) | to go for a beer |
| tou (cl) | classifier for a matching suit of clothes | yám-chàh (v-o) | to have dimsum in a tea-house |
| | | yám-gafē (v-o) | to have coffee |
| | | yám-jáu (v-o) | to go for a drink |
| tòuhsyūgún (n) | library | yāmngohk (n) | music |
| toujōng (n) | women's suit | yāmngohkwúi (n) | concert |
| tùhng (prep) | for, with | yāmtīn (adj) | overcast |
| tùhng(màaih) (conj) | and | yám-yéh (v-o) | to go for a drink |
| | | Yandouh (pw) | India |
| tùhnghohk (n) | classmate, schoolmate | Yandouhwá (n) | any of the languages of India |
| tùhngsih (n) | colleague | | |
| tūngsèuhng (adv) | usually | yānwaih (conj) | because |
| | | yāt (num) | one |
| **W** | | yātdihng (adv) | sure, surely |
| wā (i) | interjection showing surprise | yātlouh | Have a good flight! |
| | | seuhnfūng (ie) | |

# Cantonese-English glossary

| | | | |
|---|---|---|---|
| yāt yeuhng (adj) | the same | yìhgā (adv) | now |
| yāt-yuht (tw) | January | (yìhm)yiht (adj) | hot |
| yáuh (v) | to have | yìhnhauh (adv) | and then, later on |
| yáuh (v) | there is/are | yihtgáu (n) | hot-dog |
| yàuh (prep) | from | yih-yuht (tw) | February |
| yauh (adv) | also | yīnggōi (mv) | should |
| yauhbīn (adv) | on the right | Yīnggwok (pw) | England, the U.K. |
| yàuhchoi (n) | vegetables with oyster sauce | Yīngmán (n) | English (language) |
| | | yíng-séung (v-o) | to take pictures |
| yáuh géi daaih (ie) | how old? | yíngyan (v) | to make photo-copies |
| yáuh móuh (v) | is/are there? | Yínngaih-Hohkyún (pw) | Academy for Performing Arts |
| yàuh-séui (v-o) | to swim | | |
| yéh (n) | thing | yīsāng (n) | doctor |
| yehmáahn (tw) | evening, night | yiu (v) | to need, to want, to take (time), to cost |
| yeuhkfòhng (n) | drugstore | | |
| yeuhng (cl) | classifier for events, things in general | yiu (mv) | must, to have to |
| | | yúh (n) | rain |
| yeuhng (n) | kind, sort | yuhchāak (v) | to predict |
| yéung (n) | appearance | yùhdáanmihn (n) | fish-ball noodles |
| yí (i) | interjection showing mild surprise | yuhksāt (n) | bathroom |
| | | yùhláuhbāau (n) | fishburger |
| yí (n) | chair | yúhn (adj) | far |
| Yidaaihleih (pw) | Italy | yùhn (v-prt) | |
| Yidaaihleihmán (n) | Italian (language) | yuht (n) | month |
| yih (num) | two | yuhtfai (n) | monthly fee |

# English–Cantonese glossary

The respective classifiers are given in square brackets where appropriate.

## A

| | |
|---|---|
| above | seuhng(mihn) |
| Academy for Performing Arts | Yínngaih-Hohkyún |
| actually | kèihsaht |
| add, to | jāan |
| addition, in | juhng, tīm |
| afternoon | hahjau |
| again | joi |
| ago | chìhn |
| air-mail | hūngyàuh |
| airplane | fēigēi [ga] |
| airport | (fēi)gēichèuhng [go] |
| all right | dāk |
| also | yauh, dōu, tīm |
| altogether, in total | júngguhng |
| and | tùhng(màaih) |
| and then | gānjyuh, yìhnhauh |
| answer the phone, to | tēng-dihnwá |
| appearance | yéung |
| apple | pìhngggwó [go] |
| approximately | daaihyeuk |
| April | sei-yuht |
| at (a place) (to be) | hái |
| August | baat-yuht |
| Aunt | a-yī |
| Australia | Oujāu |

## B

| | |
|---|---|
| back (to go/to give) | fāan |
| bakery | mihnbāaupóu [gāan] |
| banana | hēungjīu [jek] |
| bank | ngàhnhòhng [gāan] |
| barbecued-pork bun | chāsīubāau [go] |
| barber's shop | fēifaatpóu [gāan] |
| basketball | làahmkàuh |
| bath, to have/take a | chūng-lèuhng |
| bathroom | yuhksāt [gāan] |
| be, to | haih |
| beach | hóitāan [go] |
| beard | wùhsōu [jāp] |
| be at/in (place), to | hái |
| because | yānwaih |
| become, to | jyún |
| bed | chòhng [jēung] |
| bed, to make the | jāp-chòhng |
| bedroom | seuihfóng [gāan] |
| behind | hauhmihn |
| Beijing | Bākgīng |
| below zero | lìhng hah |
| beneath | hah(mihn) |
| beside | gaaklèih |
| besides | lìhngngoih |

# English–Cantonese glossary

|  |  |
|---|---|
| better, it might be … to | jeui hóu |
| between | jūnggāan |
| bicycle | dāanchē [ga] |
| big (in body build) | gōudaaih |
| bill | dāan [jēung] |
| (the) bill, please! | mgōi màaih-dāan/ mgōi tái-sou |
| black | hāaksīk |
| blouse | sēutsāam [gihn] |
| blow, to | chēui |
| blue | làahmsīk |
| boat | syùhn [jek] |
| book | syū [bún] |
| bookcase, bookshelves | syūgá [go] |
| bookstore | syūdim, syūgúk [gāan] |
| borrow, to | je |
| boss | lóuhbáan [go] |
| bowl | wún [go] |
| boy | nàahmjái [go] |
| breakfast | jóuchāan [go] |
| breakfast, to have | sihk-jóuchāan |
| bring, to | daai |
| brother, elder | daaihlóu, gòh-gō [go] |
| brother, younger | dàih-dái, sailóu [go] |
| brown | fēsīk |
| bus | bāsí [ga] |
| bus stop | bāsíjaahm [go] |
| busy | mòhng |
| but | bātgwo |
| buy, to | máaih |
| buy food (for meals), to | máaih-sung |
| buy tickets, to | máaih-fēi |
| by the way | haih nē |
| bye-bye | bāai-baai |

## C

|  |  |
|---|---|
| called, to be | giujouh |
| can (to be able to) | sīk |
| can (may) | hóyíh |
| Canada | Gānàhdaaih |
| Canton | Gwóngjāu |
| Cantonese (language) | Gwóngjāuwá/ Gwóngdūngwá |
| cap | móu [déng] |
| car | chē [ga] |
| careful(ly) | síusām |
| casual (in dress) | chèuihbín |
| cell (mobile) phone | saugēi [bou] |
| chair | dang, yí [jēung] |
| chair, dining | chāandang, chāanyí [jēung] |
| chair, easy | ōnlohkyí [jēung] |
| change (transportation), to | jyun |
| change (money), to give | jáau |
| cheap | pèhng |
| cheeseburger | jīsí honbóubāau [go] |
| China | Jūnggwok |
| Chinese (language) | Jūngmán |
| chips, French fries | syùhtíu |
| Chiu Chow dialect | Chìuhjāuwá |
| cinema | heiyún [gāan] |
| City Hall | Daaihwuihtòhng- |
| Concert Hall | Yāmngohktēng |
| classmate | tùhnghohk [go] |
| clean | gōnjehng |
| clean the windows, to | maat-chēung |
| clear the table, to | jāp-tói |
| clothes | sāam [gihn] |
| cloudy | mahtwàhn |
| coat | lāu [gihn] |
| coffee | gafē |
| coffee table | chàhgēi [jēung] |
| cola | hólohk |
| cold | dung, (hòhng)láang |
| colleague | tùhngsih [go] |
| color | sīk |
| comb | sō [bá] |
| come, to | lèih |
| comfortable | syūfuhk |
| comparatively | béigaau |
| completely | saai, sèhng |

|  |  |  |  |  |  |
|---|---|---|---|---|---|
| concert | yāmngohkwúi [go] | drizzle | | mèihyúh | |
| congee with beef | ngàuhyuhkjūk | drugstore | | yeuhkfòhng [gāan] | |
| congee with mixed meat | gahpdáijūk | dry | | gōn(chou) | |
| continent | jāu [go] | **E** | | | |
| convenient | fōngbihn | early morning | | jī ujóu | |
| cook, to | jyú(-yéhsihk) | east | | dūng | |
| cook a meal, to | jyú-faahn | easy chair | | ōnlohkyí [jēung] | |
| cool | (chīng)lèuhng | eat, to | | sihk | |
| cost, to | yiu | eat-in | | hái douh sihk | |
| could, might | hóyíh | eight | | baat | |
| country | gwokgā [go] | eighty | | baat-sahp, baat'ah | |
| cuisine | choi | elder brother | | daaihlóu, gòh-gō [go] | |
| Cultural Center | Màhnfa-Jūngsām | | | | |
| cup | būi, chàhbūi [go, jek] | elder sister | | jèhjē, gājē [go] | |
| | | electrical appliance store | | dihnheipóu [gāan] | |
| custard tart | daahntāat [go] | | | | |
| cycle, to | cháai-dāanchē | empty the trash bin, to | | dóu-laahpsaap | |
| **D** | | England | | Yīnggwok | |
| dance, to | tiu-móu | English (language) | | Yīngmán | |
| daughter | néui [go] | | | | |
| day | yaht | entrance | | mùhnháu [go] | |
| day before yesterday | chìhnyaht | environment | | wàahnging | |
| | | Europe | | Aujāu | |
| December | sahp-yih-yuht | evening | | yehmáahn | |
| decent | hóu | evening, this | | gāmmáahn | |
| delicious | hóusihk | every (Sunday, Monday ...) | | fùhng (sīngkèih-yaht, sīngkèih-yāt ...) | |
| diagonally across | chèhdeuimihn | | | | |
| dining chair | chāangdang, chāanyí [jēung] | | | | |
| | | everyone | | daaihgā | |
| dining room | faahntēng [gāan] | expensive | | gwai | |
| dining table | chāantói [jēung] | extension, telephone | | noihsin | |
| dinner | máahnfaahn | | | | |
| dinner, to have | sihk-máahnfaahn | eyeglasses | | ngáahngéng [go, fu] | |
| dirty | wūjōu | | | | |
| do, to | jouh | **F** | | | |
| doctor | yīsāng [go] | | | | |
| documentary | géiluhkpín [chēut] | fall, to (of rain, snow) | | lohk | |
| dollar | mān | | | | |
| dozen | dā | family member | | ngūkkéiyàhn [go] | |
| dress | kwàhn [tiuh] | far | | yúhn | |
| dress shop | fuhkjōngdim [gāan] | fat | | fèih | |
| drink, to | yám | father | | bàh-bā [go] | |
| drive (a vehicle), to | jā-chē | February | | yih-yuht | |
| | | feel, to | | gokdāk | |

# English–Cantonese glossary

|  |  |
|---|---|
| ferry | syùhn [jek] |
| ferry pier | máhtàuh [go] |
| fifty | ńgh-sahp, ńgh'ah |
| finally | jeui hauh |
| fine, sunny (weather) | hóutīn, tīnchìhng |
| first (of all) | sáusīn |
| fish-ball noodles | yùhdángmihn |
| fishburger | yùhláuhbāau [go] |
| five | ńgh |
| floor | deihhá [go] |
| flower shop | fādim [gāan] |
| fog | mouh |
| food (cuisine) | choi |
| food (for cooking) | sung |
| football, soccer | jūkkàuh |
| for | tùhng |
| forty | sei-sahp, sei'ah |
| four | sei |
| France | Faatgwok |
| free, not busy | dākhàahn |
| French (language) | Faatmán |
| French fries, chips | syùhtíu |
| fresh (of fruit) | leng |
| Friday | sīngkèih-ńgh, láihbaai-ńgh |
| friend | pàhngyáuh [go] |
| from (a place) | lèih, yàuh |
| front of, in | chìhnmihn |
| fruit | sāanggwó [go] |
| fruit-stall | sāanggwódong [go] |
| fully | sèhng |
| fun, having | hóuwáan |
| furniture | gāsī |

## G

|  |  |
|---|---|
| garage | chēfòhng [go] |
| garden | fāyún [go] |
| generally | tūngsèuhng, pìhngsìh |
| German (language) | Dākmán |
| Germany | Dākgwok |
| get up, to | héi-sān |
| girl | néuihjái [go] |
| give, to | béi |
| give (as change), to | jáau |
| glass, drinking | séuibūi [go, jek] |
| glasses | ngáahngéng [go, fu] |
| glove | sáumaht [jek] |
| go, to | heui |
| go for a beer, to | yám-bējáu |
| go for a drink, to | yám-yéh, yám-jáu |
| gone out | hàahnghōi-jó |
| go out, to | chēut-gāai, heui-gāai |
| go shopping, to | máaih-yéh |
| go to school, to | fāan-hohk |
| go to work, to | fāan-gūng |
| go traveling, to | heui-léuihhàhng |
| good | hóu |
| good (of a movie or television program) | hóutái |
| good value | dái |
| grape | tàihjí [lāp] |
| gray | fūisīk |
| green | luhksīk |
| Guangzhou/Canton | Gwóngjāu |
| guest room | haakfóng [gāan] |

## H

|  |  |
|---|---|
| hair | tàuhfaat |
| half | bun |
| hamburger | honbóubāau [go] |
| handbag | sáudói [go] |
| handsome | lengjái |
| hang clothes out to dry, to | lohng-sāam |
| Happy birthday! | sāangyaht faailohk |
| Happy New Year! | sānnìhn faailohk |
| hat | móu [déng] |
| have, to | yáuh |
| Have a good flight! | yātlouh seuhnfūng |
| have to, to | yiu |
| Hawaii | Hahwāiyìh |
| he | kéuih |
| Hello! (on the phone) | wái |

|  |  |
|---|---|
| help, to | bōng(sáu) |
| her | kéuih |
| here | nīdouh |
| herself | kéuih jihgéi |
| high | gōu |
| him | kéuih |
| himself | kéuih jihgéi |
| hit, to | dá |
| hobby | sihou |
| holiday | gakèih |
| home | ngūkkéi [go] |
| Hong Kong | Hēunggóng |
| horse-racing | choimáh |
| hot | (yìhm)yiht |
| hot-dog | yihtgáu [jek, go] |
| hour | jūngtàuh [go] |
| house | ngūk [gāan] |
| how | dím(yéung) |
| How are you? | néih hóu |
| how long (a period of time)? | géinoih |
| how much, how many? | géidō |
| how old? | géidō seui/yáuh géi daaih |
| humid | (chìuh)sāp |
| hundred | baak |
| hundred thousand | sahp-maahn |
| husband | sīnsāang |

## I

|  |  |
|---|---|
| I | ngóh |
| in (a place) (to be) | hái |
| include, to | bāau |
| India | Yandouh |
| Indian language(s) | Yandouhwá |
| inside | léuihmihn |
| interest | hingcheui |
| introduce, to | gaaisiuh |
| invite, to | chéng |
| iron clothes, to | tong-sāam |
| it | kéuih |
| Italian (language) | Yidaaihleihmán |
| Italy | Yidaaihleih |

## J

|  |  |
|---|---|
| jacket | ngoihtou [gihn] |
| January | yāt-yuht |
| Japan | Yahtbún |
| Japanese (language) | Yahtmán |
| jasmine tea | hēungpín |
| jeans | ngàuhjáifu [tìuh] |
| July | chāt-yuht |
| jumper, sweater | lāahngsāam [gihn] |
| June | luhk-yuht |
| just, a short while ago | ngāam-ngāam |

## K

|  |  |
|---|---|
| kangaroo | doihsyú [jek] |
| Keep the change! | msái jáau lak |
| kind, sort | yeuhng |
| kitchen | chyùhfóng [gāan] |
| kiwifruit | kèihyihgwó [go] |
| know, to | jī(dou) |
| know how to, to | sīk |
| Korea | Hòhngwok |
| Korean (language) | Hòhnmán |

## L

|  |  |
|---|---|
| language | wá [júng], -mán |
| large | daaih |
| last night | chàhmmáahn, kàhmmáahn |
| last year | gauhnín |
| later on | yìhnhauh |
| lawyer | leuhtsī [go] |
| leave, to | jáu |
| leave (behind) (e.g. a message), to | làuh |
| leave home, to | chēut-mùhnháu |
| leave work, to | fong-gūng |
| left, on the | jóbīn |
| letter | seun [fūng] |
| library | tòuhsyūgún [go] |
| like, to | jūngyi, héifūn |
| like this | gámyéung |
| line busy (on the phone) | góng-gán |

# English–Cantonese glossary

|  |  |
|---|---|
| listen (to), to | tēng |
| listen to music, to | tēng-yāmngohk |
| listen to the radio, to | tēng-sāuyāmgēi |
| little, a | síusíu |
| live, to | jyuh |
| local (in Hong Kong) | búngóng |
| London | Lèuhndēun |
| long | chèuhng |
| long (time) | noih |
| look at, to | tái |
| look for, to | wán |
| Los Angeles | Lohkchaamgēi |
| lost | mgin-jó |
| low | dāi |
| lunch, to have | sihk-ngaan |
| Lung-ching tea | lùhngjéng |
| lychee | laihjī [lāp] |

## M

|  |  |
|---|---|
| mail, to | gei |
| man | nàahmyán [go] |
| Mandarin (language) | Póutūngwá |
| mango | mōnggwó [go] |
| Manila | Máhnèihlāai |
| manners, good | láihmaauh |
| many | dō |
| March | sāam-yuht |
| market | gāaisíh [go] |
| May | ńgh-yuht |
| may I ask | chíng mahn |
| me | ngóh |
| meeting, to be at/have a | hōi-wúi |
| Merry Christmas! | singdaan faailohk |
| message | háuseun [go] |
| message (text) | dyún seuhn [go] |
| middle, in the | jūnggāan |
| midnight, after midnight | bunyeh |
| million | baak-maahn |
| minibus | síubā [ga] |
| minute | fān(jūng) |
| Miss | síujé |
| missing | mgin-jó |
| Monday | sīngkèih-yāt, láihbaai-yāt |
| money | chín |
| month | yuht [go] |
| month before last | chìhn go yuht |
| monthly fee | yuhtfai |
| more | -dī; juhng |
| morning | seuhngjau |
| morning, early | jī ujóu |
| most | jeui |
| mostly | dōsou |
| mother | màh-mā [go] |
| moustache | wùhsōu [pit] |
| movie, film | dihnyíng, hei [chēut] |
| movie theater | heiyún [gāan] |
| Mr. | sīnsāang |
| Mrs. | (taai-)táai |
| much | dō |
| music | yāmngohk |
| must, to have to | yiu |
| myself | ngóh jihgéi |

## N

|  |  |
|---|---|
| name | méng |
| named, to be | giujouh |
| near | káhn |
| nearby | fuhgahn |
| neat | jíngchàih |
| neck-tie | tāai [tìuh] |
| need, to | yiu |
| need not | msái |
| New York | Náuyeuk |
| New Zealand | Náusāilàahn |
| news | sānmán |
| newspaper | boují [jēung] |
| next month | hah go yuht |
| next week | hah go láihbaai/sīngkèih |
| next year | hah (yāt) nín |
| night | (yeh)máahn |
| nine | gáu |
| ninety | gáu-sahp, gáu'ah |
| No problem! | móuh mahntàih |

|  |  |
|---|---|
| north | bāk |
| not | m-, -mh- |
| Not at all! (polite response to mgōi) | msái mgōi |
| not here | mhái douh |
| not in | hàahnghōi-jó |
| not that much | màh-má-déi, mhaih géi |
| not yet | meih |
| November | sahp-yāt-yuht |
| now | yìhgā |
| number | houh(máh) [go] |

## O

|  |  |
|---|---|
| o'clock | dím(jūng) |
| October | sahp-yuht |
| office | gūngsī [gāan] |
| OK | dāk |
| old | lóuh |
| on | seuhng(mihn) |
| one | yāt |
| opposite, across the road | deuimihn |
| or (in questions with two alternatives) | dihng |
| orange | cháang [go] |
| orange (color) | cháangsīk |
| orange juice | cháangjāp |
| ourselves | ngóhdeih jihgéi |
| outlying island | lèihdóu [go] |
| outside | chēutmihn |
| overcast | yāmtīn, tīnyām |
| overcoat | daaihlāu [gihn] |
| over here | nībīn |
| over there | góbīn |

## P

|  |  |
|---|---|
| packet | bāau |
| pair | deui |
| Pakistan | Bāgēisītáan |
| pantyhose | sīmaht [deui] |
| papaya | muhkgwā [go] |
| Paris | Bālàih |
| pay, to | béi-chín |
| pear | léi [go] |
| Peking | Bākgīng |
| pen | bāt [jī] |
| person, people | yàhn [go] |
| Philippine language(s) | Fēileuhtbānwá |
| Philippines, the | Fēileuhtbān |
| photocopies, to make | yíngyan |
| pictures, to take | yíng-séung |
| pier | máhtàuh [go] |
| pineapple | bōlòh [go] |
| plan (call) | gāaiwahk [go] |
| plate (measure) | dihp |
| plate (object) | díp [jek] |
| play a ballgame, to | dá-bō |
| play basketball, to | dá-làahmkàuh |
| play electronic games, to | wáan-yàuhheigēi |
| play, soccer, football, to | tek-jūkkàuh |
| play sports, to | jouh-wahnduhng |
| play tennis, to | dá-móhngkàuh |
| Please ... | mgōi ... |
| plum | boulām [go] |
| pork dumpling | sīumáai [go, jek] |
| post, to | gei |
| postcard | mìhngseunpín [jēung] |
| pot (for tea) | wùh |
| pound (weight) | bohng |
| predict, to | yuhchāak |
| prepaid (phone) card | chúhjik kāat |
| pretty | leng |
| previous (week, month, year) | seuhng |
| Pu-erh tea | bóuléi |
| purple | jísīk |
| purse | ngàhnbāau [go] |
| put on (a scarf), to | laahm |
| put on (eyeglasses, cap or hat), to | daai |
| put on a tie, to | dá-tāai |
| Putonghua | Póutūngwá |

# English–Cantonese glossary

## Q
| | |
|---|---|
| quick | faai |
| quite | géi, hóu |

## R
| | |
|---|---|
| radio | sāuyāmgēi [ga, go] |
| rail station | fóchējaahm [go] |
| rain | yúh |
| rain, to | lohk-yúh |
| read, to | tái(-syū) |
| really | jān haih |
| red | hùhngsīk |
| relative | sēungdeui-sāpdouh |
| humidity | |
| remember, to | geidāk |
| report | bougou [go] |
| return, to | fāan |
| ride a bicycle, to | cháai-dānchē |
| right, on the | yauhbīn |
| room | fóng [gāan, go], tēng [go] |
| roughly, approximately | daaihyeuk |
| rubbish | laahpsaap |
| run, to (for exercise) | páau-bouh |
| running shoe | páaubouhhàaih [jek] |

## S
| | |
|---|---|
| same, the | yāt yeuhng |
| San Francisco | Sāamfàahnsíh |
| sandal | lèuhnghàaih [jek] |
| Saturday | sīngkèih-luhk, láihbaai-luhk |
| scarf | génggān [tìuh] |
| scenery | fūngging |
| school | hohkhaauh [gāan] |
| school, primary | síuhohk [gāan] |
| school, secondary | jūnghohk [gāan] |
| schoolmate | tùhnghohk [go] |
| see, to | tái, gin |
| see a movie, to | tái-dihnyíng, tái-hei |
| See you tomorrow! | tīngyaht gin lā |
| self | jihgéi |
| sell, to | maaih |
| send something by post, to | gei(-seun) |
| September | gáu-yuht |
| servant's room | gūngyàhnfóng [gāan] |
| seven | chāt |
| seventy | chāt-sahp, chāt'ah |
| several | géi |
| shall (in predictions) | wúih |
| Shanghai | Seuhnghói |
| Shanghainese (language) | Seuhnghóiwá |
| shark | sāyùh [tìuh] |
| she | kéuih |
| shirt | sēutsāam [gihn] |
| shoe | hàaih [jek] |
| shoe, high-heeled | gōujāanghàaih |
| shoe, leather | pèihhàaih |
| shoe, sports | bōhàaih |
| shoe store | hàaihpóu [gāan] |
| shop | dim, pou [gāan] |
| shopping, to go | máaih-yéh |
| short | dyún |
| short (in body build) | ngái |
| shorts | dyúnfu [tìuh] |
| should | yīnggōi |
| shower (of rain) | jaauhyúh [chèuhng] |
| shower, to (have/take a) | chūng-lèuhng |
| shrimp and bamboo-shoot dumpling | fángwó [jek] |
| shrimp dumpling | hāgáau [jek] |
| sing, to | cheung-gō |
| sister, elder | jèhjē, gājē [go] |
| sister, younger | (mùih-)múi [go] |
| sitting room | haaktēng [go] |
| six | luhk |
| sixty | luhk-sahp, luhk'ah |
| skirt | (bunjiht)kwàhn [tìuh] |

|  |  |  |  |
|---|---|---|---|
| slacks | (sāijōng)fu [tìuh] | such | gam |
| sleep, to | fan-gaau | suit (men's) | sāijōng [tou] |
| slipper | tōháai [jek] | suit (women's) | toujōng [tou] |
| slowly | maahn-máan | summer | hahtīn |
| small | sai | Sunday | sīngkèih-yaht, láihbaai-yaht |
| small (in body build) | ngáisai | supermarket | chīukāp-síhchèuhng [gāan] |
| smart (in dress) | sīmàhn | | |
| snow | syut | sure(ly) | yātdihng |
| snow, to | lohk-syut | surface mail | pìhngyàuh |
| so | gám; gam | surname, to have the | sing |
| soccer, football | jūkkàuh | | |
| sock | maht [jek] | surroundings | jāuwàih |
| sofa | sōfá [jēung] | sweater, jumper | lāangsāam [gihn] |
| some | dī | sweep the floor, to | sou-deih |
| son | jái [go] | sweets | tòhnggwó |
| Sorry! | deui mjyuh | sweet shop | tòhnggwódim [gāan] |
| south | nàahm | | |
| Spain | Sāibāanngàh | swim, to | yàuh-séui |
| Spanish (language) | Sāibāanngàhmán | swimming pool | wihngchìh [go] |
| speak, to | góng | Sydney | Sīknèih |
| spectacles, glasses | ngáahngéng [fu, go] | **T** | |
| sports | táiyuhk, wahnduhng | table, coffee | chàhgēi [jēung] |
| | | table, dining | chāantói [jēung] |
| sports shoe | bōhàaih [jek, deui] | Taiwan | Tòihwāan |
| spring roll | chēungyún [tìuh] | take, to | daai |
| stationery shop | màhngeuihdim [gāan] | take (a means of transport), to | daap |
| stay, to | làuh | take-away | līk-jáu |
| still | dōu, juhng | take pictures, to | yíng-séung |
| store | dim, -póu [gāan] | tall | gōu |
| street | gāai [tìuh] | tall and thin | gōu-gōu-sau-sau |
| streetcar | dihnchē | taxi | dīksí [ga] |
| streetcar/tram stop | dihnchējaahm | taxi rank | dīksíjaahm [go] |
| strong | kèuhnggihng | tea | chàh |
| student | hohksāang [go] | teach (in school or university), to | gaau-syū |
| study | syūfóng [gāan] | teacher | sīnsāang, lóuhsī [go] |
| study, to | duhk-syū | | |
| subway (in Hong Kong, MTR or Mass Transit Raiway) | deihtit | telecom | dihnseun |
| | | telephone | dihnwá [go] |
| | | telephone, to | dá-dihnwá |
| | | telephone extension | noihsin |
| subway (MTR) station | deihtitjaahm [go] | television | dihnsih |

# English–Cantonese glossary 289

|  |  |  |  |  |  |
|---|---|---|---|---|---|
| television drama | dihnsihkehk [chēut] | total, in | júngguhng | | |
| television set | dihnsihgēi [go, ga] | train | fóchē [ga] | | |
| tell, to | wah ... tēng | tram | dihnchē [ga] | | |
| temperature | heiwān | tram stop | dihnchējaahm [go] | | |
| ten | sahp | transport | gāautūng | | |
| tennis | móhngkàuh | trash | laahpsaap | | |
| tennis racket | móhngkàuhpáak | troublesome | màhfàahn | | |
| ten thousand | maahn | trousers | (sāijōng)fu [tìuh] | | |
| thank you (very much) (for a favor) | mgōi (saai) | T-shirt | tīsēut [gihn] | | |
| | | Tuesday | sīngkèih-yih, láihbaai-yih | | |
| thank you (very much) (for a gift) | dōjeh (saai) | twenty | yih-sahp, y'ah | | |
| | | two | yih, léuhng | | |
| that | gó | type, to | dá(-jih) | | |
| them | kéuihdeih | typhoon | tòihfūng [go] | | |
| themselves | kéuihdeih jihgéi | | | | |
| then | gānjyuh, yìhnhauh, jauh | **U** | | | |
| | | UK, the | Yīnggwok | | |
| then, only then | sīnji | umbrella | jē [bá] | | |
| there, over there | gódouh | uncle | sūksuk | | |
| there is/are | yáuh | under, beneath | hah(mihn) | | |
| they | kéuihdeih | underground railway (in Hong Kong, MTR or Mass Transit Railway) | deihtit | | |
| thin | sau | | | | |
| thing | yéh [yeuhng] | | | | |
| thirty | sāam-sahp, sā'ah | | | | |
| this | nī | | | | |
| this evening | gāmmáahn | underground (MTR) station | deihtitjaahm [go] | | |
| this year | gāmnín | | | | |
| thousand | chīn | university | daaihhohk [gāan] | | |
| three | sāam | unlimited | móuhhaang | | |
| thunderstorm | lèuihbouh [go] | us | ngóhdeih | | |
| Thursday | sīngkèih-sei, láihbaai-sei | U.S., the | Méihgwok | | |
| | | usually | tūngsèuhng, pìhngsìh | | |
| ticket | fēi [jēung] | | | | |
| tidy up, to | jāp | | | | |
| tie | tāai [tìuh] | **V** | | | |
| time | sìhgaan | vacuum-clean, to | kāp-chàhn | | |
| time, a | chi | value | jik | | |
| today | gāmyaht | Vancouver | Wāngōwàh | | |
| toilet | chisó [go] | vegetables with oyster sauce | yàuhchoi | | |
| Tokyo | Dūnggīng | | | | |
| tomorrow | tīngyaht | very | hóu | | |
| tomorrow evening/night | tīngmáahn | video-recorder | luhkyínggēi [go, ga] | | |
| | | video-tape | luhkyíngdáai [béng] | | |
| tonight | gāmmáahn | violet | jísīk | | |
| Toronto | Dōlèuhndō | visit friends, to | taam-pàhngyáuh | | |

## W

| | |
|---|---|
| wait, to | dáng |
| wait a minute, to | dáng yāt jahn/dáng |
| waiter | fógei [go] |
| walk, to | hàahng(-louh) |
| want, to | yiu |
| want to, to | séung |
| warm | (wān)nyúhn |
| wash, to | sái |
| wash clothes, to | sái-sāam |
| wash the dishes, to | sái-díp |
| wash up, to | sái-wún |
| watch, to | tái |
| watch a movie, to | tái-dihnyíng, tái-hei |
| watch football, to | tái-jūkkàuh |
| watch television, to | tái-dihnsih |
| water | séui |
| water-melon | sāigwā [go] |
| we | ngóhdeih |
| wear, to | jeuk |
| weather | tīnhei |
| Wednesday | sīngkèih-sāam, láihbaai-sāam |
| week | sīngkèih, láihbaai [go] |
| week before last | chìhn go láihbaai/ sīngkèih |
| Welcome! | fūnyìhng (gwōnglàhm) |
| west | sāi |
| what? | mātyéh, dímyéung |
| what is the price? | dím maaih a |
| what time? | géidímjūng |
| when? | géisìh |
| where? | bīndouh |
| which? | bīn(+ classifier/ demonstrative, e.g. bīn jek, bīndī) |
| white | baahksīk |
| who? | bīngo, bīnwái |
| why don't we ...? | bātyùh |
| wife | taai-táai [go] |
| will (in predictions) | wúih |
| wind | fūng [jahng] |
| window | chēung [jek] |
| window-shopping, to go | hàahng-gāai |
| windy | daaihfūng, fūngsái kèuhnggihng |
| winter | dūngtīn |
| wish to, to | séung |
| with | tùhng |
| woman | néuihyán [go] |
| wonder, to | mjī |
| won-ton noodles | wàhntānmihn |
| wrong number (on the phone) | daap cho sin |

## Y

| | |
|---|---|
| year | nìhn |
| year, last | gauhnín |
| year, this | gāmnín |
| year before last | chìhnnín |
| years of age | seui |
| yellow | wòhngsīk |
| yesterday | chàhmyaht, kàhmyaht |
| yesterday evening | chàhmmáahn, kàhmmáahn |
| you (plural) | néihdeih |
| you (singular) | néih |
| young | hauhsāang |
| younger brother | dàih-dái, sailóu [go] |
| younger sister | (mùih-)múi [go] |
| yourself | néih jihgéi |
| yourselves | néihdeih jihgéi |

## Z

| | |
|---|---|
| zero | lìhng |

# Further reading

## Dictionaries

Chiang Ker Chiu (n.d.) *A Practical English–Cantonese Dictionary*. Singapore: Chin Fen Book Store.
Chik Hon Man and Ng Lam Sim Yuk (1989) *Chinese–English Dictionary: Cantonese in Yale Romanization, Mandarin in Pinyin*. Hong Kong: New Asia, Yale-in-China Language Centre, Chinese University of Hong Kong.
Cowles, Roy T. (1965) *The Cantonese Speaker's Dictionary*. Hong Kong: Hong Kong University Press.
Cowles, Roy T. (1986) *A Pocket Dictionary of Cantonese*. 3rd ed. Hong Kong: Hong Kong University Press.
*English–Cantonese Dictionary: Cantonese in Yale Romanization* (1991) Hong Kong: New Asia, Yale-in-China Chinese Language Centre, Chinese University of Hong Kong.
Huang, Parker Po-fei (1970) *Cantonese Dictionary: Cantonese–English, English–Cantonese*. New Haven, CT, and London: Yale University Press.
Kwan Choi Wah (1989) *The Right Word in Cantonese*. Hong Kong: Commercial Press.
Lau, Sidney (1973a) *A Cantonese–English and English–Cantonese Glossary to Accompany "Elementary Cantonese" (Units 1–20)*. Hong Kong: Government Printer.
Lau, Sidney (1973b) *A Cantonese–English and English–Cantonese Glossary to Accompany "Intermediate Cantonese" (Units 21–40)*. Hong Kong: Government Printer.
Lau, Sidney (1977) *A Practical Cantonese–English Dictionary*. Hong Kong: Government Printer.
Matthews, Stephen and Virginia Yip (2011) *Cantonese: A Comprehensive Reference Grammar*. London and New York: Routledge.
Meyer, Bernard F. and Theodore F. Wempe (1978) *The Student's Cantonese–English Dictionary*. 4th ed. Hong Kong: Catholic Truth Society.

# Appendix

Here are two graphic representations of the contours of the six tones of Cantonese, made using *VisiPitch®*, a system which displays pitch traces of spoken language.

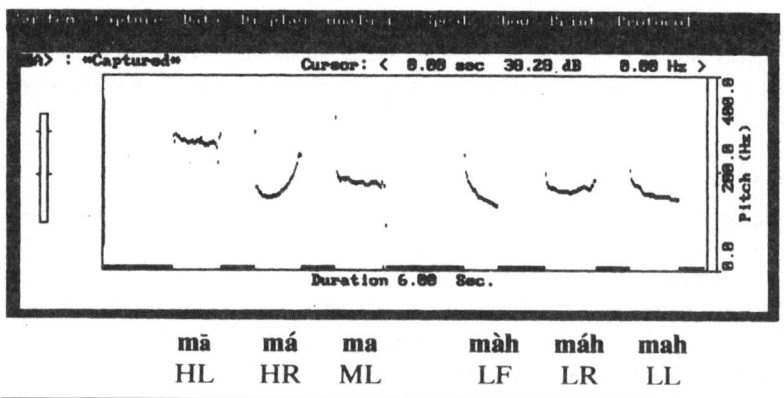

Figure 1 Reproduced by courtesy of Kay Elemetrics Corp.

In Figure 1, the black lines represent the syllable **ma**, pronounced on each of the six tones, in the traditional Chinese sequence. If you have the audio, you may want to listen to the recorded demonstration.

The first tone (**mā**) is the high level tone, on a consistent high pitch.

The second tone (**má**) is the high rising tone. Notice the curve, which rises from a fairly low pitch almost to the pitch of the first tone.

The third tone (**ma**) is the mid level tone, the tone of one's normal voice.

The fourth tone (**màh**) is the falling tone, falling from a medium pitch to a lower pitch.

# Appendix

The fifth tone (**máh**) is the low rising tone, but the rise is far less obvious compared with that of the second tone.

The sixth tone (**mah**) is the low level tone, which stays more or less at the same pitch. But notice that the difference in pitch between this tone and the third (mid level) tone is smaller than that between the first (high level) tone and the third (mid level).

Note that each of these tones is relative to the other. There is no absolute pitch as, of course, no two people's voices are identical. The important thing to remember is to differentiate the relative levels and contours of the tones, with particular respect to the "benchmark" third tone, your normal, or neutral, voice level. Provided that each tone is appropriately distinguished in this way, your Cantonese speech will be readily understood.

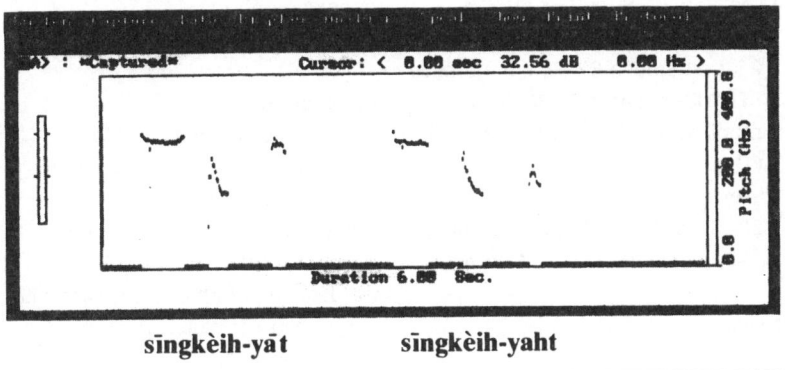

Figure 2 Reproduced by courtesy of Kay Elemetrics Corp.

Figure 2 displays a representation of the words **sīngkèih-yāt** (*Monday*) and **sīngkèih-yaht** (*Sunday*). In both, the first syllable, **sīng**, is pronounced on the first, high level, tone. The second syllable, **kèih**, is pronounced on the fourth, low falling, tone. The words **sīngkèih-yāt** and **sīngkèih-yaht** are distinguished only by the tone of the third syllable. In **sīngkèih-yāt**, the **yāt** is pronounced on the first tone (on the same tone as **sīng**, but note that it is much shorter because of the unexploded final consonant **-t**). In **sīngkèih-yaht**, the **yaht** is pronounced on the sixth, low level, tone. Again, notice how short the word is. However, despite its shortness, its tone is still significant.

# Index of grammatical structures

address, forms of 84–5, 133
adjectival phrase construction with **ge** 83
adjective phrases 80
adjectives 20, 80, 82–3, 103–4, 119, 124, 133, 168, 182, 207, 210, 237; attributive 82–3; comparative 82, 103; possessive 85, 133; predicative 82; reduplicated 80,168; superlative 103, 108
adverbs and adverbial phrases: 4, 22, 50–1, 84, 153, 219; manner 197; place 83, 161–2, 178; time 54, 124
advice 194–6, 201
age 85–6, 93, 134, 148
alternatives ("or") 80, 82–3
anticipation 37, 152
aspect markers: **-gán** (progressive) 137; **-gwo** (experiential) 218–20, 223; **-háh** (delimitative) 238; **-jó** (perfective) 100–1, 152–3, 160, 208, 223

"be" **(haih)** 16–17, 20–1

classifiers 22, 34, 43, 52, 65, 96, 114–15, 118, 131, 133, 159, 161, 164, 167, 206, 217; with demonstratives 83–5, 89
color 208

comparison 103, 108, 183,
completion of action 100, 160; anticipation of 152
concession 133
conditions 50
confirmation, requests for 223

dates 59, 61, 194
definite determiners 36, 161
delimitative aspect marker (**-háh**) 238
demonstrative pronoun 84, 89
destination 101, 123–4, 169, 220
**dī**: definite determiner 36; indefinite pronoun 49; plural 36, 89; possessive 192
**-dī**: comparative 108, 182
distance 168–9
**dō** and **tīm** 178–9
**dōjeh** and **mgōi** 37, 177
**dōu** and **yauh** 49–50

elision of number expressions 13, 86
emphasis 84, 138, 162–3, 179
experiential aspect marker (**-gwo**) 218–20, 223

**fāan** 115–17, 122–4, 135–6, 182, 196, 210–11, 231
forecasting, weather 189–91

# Index of grammatical structures

frequency 54–5, 219, 225
future, expression with **wúih** 192–3, 196

**-gán**: progressive aspect marker 137
**ge** in adjectival phrase construction 83
greetings and introductions 20, 22–3, 193, 231
**-gwo**: comparative 108, 182–3; experiential aspect marker 218–20, 223

**-háh**: delimitative aspect marker 238
**hái**: locative marker 50, 72, 136, 138
**haih** ("be") 20–2, 207–8

indefinite pronoun 35, 49
interjective **nē** 84
invitation 237

**jauh** (conditional adverb) 50
**jeui**: superlative 103, 108
**-jó**: perfective aspect marker 100–1, 134, 152–3, 160, 208, 223
**jouh** 72

kinship 87

**léuhng** and **yih** 34, 53, 64, 85, 104
likes and dislikes 48, 51, 138, 183
locatives 50, 72, 120, 136, 138, 161–2, 166, 178
look like 81–2

measures 34, 43
**meih** 147, 153, 218, 223
**mgōi** and **dōjeh** 37, 177

money and prices 35–7, 42, 44, 67, 96–100, 103–4, 111, 177, 179, 183–4
**msái** 115, 118, 123, 151, 179, 196, 210
"must, should" (**yiu**) 67, 103, 196–7, 210

negatives 14, 21–2, 49, 51, 72, 118, 148, 160, 162, 207, 218–19
numbers 33–5, 42, 49, 54, 58, 65, 86, 97, 104, 110, 113, 115, 118–20, 194; elided forms of 13, 86

obligation 67

particles: **ā** 237; **ā ma** 163; **a** 22, 36, 72, 82, 148, 161, 220; **àh** 84; **dāk** 72, 124, 210; **dou** 124; **dóu** 162–3; **fāan** 182, 211; **ga** 82, 182, 220; **ga la** 133; **ga laak** 137; **ge** 83, 220; **ja** 87; **jēk** 103; **lā** 35, 134, 148; **la** 67; **laak** 84; **làh** 89; **lō** 9, 162; **nē** 21, 83; **saai** 152, 167; **wo** 85, 207; **yùhn** 153
percentages 191
perfective aspect marker (**-jó**) 100–1, 152–3, 160, 208, 223
personal pronouns 36
"please" 148, 177–8, 231–2
plural modification 89
possessive **dī** 192
possessive (genitive) pronoun 85
possibility 72
prediction 192–3
preference 190
progressive aspect marker (**-gán**) 137
pronouns: demonstrative 84, 89; inclusive ("everyone") 197; personal 36; possessive 192

questions 8–10, 21–2, 24, 36, 54, 81, 84, 89, 116–18, 124, 135–6, 147–8, 152, 161–2, 166, 192, 219–20, 223, 237; choice-type 21–2, 72, 82, 147, 163, 168, 192, 218, 237; with **àh** 84, 118, 163, 207
question-words 21, 219

reduplicated adjectives + **déi** 80
requests 36–7, 147, 152, 156

sequence, conjunctions of 120
serial construction 167
**séung**, modal ("want to") 151–2
"several" 88–9, 99, 149, 151
**sīnji** 123–4, 169
size 182
superlative 103, 108
surprise 8–9, 118, 207

telephone conventions 230–3
texting 237
thanks 37
**tīm** and **dō** 178
time: duration of 114, 118–19, 224; frequency of 54–5, 219, 225; point of 72; telling the 64–5, 71

time expressions 52, 55, 68, 72, 220, 224
topic–comment constructions 36, 119; with **syun** 133

verbal particles: **dāk** 72, 124, 210; **dóu** 124, 162–3; **fāan** 182, 211; **saai** 152, 167; **yùhn** 153
verb–object constructions 13, 47, 54–5, 68, 101, 103, 114, 124, 146, 190, 210; split 117

"want to" (**séung**) 151–2
**wúih**, modal of prediction and futurity ("will, shall") 5, 192–3, 196, 232

**yáuh**, verb of possession and existence 49, 193, 218, 224, 237
**yáuh móuh**, choice interrogative 71–2, 81, 151–2, 160, 163, 192, 218, 236
**yauh** and **dōu** 50
"yet" 147
**yih** and **léuhng** 34, 53, 64, 85, 104
**yiu**, modal of obligation ("must, should") 67, 103, 196–7, 210
**yiu**, verb of necessity 100, 116–18, 122–4, 169